ELEMENT CLASSIC EDITIONS

CONCENTRATION AND MEDITATION
A Manual of Mind Development
Christmas Humphreys

THE GREAT PYRAMID DECODED
Peter Lemesurier

THE LAST BARRIER
A Sufi Journey
Reshad Feild

THE CHASM OF FIRE

Born in Russia in 1907, Mrs. Tweedie was educated in Vienna and Paris. Eventually she moved to England where she was happily married to a naval officer. Distraught by his premature death in 1954, she looked for consolation and meaning in her life. She worked as a librarian in the Theosophical Library in London, and eventually her search took her some five years later to India where, in 1961, she found her way to a Sufi Master who was to change her life forever. She returned to England after his death in 1966.

Until her retirement in 1991, Mrs. Tweedie held meditation meetings in her home where her group worked extensively with dreams, as her Teacher had done. She has lectured in England, Europe and throughout the United States and, from its base in California, the work of her Teacher continues under the auspices of 'The Golden Sufi Center' which can be contacted at PO Box 428, Inverness, Ca. 94937–0428, USA.

BY THE SAME AUTHOR

DAUGHTER OF FIRE
A Diary of a Spiritual Training with a Sufi Master
(The complete unabridged edition of *The Chasm of Fire*,
Blue Dolphin Publishing, Inc)

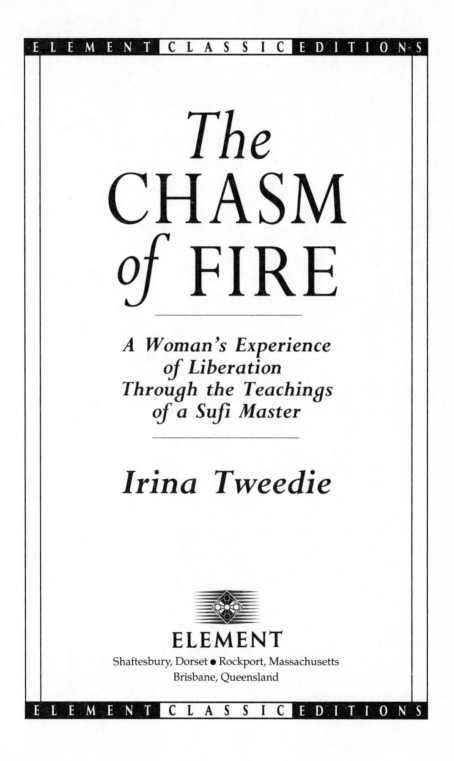

The
CHASM
of FIRE

*A Woman's Experience
of Liberation
Through the Teachings
of a Sufi Master*

Irina Tweedie

ELEMENT

Shaftesbury, Dorset ● Rockport, Massachusetts
Brisbane, Queensland

First published in Great Britain in 1979
© Irina Tweedie 1979

Element Classics Edition published in Great Britain in 1993
by Element Books Limited, Longmead, Shaftesbury, Dorset
© Daughter of Fire Trust 1989

Published in the USA in 1993 by
Element, Inc.
42 Broadway, Rockport, MA 01966

Published in Australia in 1993 by
Element Books Limited for
Jacaranda Wiley Limited
33 Park Road, Milton, Brisbane 4064

Text designed by Humphrey Stone
Cover design by Max Fairbrother
Printed and bound in Great Britain by
Dotesios Ltd, Trowbridge, Wiltshire

British Library Cataloguing in Publication data
Tweedie, Irina
The chasm of fire.
1. India.Sufism – Diaries
I. Title
297′ .4′ 0924

Library of Congress Cataloging in Publication
Data available

ISBN 1–85230–040–X

Preface

This book is an account of spiritual training according to the ancient Yogic tradition.

"Keep a diary," said my Teacher. "One day it will become a book. But you must write it in such a way that it should help others. People say, 'Such-and-such things did happen thousands of years ago because we read in books about them.' This book will be a proof that such things as are related do happen today, as they happened yesterday and will happen tomorrow – to the right people, in the right time and the right place."

I have preserved the diary form. I found that it conveys better the immediacy of experience and, for the same reason, I have used throughout the first person singular. When I tried to write it in an impersonal way, rather like a story, it seemed to lose its impact. *It happened to me*; I am involved in it day by day.

The first draft was begun in September 1971 in Sutherland, Scotland, nearly ten years after the first meeting with my Teacher. I could not face the attempt before that; could not even look at the entries in my diary. It was like a panic; I dreaded it; too much suffering is involved in it. The slow grinding down of the personality is a painful process.

The reader may find the account a little repetitive at times. Naturally so. For it is the story of a teaching, and teaching is continual repetition. The pupil has to learn the lesson again and again in order to be able to master it and the teacher must repeat the lesson, present it in a different light, sometimes in a different form, so that the pupil should understand and remember. Each situation is repeated many times but each time it triggers off a slightly different psychological reaction leading to the next experience, and so forth.

When I went to India in 1961, I hoped to get instruction in Yoga, expected wonderful teachings; but what the Teacher mainly did was force me to face the darkness within myself, and it almost killed me. It was done very simply – by using violent reproof, even aggression. My mind was kept in a state of confusion, unable to function properly. I was beaten down in every sense until I had to come to terms with that in me which I had been rejecting all my life.

Somewhere in one of the Upanishads – I do not remember which one – there is a sentence which puts our quest for spirituality in a nutshell : 'If you want Truth as badly as a drowning man wants air, you will realise it in a split-second.' But who wants Truth as badly as that? It is the task of the Teacher to set the heart aflame with an unquenchable fire of longing; it is his duty to keep it burning until it is reduced to ashes. For only a heart which has burned itself empty is capable of love. It is my sincere and ardent desire that this work should be a pointer on the Way, at least for some of us, for, as a well-known saying goes, 'We are both the Pilgrim and the Way.'

Finally, as the story is at last about to be printed, I would like to express my gratitude to Jeanine Miller and John Moore for all their help in its preparation for publication.

London 1978   IRINA TWEEDIE

PART I

⚹ 1 ⚹

2 *October* 1961

Coming home ... My heart was singing. This feeling of joy seized me as soon as I left the train.

The large railway station was like so many others I happened to see during my travels in India – the steel rafters; the roof blackened by smoke; the deafening noise of hissing railway engines; the usual crowd of squatting figures surrounded by their belongings, patiently waiting for the departure of some local train; coolies fighting for my luggage; the flies; the heat. I was tired and very hot but somehow, and I did not know why, I loved this station. Just the feeling of having arrived made me feel glad.

Drawn by an old horse, the *tonga* [two-wheeled carriage] was plodding along the way to Aryanagar, the district of my destination. This part of the town seemed fairly clean, even at this time of day. It was nearly 5 p.m. and still very hot.

I felt light, free and happy as one would feel when coming home after a long absence. Strange ... This wonderful sensation of coming home, of arriving at last ... Why? It seemed crazy. I wondered, how long am I destined to stay here? Years? All my life? It mattered not: it felt good. That was all I knew for the moment.

We were trotting along a wide avenue flanked with trees. Large bungalows, gleaming white, announced in bold letters the names of banks, insurance companies, engineering firms. A main post office to the right, a hospital on the left, then a large bazaar. Passing glimpses into the side-streets lined with shops and barrows, goods displayed on the pavements and all the noise, all the typical smells composed of fried oil, garlic, spices and incense. I sniffed the air ... it was good. Kanpur. It was just one more Indian city such as I had seen many a time before. And still ... this glorious feeling of coming home; there was no earthly reason for it.

True, I had come to meet a great Yogi, a *guru* [the Hindu, also Sanskrit, word *guru* means teacher], and I expected much from this encounter. But surely this was no reason to feel so light, so childishly happy. I even caught myself laughing aloud and thinking 'For the rest of my life it will be ...'; and immediately I was amazed at this idea.

After repeated enquiries from the street vendors and shopkeepers on our way my driver delivered me at last to my destination. It was a low, sprawling, terra-cotta-red bungalow set in a large open garden with flower beds in front and plenty of trees at the back. The street was fairly wide; a tiny post office in a garden amongst palm trees stood just opposite and next to it I noticed a bakery. After a hot, dusty journey it looked like heaven – all so fresh and peaceful.

But my joy was short-lived. Mrs Ghose, the proprietor, told me that she had no accommodation. She said she had written about it and seemed surprised that I knew nothing. 'But I will take you along to Miss L.'s friend, Pushpa; there you will be sure to find a place to stay for the time being.'

Stout and middle-aged, she climbed into the tonga beside me and seated practically on top of my suitcases gave instructions in Hindi to the driver. She then kept talking rapidly to me – something about tenants and some letters – but I hardly listened. Here was I, not knowing where I would spend the night. There were no hotels in the vicinity, that I knew about.

Mrs Ghose suddenly ordered the driver to stop. 'Here lives Miss L.'s *Guru-ji*' [the particle '*ji*' is a sign of respect]. She turned to me, 'Would you like to meet him?'

It was the most unsuitable moment to meet anyone, least of all an important person like a guru! But my protests were of no avail; she was already disappearing through a wide wooden gateway leading into a rather dry-looking garden with several shrubs and a few trees. In the background stood a long white bungalow; a large, tall doorway with wooden shutters led, presumably, into an inner courtyard.

Before I even had time to collect my thoughts, three bearded Indians emerged from the door opposite the gate and were advancing towards me, followed by Mrs Ghose. All three were elderly; all three were dressed in white. I jumped down from the tonga and joining my palms in the Indian way of greeting, looked at each of them in turn, not being sure which one was the guru. The oldest and tallest of the three, who looked exactly like an Old Testament prophet – long, grey beard; blazing, dark eyes – walked ahead of the other two and, as if in answer to my thoughts, pointed to the one walking closely behind him. This was the guru.

Next moment he stood in front of me, quietly looking at me, with a smile. He had a kindly face and strange eyes – dark pools of stillness, with a sort of liquid light in them.

I had just time to notice that he was the only one to be wearing wide trousers and a very long *kurta* [a collarless, India-style shirt] of immaculate whiteness; the other two were clad in rather worn kurtas and *longhi* [a straight piece of, usually, cotton material, tied round the waist and reaching to the ankles.]

My mind had hardly time to register this; and then it was as if it turned a somersault. My heart stood still for a split-second. I caught my breath. It was as if *something in me* had stood to attention and saluted. I was in the presence of a Great Man.

'There is no accommodation for me with Mrs Ghose,' I said quickly, looking at him, confused and feeling insecure. I was aware that I was speaking just to say something – anything – for I felt completely lost. Deep down in me there was a sort of terror, a kind of excitement and, at the same time, a feeling of being annoyed with myself for being shy and confused like a child.

"Miss L. wrote to me that you will be coming," he said, and his smile deepened. It was a pleasant, baritone voice; it suited well the general aura of peace which seemed to surround him.

Mrs Ghose stepped forward and began to tell her story all over again – that she had written to Miss L., she had nothing free, letters going astray, and so on. He nodded slowly.

"You will be able to stay with Pushpa. And," he added, "I expect you tomorrow at 7 a.m."

Some more polite words were exchanged but I hardly understood anything.

Shortly afterwards, we arrived at Pushpa's place. It was a large, two-storey house, with a very small garden. She herself was pleasant looking, plump with a pretty face. Mrs Ghose once more began her explanations. But soon I found myself installed in the guest room on the ground floor. In front of the two windows was a high brick wall, covered with a flowering creeper. The light filtering through the leaves made the room seem green and cool.

The bliss of a cold shower; a short rest; and then a lovely Indian meal with the whole of the family, seated around a large table in the dining room. Under the table a dog licked itself, and smelled to high heaven, but it fitted into the frame of the whole experience and I accepted it.

3 *October*

How well I slept under the humming fan.

But I could not go to him at 7 in the morning as he had told me. Breakfast was at 9. All the family kept piling questions on me – about England, my travels, myself; everybody had something of special interest to ask and it was after 10 when, at last, I was free to go. Pushpa sent her boy-servant to show me the way.

Already, when passing through his garden gate, I could see him seated in his room, in a very large chair opposite the open door from where he could see part of the garden and the entrance gate. He looked steadily at me approaching him. With a brief nod he acknowledged my greeting.

"I expected you at seven," he said, fingering his *mala* [a kind of rosary, much used in the East]. "It is not exactly seven now."

I explained that the breakfast was late and that I could not get away earlier. He nodded. "Yes, it would have been discourteous," he remarked, and told me to sit down.

The room was silent. He seemed to pray; bead after bead of the mala sliding through his fingers. I looked around. It was a corner room, rather narrow. Another door to the right flanked by two windows led into the garden. Two large wooden *tachats* [a wooden bench used as a bed] were standing along the left wall which had two recesses built into it, filled with books. A row of chairs and a small divan for visitors stood facing the tachats, with their backs to the windows and the side door, leaving only a narrow passage to the third door at the opposite end of the room. It was covered by a green curtain and led to the next room from which one could reach the inner courtyard. All was clean and orderly. His name, executed by naive, infantile hands, hung in three frames on the wall over the tachats.*

While looking at the frames I mused over this name, and was glad that I saw it written before me and did not need to ask him or anybody else. I remembered vividly how I told L. in a sudden panic, as she was giving me his address, that I did not want to know his name. It was baffling and I had no explanation why I had felt then that he had to remain without a name, without even a face for me. L. told me that the fact of not wanting to know his name had a deep meaning but refused to clarify the point. 'You will know one day,' she said rather mysteriously. And now here it was: right in front of me, written three times, hanging on the wall ...

"Why did you come to me?"† He asked quietly breaking the silence. I looked at him. The beads in his right hand were resting on the arm support of the chair and all at once, as if waiting for this very question, I felt a sudden irresistible desire to speak, an urgency to tell everything, absolutely, about myself, my longing, my aspirations, all my life ...

It was a compulsion. I began to speak and talked for a long time. I told him that I wanted God, was searching for Truth. From what I had learned from L., I knew that he could help me. I went on and on. He kept nodding slowly as if the torrent of my words was a confirmation of his own thoughts, looking at me, no, rather through me, with those strange eyes of his, as if to search out the very intimate, hidden corners of my mind.

'I want God,' I heard myself saying, 'But not the Christian idea of an anthropomorphic deity. I want the Rootless Root, the Causeless Cause of the Upanishads.'

"Nothing less than that?" He lifted an eyebrow. I detected a slight note of irony in his voice. He was silent again, fingering his mala. I too was silent now. 'He thinks I am full of pride,' flashed through my mind. Indistinct feelings of resentment surged from the depth of my being and went. He seemed so strange, so incomprehensible. His face was expressionless. I noticed that his eyes were not very dark, rather hazel brown, with small golden sparks in them.

I began telling him that I was a Theosophist, a vegetarian, and ... "Theosophist?" He interrupted enquiringly. I explained. "Oh yes, now I remember; long ago I met some Theosophists." Again the silence fell. He closed his eyes. His lips were moving in silent prayer. But I still went on explaining that Theos-

* According to the ancient tradition, the disciple never pronounces the name of the guru. I could not pronounce it and always felt loath to write it.
† The traditional question of every spiritual Teacher to an aspirant or a would-be disciple. According to Spiritual Law, the human being must clearly state his case himself. The Teacher will do nothing against the free will of the individual.

ophists do not believe that a guru is necessary; we must try and reach our Higher Self by our own efforts. "Not even in a hundred years!" He laughed outright. "It cannot be done without a Teacher!"

I told him that I did not know what Sufism was.

"Sufism is a way of life. It is neither a religion nor a philosophy. There are Hindu Sufis, Muslim Sufis, Christian Sufis. My Revered Guru Maharaj was a Muslim." He said it very softly, with a tender expression, his eyes dreamy and veiled. And then I noticed something which in my excitement and eagerness I had not observed before; there was a feeling of great peace in the room. He himself was full of peace. He radiated it; it was all around us and it seemed eternal. As if this special peace always was and always would be, forever ...

I looked at his face. He could be said to be good looking in a masculine sort of way. There was nothing feminine in his features – the rather strong nose, the very high forehead. The grey beard and moustache gave him a dignified and distinctly oriental appearance. His hair was short-cut, Western style.

'How shall I address you? What is the custom?' I asked.

"You can call me as you like; I don't mind. People here call me *Bhai Sahib*, which in Hindi means Elder Brother." So, 'Bhai Sahib it is going to be for me too,' I thought. 'That is what he really is; an Elder Brother.'

'When I arrived I had a feeling of coming home; and now I cannot get rid of the impression that I knew you before. That I knew you always. Bhai Sahib, where did we meet last time?'

"Why ask?" He smiled, "Some day you will know yourself. Why ask?"

At 11.30 he sent me away.

"For the first few days only (he put special emphasis on the word 'only'), you will not stay here for long periods of time. Be back after six p.m." I left and took with me the haunting memory of his face, full of infinite sweetness and dignity, and this impression remained with me for quite a while.

We had lunch. Much talk at table; all the family present. Grandfather is lovely, quite a character.

After lunch I went to have a rest in my room. Everybody else went for a rest also, as is the custom in every hot country. The room was cool and tranquil, full of green light like a secluded greenhouse. Suddenly I realized that I could not remember his face; could not recollect what he looked like! It gave me such a shock that I literally gasped. His garment, his mala, his hands, the room and the furniture I remembered well, and a good part, though not the whole, of our conversation; his slender feet in brown strap-sandals. The feet, those sandals, where had I seen them before? I remembered. It was in a dream long ago I was looking at them, trying to follow them, being led down a stony desert road by a tall Indian whose face I did not remember. They were the same feet, the same sandals. But his face, seen only a few hours ago, I could not recollect ...

I could hardly wait till 6 p.m. When I arrived he was sitting cross-legged in his chair in the garden talking to some men seated around on chairs. I felt very relieved. Of course, how stupid of me! Here he was in the flesh, looking very real and solid like everyone else. And sure enough he had a face, and he was laughing at this very moment for he was telling a funny story in Hindi. Everbody laughed and I was looking fixedly at him. How could I be so foolish as to forget something so memorable! I looked at his features to impress them well on my mind. After a while he turned to me and said in English:

"I would like you to keep a diary; day by day entries of all your experiences. And also to keep a record of your dreams. Your dreams you must tell me, and I will interpret them for you. Dreams are important; they are a guidance."

4 October

Went to Bhai Sahib in the morning after breakfast. And in the evening after 6 p.m. When I am at his place, the thinking process seems to slow down considerably. Thoughts come and go, lazily, slowly, just a few, and far between. I see people come in, touch his feet, sit down quietly and fall into a 'deep state', completely oblivious to the surroundings. I was told that this was the state of *dhyana* [contemplation followed by complete abstraction of all outward impressions]; but what this dhyana is supposed to be he did not tell me; only smiled and said that I will know it myself one day ... I have heard this one before, so it seems.

Perhaps, after all, it is of no importance if he is a great guru or not. Perhaps it does not even matter for me to be able to understand who he is. If he can teach me to abstract the senses (because this is what dhyana seems to be), to be able to meditate like this, oblivious to everything, I would not ask for more. After all, it is supposed to be a desirable state to which all Yogis aspire; and it is the most difficult state to achieve, especially for we Westerners who are used to living and functioning on the mental level; to go beyond it appears a sheer impossibility. But here I see it done, seemingly so easily, so effortlessly. He tells me that I will be able to do it too, one day. I can hardly believe it.

5 October

On the first morning, three days ago, he had said; "If you say to a human being: 'Sit in this *asana* (posture), or that one; meditate in this way or that,' you are putting the human being in prison. Leave the man alone and he will find God in his own way."

Asked him this morning if it was true, as I read in a book, that the *Atma* [Higher Self], when in incarnation, assumes the features of the physical body and can be seen more or less one foot above the head of the person; and the eyes are the same as the physical eyes.

"The eyes and the forehead are the same; and, yes, it is true, it can be seen above the head of the person."

Then I asked why on the second day of our meeting he had wanted to know if I was free, completely free, that I had no dependants, no one to look after, nor any obligations to bind me. 'You know that I am free; so why did you ask?'

"Yes I know of course that you are free. But I wanted a confirmation from yourself. Sometimes in this physical world we have to behave and to speak as if we know nothing." It seemed a strange answer but I did not ask further. Looking at me thoughtfully he said: "It takes time to make a soul pregnant with God. But it can be done; IT WILL BE DONE ..." This too seemed a strange statement. I kept very still. Gazing at him, and wondering.

Later came a young man whom I had already seen here. A handsome, tall Indian with a severe face; he could be about thirty I thought. This time he brought his three-year-old girl with him. The young man touched the Guruji's feet, bowing down very low. He then sat down and immediately fell into deep dhyana, sitting there perfectly motionless, unconscious of everything, his child standing between his knees, playing quietly with a flower.

"He is a highly evolved human being," said Bhai Sahib, as soon as the man had left. "He works on the railway and comes here when he can."

⊰ 2 ⊱

6 *October*

Doubts kept creeping into my mind. Many doubts. Such ordinary surroundings. Such ordinary people around him. Is he a Great Man? There seems to be none of the glamour of a great guru about him as we are used to reading in books. He seems so simple, living a simple, ordinary life. Clearly, he takes his household duties seriously. I could see that he was the head of a large family – six children, and his brother and his family living also in the same house, all sharing the same courtyard. And I saw also other people there, a few other families. The place was full of comings and goings, all kinds of activities, not to count his disciples of whom there seemed to be many.

Decided to speak to L. about it. She will soon be back. In the meantime, I resolved to stay away as much as possible. Went there after 6 p.m. He was writing letters seated cross-legged on his tachat. I tried to read a book I had brought with me. Soon he looked up and asked me if I felt uneasy, if I felt any pain. Told him that if my foot is not better, I will not come tomorrow. (I could hardly walk because of an infection.) He made some sympathetic noises. While speaking, I secretly hoped that he would cure it instantly. He looked at my foot; "It will come right by itself," he said as if aware of my thoughts. "Rest is useful," he added, and continued to write. Did not stay long and went home.

9 *October*

Pushpa's house is roomy and comfortable. Ceiling fans are in every room. With my infected foot as an excuse, I did not go to the guru last night. But I went this morning. He was talking nearly all the time about his guru, and how much money he spent on him. I wonder if he knows my thoughts about him and talks like this because of it. I have now every possible suspicion about him. Stayed for a very short while. I did not return in the afternoon as it was raining heavily. Will try to keep away from him until L.'s arrival. So much hope shattered ... Did I expect too much perhaps? It all seems so commonplace; and he hardly bothers to answer my questions.

"You will know one day."

Why and how? What prevents him from explaining? What an attitude!

A feeling of great loneliness ... Dark, endless longing. I do not know for what. Much disappointment and much bitterness. 'Who are you, Bhai Sahib? Are you what L. told me? A Great Teacher, a man of great spiritual power? Or are you just one of so many pseudo-gurus one meets here in India? Are you a Teacher at all? You seem to have many disciples. From what I have heard from L., you must be a Great Man. But are you?'

10 *October*

It was raining in the morning. Went about 5 p.m. There were no visitors. Then a professor of mathematics arrived and sat with us. Later Bhai Sahib suggested that we might like to go to a learned discussion which was being held in the park. I refused. I wanted to be punctual at the *Kirtan* [singing of devotional hymns in praise of the Deity] which was being held at Pushpa's place at 7 p.m.

Left with the professor of mathematics, who was also going to the Kirtan. Walking along he asked me what this discussion at the park was supposed to be about. I said it concerned the Avatar [divine incarnation] of Ram, one theory being that he was the only real incarnation of Vishnu [the Second Person of the Hindu Trinity: the Preserver].

Then I began to tell him about my doubts. 'Is there any purpose in going to Bhai Sahib at all? Is it not a waste of time?' He listened with great seriousness.

'If you are convinced that your guru is always right, that he is the only Great Man, then you will progress. Your guru may not be great at all, but you think that he is, and it is your faith which will make you progress. It is the same with Ram; what does it matter if he is the only incarnation of God or not? For the man who believes it, he is. So why discuss? I refuse to participate in intellectual acrobatics.'

I agreed with him. 'What disturbs me most with Bhai Sahib,' I went on, 'is the fact that he does not answer questions. Every time I want to know something, he will say, "You will know it one day yourself." Now who can tell me if I will really know? Maybe I never will; so why not simply answer it? I want to know NOW, not sometime in a hypothetical future! I begin to wonder if I am wasting my time!'

'You know,' he said, 'just to give an example: a son of a rich man inherits the wealth of his father and then he will have more than you or me. Now, here it is the same in this place. This man has a certain power which will reveal in time something very wonderful within yourself. It happened to others, it happened to me. I have been here for the last twelve years, I speak from experience. I don't know how it happened: I have no explanation for it. I don't know how one can inherit such a thing, but it is a fact. Stay here for a month and you will be in the state L. is in, and we all are, and then you will think differently. L., when she came years ago, spoke as you do now.' I said I was sure it would take longer than one month.

'Of course, it takes years;' he agreed, 'but after one month you will be able to form a judgement.'

I told him I had decided at any rate to stay here until March, and he answered that it would be wise to do so.

'I have seen strange and wonderful things happen to human beings here. Dhyana is definitely NOT a mediumistic trance; it is a Yogic state; it has nothing to do with mesmerism either.'

We were entering Pushpa's gate. The veranda was brightly lit; many people were already there. 'Dhyana is complete abstraction of the senses.' He repeated, 'A Yogic state.'

As we entered the music started. I was in deep thought. So, that was it. Somehow I felt that this conversation represented a turning point An intelligent man with a balanced mind, normal and reasonable, gave me his opinion. I liked and trusted him from the first moment I saw him, a few days ago. In my heart I felt I should give it a try, accept the situation as it presents itself and see what will happen . . . Why not?

Lights were burning in front of the pictures of Rama, Shiva and Parvati [Hindu deities]. The room was crowded, everyone seated on the floor, their faces full of devotion; my heart kept rhythm with the ancient melody . . . 'Hari Rama, Hari, Hari . . .', and I was thinking and thinking . . .

And I was still thinking deeply when in my room, hardly aware of howling dogs roaming the streets and the evening noises of a busy Indian street. 'Is dhyana just sleep?' I asked.

"If you think that it may be sleep, then it is sleep. If you think it is not, then it is not." His face had been stern, but with a faint suspicion of a twinkle in his eye, a hidden laughter.

12 *October*

I feel well and my foot has healed completely.

Arrived about 5 p.m. Nobody was in the room. Sat down in my usual place in the chair opposite his tachat. His wife* came in, searching for something in

* Sufis lead the normal life of a householder and marriage for them does not represent a barrier to reaching the higher states of consciousness.

the recess amongst the books. Then he entered. I do not remember how we started to talk about dhyana, but probably I began because it kept worrying me. As soon as I had stepped into his room, the thinking process had slowed down and I felt sleepy; I told him so and he translated it to his wife. She said that I was not the only one; it happened to her too.

"I never sleep during the day," he remarked.

'How can you keep awake in this place?' I wondered; 'I feel sleepy as soon as I sit down!' He laughed. Then he began to tell me that in 1956 he was very ill, desperately ill, and many people came who could be of some help, in one way or another. But they all sat there fast asleep, and his wife used to ask: 'What have they all come for – just to sleep?'

'So dhyana does mean to be asleep after all? Are dhyana and sleep the same thing?'

"No they are not. They could be similar at the beginning. But if you remain too long unconscious, without being conscious somewhere else, then you are not normal, then something is wrong with you."

'Do you mean to say that one becomes conscious somewhere else when unconscious on the physical plane? You may remember that I asked you several times about it but you never answered!'

"Of course!" He laughed merrily. "It comes gradually, little by little. It takes time. But before you can do it you must forget everything. Leave everything behind."

It seemed to be a frightening thought. He laughed again softly and gave me a look of kindly amusement. "How do you swim?" he began after a silence. "You throw water behind and behind you; that's how you propel yourself. Spiritual life is the same; you keep throwing everything behind, as you go on. This is the only way; there is no other."

'Is there not a danger of becoming stupid by forgetting everything?' I wondered.

"Why?" he retorted; "If you have ten rupees in your bag and you get ten thousand, you will forget the ten rupees will you not? The ten rupees are still there aren't they? But you don't think of them any more." I could see what he meant and also that he was right.

Later I mentioned a discussion I had with L. about spiritual life. She was of the opinion that I could not go on further by myself alone, or progress more than I had already done; that a guru was absolutely necessary.

"A guru is a short-cut, a short-cut and a sharp one. But not a guru; a friend, a Spiritual Guide. I have nothing to teach."

'What do you mean by a system?' He often used the expression in conversation. I was not quite sure if I understood its meaning.

"A system is a school of Yoga, or a path to Self Realisation; the meaning is the same. We are all called Saints but it is the same as Yogis; in Wisdom there is no difference. The colour of our line is golden yellow, and we are called the Golden Sufis or the Silent Sufis, because we practise silent meditation. We do not use music or dancing or any definite practice. We do not belong to any country or any civilization, but we work always according to the need of the people of the time. We belong to Raja Yoga, but not in the sense that it is practised by the Vedantins. Raja means simply 'Kingly', or 'Royal' – the Direct Road to Absolute Truth."

'And why is it that one cannot go on by oneself any further and one needs a guru?'

"Because by yourself alone you can never go beyond the level of the mind. How can you vacate?"

'You mean to empty the mind, to clear it of any thought?' I asked, not being sure what he meant by 'vacate'.

"Yes, how can you vacate, clear out your mind, if you are constantly working through the mind? How can the mind empty itself of itself? You must be able to leave it, to forget everything and this one cannot do alone. For the mind cannot transcend itself."

'Will I ever be able to do it, as I am afraid of this idea?' I said, doubtfully. He laughed again looking at me sideways.

"If you are ill, who does the work? Others, of course! If you are unconscious, be sure there will be many people to look after you!" I said that it may be true in theory; but if, for instance in deep *samadhi* [a superconscious state; a merging into Universal Consciousness], I could easily be robbed.

"No," he retorted; "then you are not in samadhi. If you are in samadhi, you go to your Creator, and the Creator will look after you. And even if you are robbed, it is not because you were in samadhi, but because it was your destiny to be robbed, and it is of no importance to you once you have reached this state of consciousness. When we travel together, you will see that I take nothing with me, I am not afraid."

'But if you travel and have no money, somebody has to travel with you and keep the money and be careful that it is not lost; otherwise both of you will be in trouble,' I insisted.

"Yes, that could be true; but not necessarily so. Perhaps I could travel free, or the money will be forthcoming; God works through many channels. At any rate, I affirm; that to him who is in samadhi nothing happens, and if it does, he does not care." He fell silent. After a while he said thoughtfully: "You have your knowledge. You will forget it all. You MUST forget it before you can take any further step."

I wondered if this is what the scriptures mean; one should forget all books and leave all acquired knowledge behind; only then can one make the big leap into the Unknown beyond the mind? He agreed.

"There are only very few people in the world nowadays who can teach you the Sufi method. The Sufi method represents complete freedom. You are never forced. To put somebody in dhyana can be done, but it would only show that my will is stronger than yours. In this case it would be mesmerism; there is nothing spiritual about that; and it would be wrong. When the human being is attracted to the Spiritual Guide and wants to become a *shishya* [disciple], there are two ways open to him: the path of dhyana, the slow but the easier way;

or the path of *tyaga* (complete renunciation, the Road of Fire, the burning away of all dross). And it is the Guide who has to decide which way is the best suited in each individual case. The path of dhyana is for the many, the path of tyaga is for the few. How many would want to sacrifice everything for the sake of Truth? The shishya has every right to test the Guide, (here he laughed his young and merry laugh) then the Guide can take over and the disciple has no free will for a while."

He contradicts himself, I thought, but said nothing. Then he began to speak about his guru, the Great Sufi.

"He is always with me," he said.

'Do you mean that you see him?' I asked.

He had a tender, far-away look. "If I say that I see him with these physical eyes, I would be lying; if I say that I don't see him I also would be lying," he said, after a brief silence. I knew what he meant: he could reach him in his higher states of consciousness.

Well perhaps it is a good thing after all, that I came here. And I was thankful for the opportunity of this conversation.

⤞ 3 ⤝

15 *October*

Went to the Gita class this morning. Of no interest. When I arrived at Bhai Sahib's place, he was asleep. His lean figure in a white *dhoti* [Indian dress: a kind of sarong] looked strange and contorted. I sat down quietly, in the corner near the door. All was still. Some noises from the street; a child was crying somewhere in the courtyard.

Then I became aware of a great power in the room. A tremendous power. I could scarcely breathe; the force was terrific. I felt a great disturbance in the throat and my heart ached and beat irregularly.

After a while, perhaps an hour or more, Bhai Sahib sat up, looked around with glazed eyes and then sat, cross-legged and motionless, in deep meditation, looking ahead with unseeing eyes. And the force in the room seemed greater and deeper, increasing all the time so that the room seemed to vibrate and hum with it. One could literally hear it like a great sound, high and low at the same time.

I sat with closed eyes, trying to endure it, for it was difficult to bear. The mind? It was hardly present at all. Lost somewhere, swallowed up, dissolved, or rather absorbed by the charged atmosphere of the room. Opened my eyes after a while and saw that he was looking directly at me. It gave me a kind of jerk, like an electric shock. The expression in his eyes ... it frightened me; but then I realised that he was not really looking at me at all. His eyes were wide

20

open, unseeing; he was evidently not in this world. I began to feel so sleepy and had to fight with all my might against it.

After a while, his wife came in and told him that tea was ready. He took the small towel which he always carried with him and went out. Not a word was spoken.

A young man, who until then had been sitting there silently, now said something to me. I could not reply, could not utter a word – too great was the peace, the seemingly eternal stillness.

Went home, fell on my bed and plunged into a deep sleep.

16 *October*

Went to him in the morning. I did not speak, neither did he. He kept walking up and down on the brick elevation in front of the house, repeating his prayers, mala in hand.

17 *October*

Arrived in the evening about 6 p.m. *Durga Puja* [devotional service in honour of the goddess Durga] was going on in Deva Singh Park across the street, opposite the house. Loud music was pouring out from a large, brilliantly illuminated marquee, a rhythmic sing-song of devotional prayers. He was not in the garden but somewhere in the street, so I was told. Something had happened, a fight or a disturbance of some sort, and he was talking to a police officer.

His wife and the women of Bhai Sahib's household stood in a group discussing the event. A bright lamp was fixed on one of the trees in the garden. Thousands of moths and insects were dancing madly round it. What was attracting them so much to the brightness of the light? Though half-burned, they returned again and again in ecstatic dance until they fell to the ground in the last convulsions of death.

To die burned by Thy Light . . . what a wonderful death!

Bhai Sahib came striding back followed by gesticulating men in dhotis. The atmosphere became more and more charged with excitement, everyone, shouting except him. Could not bear the noise. Went into the room and sat alone in the dark.

Soon, chairs were brought in; men filed into the room and I left. It was too much for me. It was raining softly, the air was so fragrant as only the air of India can be; all the year round shrubs are flowering in the gardens. I walked swiftly, lifting my face to the moist air, breathing deeply.

18 *October*

Went in the evening. Did not speak. Neither did he. He was writing letter after letter and his wife kept coming and talking and interrupting him. There is no privacy in India. How difficult it must be for him, never alone, disturbed at all times during the day, even when in deep meditation. I wondered how he could bear it; perhaps he was used to it and did not mind at all?

19 October

Soon after my arrival, a man came in and began to talk to him in Hindi. After a while, Bhai Sahib turned to me, introduced the man as a professor of history and told me that he would like to speak with me. Did not feel like talking at all, but could not refuse.

After a few preliminary exchanges of polite sentences, the professor told me that he knew exactly my state of mind. I retorted, slightly ironically, that, if he did, why did he not explain it? I was, he said, thinking that what I see here is mesmerism, or sleep, and I keep doubting if it is a good thing or just nonsense, and if I should remain here or go away. Admitted that this was in fact my state of mind. An interesting conversation followed of which I remember hardly anything, which is a pity. At the end of it, I asked what would be the correct attitude according to him.

'First, faith; absolute faith in the guru. One must have faith that he knows the right road which will lead to the Truth. Without absolute faith in the guru, it is impossible to achieve anything.' He was speaking seriously, with utmost conviction. 'Should one feel sleepy, one should relax, close the eyes and wait for something. Mind you, for a long time you may wait and nothing will happen. It is here where faith will help you. Feel deeply that you are in the presence of God; and wait for His Grace, full of alertness and surrender. Then you will not fall asleep, not really; and one day His Grace will strike you.'

I asked him how long it takes, as a rule, for such a thing to happen.

'I think not more than two years. This is the average.'

'Do you mean that I have to stay here all the time? Endure the heat of the plains? I will surely die!'

'By no means,' he replied. 'I feel that you should not stay here too long at a time. A little in the morning and a little in the evening. Then go away and come back after one week or two; and go away for a few months in the summer when the heat becomes unbearable.'

I could not agree with him. If I have decided to come here for the training, to go away again and again would be a waste of time! Surely if I want spiritual life, the only important thing would be to take the greatest advantage of the opportunity, in spite of the difficult circumstances.

20 October

Went in the evening. His wife was talking non-stop all the time. There was nobody except myself. It is all so empty and banal. Who is he? How can I know? Perhaps a sign will be given to me? I know that it happens sometimes that a sign is given . . .

Feel restless and afraid. How can I trust him? Have faith? How is it possible? What shall I do? This man has power; there is no doubt about that. What does it all mean?

21–24 October

Did not go to the house at all. What is the use? Better wait for L.'s arrival.

And still ... still, somehow, I feel that he can take me 'there' – where love is, and stillness, and the mind is not ...

25 October

Looking after Pushpa's garden! Re-arranging flowers. Planting, watering. Being frantically active. Better not to think. Work and work, just that. Such a disappointment, the whole affair ... I had hoped for so much. Oh please my mind, stop thinking.

There is a kind of power at his place – it is not just imagination; very disturbing it is. Must wait for L. She must help me clear some points and, if she cannot, then I will go to Madras, have a look at South India and Ceylon, then forget the whole affair, if I can. But it will not be easy. At the idea of going away something in me cries. It is so deep I am hardly conscious of it; it is just on the threshold of comprehension. A deep yearning.

27 October

Woke up in the middle of the night (have restless nights lately, crammed with dreams). Awoke with a sentence so resounding in my ears that I could still hear it. 'There is no other Way at all to go.' No other way. Only this was important. It was as if someone else was thinking it, not me. The finality of it ... I knew, to my profound dismay, that I *could not go*. Will never be able to go. It was like the very act of dying.

30 October

L. arrived on Saturday in the morning. Had a long talk with her. Several discussions since then. She did not prove to be much help.

Told her how disappointed I was. I even cried. Did hope she would ask him for an explanation as to what happened to my mind; and what about my heart condition (it keeps beating very fast as in a fever, often missing beats out).

Apparently she did ask him. All that he had said, she told me, was that I was suffering from a too restless mind and fearful imagination. But, she added, she quite understood my state of mind, the state of doubt and uncertainty. 'Stay for a while,' she said, 'and see what happens. At the beginning, it is not necessary to have implicit faith. Later on, it is necessary.'

Went to the house again. Ten days since I last went. Realized how much I had missed the atmosphere.

I asked him myself about the wild activity of my heart. He told me that there are two hearts – a physical one and a non-physical one – and when the latter is activated, the former is bound to feel it.

"Nothing will happen to you," he smiled. "Don't fear; no harm at all. I am here to see to that."

After a while, he turned to me and asked, "Now you have no disturbance at all, is it so?" I realized to my astonishment that my heart was quite alright. "It is because I have it now."

'Oh no!' I exclaimed. 'Give it back to me, please. I don't want you to have it; it would be unfair to you!'

"Am I a juggler – to let it go backward and forward?"

He was laughing now, obviously amused. But I asked him seriously to give it back to me again. 'I challenge you to do it; I want to see if you can; I want to believe that you have the power to do so!'

Conversation then resumed about the *Vedas* [holy texts of Hinduism]. Then there was silence. When I happened to look at Bhai Sahib, he was far away. I was fascinated by the expression on his face – like carved stone, antique and cruel, as old as humanity.

All of a sudden, I got the heart trouble again – and not only that but giddiness and headache as well. But I still did not believe that he had done it; surely it was just coincidence?

Sitting in his customary cross-legged position, Bhai Sahib was rocking himself gently, in samadhi.

'Do you know how you look in samadhi?' I asked when he opened his eyes. 'Tibetan, and as old as the hills!'

"Tibetan?" He repeated the word slowly, his voice strange and monotonous, looking straight at me. "If you know it, why do you still doubt?"

It took my breath away. I knew what he meant and silently I bowed to him with joined palms.

≮ 4 ≯

1 *November*

Last evening we went for a walk – the three of us, he, L., and myself. I hoped to see the Ganga (Ganges) but it was already getting dark and I feared that we would not see much. He walked very fast; we could hardly keep pace with him.

Arriving at the *ghat* [elevated bank of the river where ritual bathing takes place and also cremation], I could just see that there was hardly a river at all at that point. In the rapidly fading light of dusk, I could just detect puddles of stagnant water amongst banks of sand stretching far into the distance. We turned back. He was talking to L.; I was half-listening. Suddenly I was struck by one of his sentences.

"We who are pledged to the service of humanity."

I pricked up my ears. This was the sign I was waiting for; I was sure I knew the meaning of that, I thought, with gladness and relief. It means that he belongs to the Hierarchy, the Great Brotherhood who help the evolution of mankind. Tried to reflect upon it but they began talking about the states of dhyana, and L. kept teasing me, making comments about my fear of it.

Back in his garden, we sat in front of the house. A few people came – mostly men from the neighbourhood. At 8 o'clock L. got up.

'I am leaving you,' she said with a smile.

"Can you leave me?" His voice had hidden laughter in it.

'It is time to go for our supper.'

"No. I mean, can you, could you, leave me?"

'No, never!' replied L., with emphasis.

"And you could leave me?" he said, turning towards me.

'Oh, yes, I can!' I realized I had reacted too quickly – suspiciously so.

"*Try*," he said, very quietly, looking me straight in the eyes.

I nearly said to him, 'Switch off the Light!' When he has that strange, unearthly light in his eyes, I cannot look at him.

We left. I felt disturbed and asked L. what she made of this last remark of his.

'I'm not quite sure. But did you not say yesterday that your greatest trouble seems to be that you know you will not be able to go away? I think his remark alluded to that.'

She could be right.

'I did not tell him about our conversation,' L. continued. 'I never tell anything.'

So that means that he *knew*. He knows that I cannot go away.

He told L. that I do not want dhyana; so I am not going to have it.

Did I want dhyana, I wondered? Somehow I recoiled from the idea of becoming unconscious. But was the reason for my being uneasy about it really because I did not trust him completely? Had he spoken to L. like that because he intends to put me on the other road, the path of tyaga (complete renunciation)?

Not once, but several times, I have told him that I want to become like him, to have samadhi in full consciousness, the highest Yogic state. 'Make the highest Ideal your goal, and then try to reach it,' I remember saying.

He answered gravely: "In order to become conscious on all levels of being, we have to go through a period of unconsciousness. How will we transcend the physical plane otherwise? Complete abstraction of the senses, complete elimination of the thinking process – that represents a temporary loss of consciousness."

So I think I will come to *know* dhyana, but my path will be a different one.

When L. and I reached his place this morning, he was already in the garden.

Asked him about the meaning of the last remark he had made when we were leaving yesterday evening. Told him that a few days ago, in the morning, still between sleeping and waking, I had realized with a certain shock that I will not be able to go away. Could he have meant the same thing? He laughed gaily and said that that was precisely what he had meant.

"It is your Higher Self who prevents you from leaving, who told you to stay."

He took some writing paper and began to write letters. I sat quiet for a while. Then a conversation began during which L. was saying that the disciples of Socrates had complained bitterly that they were at a disadvantage – that it was not fair to them that in his presence their minds did not work and they could not discuss properly, as they were expected to. Just like me, I thought. Well, that settles it . . . I stay.

"Some force has been used on you; something had to be forced – and it will go on, not only now, but for years, for always, while the physical body lasts."

I asked how it was that I had not noticed it, and when was it?

"It was one day when we were left alone for a while, right at the beginning." His eyes seemed to pierce right through me. "This force which has been used on you will make you doubt, will cause disturbances of many kinds, but it was necessary."

I sat there wondering, my heart hammering wildly. Perhaps the Road will be free now? Perhaps the Road to Freedom will open?

In the evening, L. was asking questions on how the guru gives to the disciple, according to the Sufi system. Is it the same in all Yoga schools. Apparently, yes. It is done through *prana* [life force] and mainly through the heart *chakra* [centres of psychic energy associated with locations along the spine]. In all great schools, it is the same.

2 *November*

Was alone with him this morning. He was sitting on the tachat; I was opposite him on a chair. With half-closed eyes and fingering his mala, he fired question after question at me concerning my life and myself. Ideas kept rushing clearly and sharply into my mind. Could not help feeling flattered that he should take interest in me.

The subject of *kundalini* [an 'inner fire' that is coiled like a serpent at the base of the spine] was raised.

"It is of no importance if you believe in the existence of kundalini or not; kundalini *is*. Kundalini is not sex-impulse alone; but sex power forms part of kundalini. As a rule, this energy at the base of the spine is more or less dormant. By our system, it is awakened gently; it will not give you much trouble." After a moment, "Not much," he added thoughtfully. "With L. it was different. Kundalini was awakened in her with Hatha Yoga practices. That is why she has much trouble. I do what I can to help her, but," he shrugged, "it is in the Hands of God.

"When it is awakened by Hatha Yoga, it becomes a great problem. It is a difficult way. One has to know how to take it up and take it down again through all the chakras, and it is troublesome. But with us, we begin to notice it only when it reaches the heart chakra: it means peace, bliss, states of expanded consciousness. We awaken the 'king', the heart chakra, and leave it to the 'king' to awaken all the other chakras."

In the evening, all was still. The garden seemed to sleep, hardly any traffic sound from the quiet street. He sat on the tachat in a deep state of samadhi. I noticed that he was in a different posture from the usual – not cross-legged but seated on his heels. He stared at me with unseeing eyes, a strange smile playing on his lips. My heart made one big leap in sudden fear ... Have never seen him like this before. Difficult to describe his face – composed of sheer energy. *Devic* [derived from *deva* and meaning 'angelic'] perhaps? Certainly a human face can never have such an expression. The feeling of dynamism, of tremendous power, increased more and more.

I just sat there, my mind not working much. Thoughts, insignificant thoughts, came and went in a kind of slow motion. Perhaps he was doing something to my 'higher vehicles'? But I did not feel anything.

An hour, or even more, passed. A calendar hung on the wall opposite. Could not remember what day it was. On 2 October I came here – seven years after I had learned about Theosophy for the first time. Exactly seven years ... strange.

An ant was crossing the floor – black, very large, about an inch long. Many insects grow to a large size here in India. I watched it for a while, until it disappeared under a chair.

"What thoughts are in your mind?"

His voice startled me. 'Nothing in particular. Just a few silly thoughts.'

"Go home and lie down," he ordered. "Speak to nobody, try to rest; give your mind a rest."

I did not feel that my mind needed a rest but I got up ready to go. 'For how long shall I rest?'

"Oh, half an hour or so; more if you can."

His voice was full of indifference, quite casual. But I understood that something very special had happened. What? There was no way of finding out. Mind was peaceful, body was peaceful. Did not feel sleepy at all.

27

Decided to have an earnest talk with him.

"And how do you feel this morning?" he asked as soon as I sat down.

'May I ask something?'

"You may ask."

'What happened last night?'

"What do you mean by that?" He smiled faintly.

'You must know what I mean'.

"I was out of my body and know nothing."

Told him that I had not slept. He said that he had not slept either and added that he usually only sleeps for about twenty minutes, not more than half an hour. (I knew from L. that the rest of the night he is in deep samadhi.) Told him how fine I felt this morning and explained the meaning of the English expression 'keyed up' – like the strings of a musical instrument which, when given a few turns of the keys, are able to respond to a higher pitch of sound. He nodded.

"It is like that," he said. "Very wonderful things did happen yesterday and this morning." He spoke slowly, looking out of the window. "But the physical body cannot have cognition of them."

In the afternoon, I was alone with him. He was seated cross-legged on the tachat writing letters. When I came in, he gave me one of his faint smiles and continued to write. I waited for an opening and, when he sealed up two envelopes, I offered to post them on my way home. He nodded. "They must go today. Someone is in need of help."

Then I told him what a relief it was for me to know that he belongs to the Hierarchy.

"Hierarchy?" He lifted his eyebrows.

Clearly he did not know what I meant. Though his English was very good, slightly biblical, he had hardly any opportunity to practise it and there were English expressions that he did not know.

I explained what I knew from books about the Great Brotherhood and its function in the world to help with the evolution of mankind. He sat motionless, looking at me. His face was expressionless. I took a deep breath – how my heart pounded. I could not think clearly. I could see that he was listening with the utmost attention.

"And who are they?" He glanced at me sideways with a stern look. A swift feeling of terror came and went; but the abruptness of the question made me laugh.

"Why are you laughing?" He stared hard at me.

I leaned forward. 'Because I do not need to answer this one! Here is one of its members right in front of me!'

He smiled. Then quite unexpectedly, he threw his head back and laughed his boyish laughter. How young he can look, I thought, how amazingly young.

"Yes," he said, still smiling. "But we usually do not mention these things; it is not done."

He carefully and deliberately poised the point of his pen on the sheet of paper and continued to write. Great stillness was in the room. Only the scraping of the pen, the swoosh of the ceiling fan and the wild pounding of my heart.

At last he finished, put the writing material into the recess and reclined, stretching himself comfortably on his back, crossing his hands on the pillow supporting his head.

I knew I could speak. Told him that I had been doubting so much who he was and if I could, if I should, trust him. 'I trust you now; I will not resist anymore – will try not to consciously at any rate. Unconsciously, of course, I cannot know . . .'

"I will take care of that." He closed his eyes.

'Do with me everything that you deem necessary to make me fit for the work because I well realize, as I am now, I am useless for the work you may want me to do.'

"All I can say is that you *are* being prepared for the work."

Suddenly his face assumed the strange look he always has when functioning on a different plane of consciousness – the bottomless depth of his eyes, the inward look, which does not see things of this world.

"Do you remember your previous life?"

'No.'

The reflection of infinitude in his eyes, endless space, divorced from time, seemed to penetrate through my very being.

'But it must have been a bad one,' I continued, 'because I came with bad tendencies into this one.'

"We all have bad tendencies," he replied, and then, as if speaking from very far away, his eyes completely veiled with a kind of blue mist, he added very slowly, "The time may come – I don't say that it will come, *but it may come* – when you will have powers and know many things."

I said that I suspected that I had been evolving on Hatha Yoga lines because in this life, elderly as I am, my body could do all the exercises relatively easily without ever having learned them and that I loved doing them.

"That's why you forgot everything!" Again the boyish laughter.

I knew what he meant. But for some reason I felt hurt.

"You told me that you understand that you will have many difficulties and are prepared to face them. So, you do it from *your own free will*. Remember that. You will suffer injustice and will be hurt where it hurts most – where you are most afraid of being hurt. You do realize that?"

I said that I did. I knew what I was doing but I also felt that *I had no choice.* Then he asked me why I had pledged myself; was it a vision?

'If you mean by a vision that I saw or heard something with my senses, no. But if you mean by vision a clear mental image and a certitude, without any possibility of doubt, then, yes.'

"This must be a link from a previous life – not necessarily the last."

Again his face took on the special expression which so much fascinates and even slightly frightens me.

4 November

Slept badly and restlessly – but it was much better than the previous night.

When reading a book sitting on the veranda after lunch, quite out of the blue, a strange sweetness pervaded my heart. It was such a subtle feeling. As soon as I tried to analyse it, it vanished; and then reappeared again. This feeling – so light, so elusive – had nothing to do with my environment; and it had nothing to do with him either – at least, not directly. Closer to me than breathing, I thought. Yes, that's what it is like. And it is just like the beginning of falling in love. Falling in love with what?

6 November

'How does one get love, Bhai Sahib? How does one get humility?'

"How do you smell the scent of flowers? There is no effort on the part of the flower; neither on your side; just smell it, effortlessly."

'L. told me that since she has known you, she always sleeps well. I have hardly slept for the past three nights.'

"The way of training is different. The time will come when you will say, 'I did not sleep for years'."

'Can one see prana?'

"Yes; but not with the physical eyes. In dhyana, the flow of prana is reversed; but not so in sleep. Reversed in the sense that all the sensory energies are introverted, absorbed in the heart, instead of being extroverted. It is a movement within instead of without, as in the waking state of consciousness or in sleep. For the first few times, the Teacher has to do it and put the shishya in dhyana. Later he learns how to do it himself. Realising Atman is one thing; but to realize Brahman [the Absolute] is something else."

'Can it be done in one life?'

"It can be done, *and it is done*, in one life. From the moment the training begins, the progress continues. Sometimes one gets the realization on one's deathbed. When I misunderstood you yesterday and thought that you were sixty-five and not fifty-five as you really are, I had a doubt in my mind . . ."

'What doubt, Bhai Sahib?'

"You understand, of course, that it is not appropriate to tell people how long they are going to live . . ."

'Oh, Bhai Sahib!' I interrupted. 'Please do not make the training much longer now that you know I am ten years younger! Do not give me the realization on my deathbed!'

"No. For those who are pledged to the work it is done quicker. You know, of course, that all the *karma* [law of cause and effect] has to be burned up; I told you that before. You will have to suffer injustice, you will be attacked, it will hurt."

'Yes, I know. And I am prepared for it.'

✕ 5 ✕

7 November

Today we went to the *Samadhi* [here meaning 'grave, place of rest'] of his father, seven miles from Kanpur. It was fun, the whole of his family and many others, all in lorries.

The Sufi's tomb in a white mausoleum of simple and sober proportions is rather large, open on all sides, the roof supported by columns. The floor is paved with red tiles. It was lit with candles and small butter lamps. The site is surrounded with fields and distant groups of trees. The sky was still pink after the sunset, softly so, with grey clouds. A strong, spicy fragrance, typical of the Indian plains, was in the air.

The atmosphere was very good but not so dynamic as sometimes in the guru's place. Too many people and too much disturbance – children running about making noise. L. said that I think this way because I do not understand. The grave of a Sufi is a highly magnetic place.

8 November

Becoming aware of much peace lately. It has come gradually, creeping up like a thief. I hardly noticed it at first. It is a different kind of peace from the one experienced during the last few years. Before, it used to be a feeling of peace plus joy – life was good. Now it is like a deep, still pool, full of silence and darkness. It could be the background to anything at all – joy can be impressed on it, or love or spiritual dryness or loneliness. It makes me think of the depth of the ocean, always calm in depth even when huge waves are raging on the surface.

9 November

Slept very well. I wonder if the effect of what the guru gave me a few days ago is wearing off? Peace is with me though.

In the last few days, when I have not been able to sleep properly, I have been in a sort of 'half-state' which seems to be a preliminary state of samadhi. It was filled with images – mostly of him or his face, but chiefly of his eyes – all sorts of confused dreams which seemed so real, so intense, larger than life.

31

There was great restlessness in the physical body. In the mornings there has been no tiredness whatsoever; on the contrary, great energy. Every day at dawn I have been on the flat roof doing yogic exercises and have watched the sun rise serenely behind the feathery crowns of distant palm trees.

"You think your kundalini is asleep, but it can wake up at any moment." He gave me one of those penetrating 'unseeing' looks of his.

Then he began to sing. I love it. It is so disturbing. I do not know why. He has a pleasant voice and always sings in Persian or Urdu. As soon as his voice fills the room it is as if I am transported to another place of being. The brain stops working. I do not seem to listen with the mind. These songs of his, monotonous and in a language I do not understand, disturb something very deep within. It is like trying to get hold of long-forgotten memories; just glimpses, which are awakened by his voice and are somehow connected with him. It is as if I know the sound so well – as if it is a part of myself that I cannot understand. When I try to pin it down, it dissolves into nothing, just like mist which disappears before it reaches you.

He translated the song:

"When you are burning with thirst, do not search for water; remain thirsty."

It made me smile. Since yesterday I have had a burning desire for Truth. Deep and strong as never before.

He began another song, a long sad one with a beautiful melody.

"The body of Mohammed threw no shadow. His body was not really physical. Those who are Saints need no garments for they are Beloved of God. *Suf* means wool. Wool is warm. If the heart is warm then there is love. When you see a Saint whose heart is soft and warm, he is a Sufi.

"The Teaching is given according to the state of evolution of the disciple and according to his temperament and conditioning. As he progresses, more aspects of the Truth are revealed."

10 *November*

About midday, there was a wonderful fragrance in the air. As if carried from flowering trees by a gentle breeze, it was all around in the garden. I drew his attention to it and he told me to see if I could find where it came from. But everywhere I went it eluded me. He wanted to know what kind of scent it was and asked if I had ever noticed it before.

I told him that I had smelled it in Kushinagar, the place where Lord Buddha died; and also' at the Samadhi of his father, the other day. Then I had thought it was the smell of the Indian plains. But never had I smelled it in his garden before.

14 *November*

If I knew how painful Love is,
I would have stood at the entrance of the Lane of Love;

I would have proclaimed with the beat of the drum:
Keep, keep away, keep away!
It is not a thoroughfare, there is only one way in;
Once entered, I am helpless, I stay here;
But you who are outside, look out!
Think before entering how painful it is,
Full of sorrow, to walk the Lane of Love!

He looked radiant, singing this Persian song, beating the time on his thigh with the palm of his hand.

L. told me afterwards that Sufis rarely speak directly; they will tell a story, sing a song or tell a parable. It is their way of teaching. 'He might, for instance, speak to me and mean you,' she said. 'One has to learn how to listen. A Teacher has no right to test a disciple, or subject him to any trouble, without a previous warning. The warning is never given directly. Often the disciple does not understand it or is made to forget. But the warning is always given, for Sufis believe in the free will of the individual. The human being must consent. His consenting gives the Teacher the right to act according to the needs of the disciple who, himself, by consenting, draws down the Grace.'

It made me think. Are those songs for me or L.? The one about the painfulness of love . . . I wonder.

16 *November*

"In our system, the Realization is achieved in one life. One need not come back.

"You have been here six weeks. Do you notice how much progress you have made?"

'The mind does not know about it, so how can I know?'

"I didn't ask your mind. I asked *you*."

I thought for a while. 'Yes, Bhai Sahib, there has been a change. I always thought that I wanted Truth badly enough; but now it is like a burning fire inside me, a longing, an obsession.'

Thoughtfully, he looked out of the window. The light through foliage reflected in his eyes and made his skin greenish.

'I suffer lately from heat waves. It usually starts in between the shoulder blades, radiates over the thorax, never lower than the stomach, then mounts to the head making my forehead perspire. It never lasts long – perhaps half to one minute. Is the heart chakra responsible for it?'

"Perhaps it is, but maybe it is not. As a rule, I don't tell which chakras are activated and which are not. The whole of one's life would not be long enough to open all the chakras. In our system it is done by dhyana. I, myself, have changed the system somewhat. I did it with the knowledge of my superiors of course; my Revered Father and my Revered Guru Maharaj. I discovered new chakras; in the Scriptures not all the chakras are mentioned. Not all the occult knowledge is given out at one time. Humanity progresses. The

Teaching, once secret, is now for everyone. At one time, in the past, rich people were not supposed to know about it. But nowadays everyone is taught who wants to know and is earnest about it. *Sannyasis* [ascetics or devotees who have renounced the world], for instance, work mainly through the brow chakra. There is not much love in Sannyasis. In our system the heart chakra is mainly used. Of course, when the heart chakra is open, such force, such power is flowing through it that one forgets everything. One day, my Revered Father got an order from his Guru Maharaj to go and search for Saints and Yogis and ask them one question: 'Can you give me something without an effort on my part?' 'No,' every one of them answered, 'we cannot. Nobody can. Go away.' Have you ever heard of a system like ours where the shishya does not need to make any effort at all?"

He looked at me with a smile and I had to admit that I had never heard of one.

"No effort needed: just come here and sit. Everything is done for you. Why make an effort? Effort does not lead anywhere. If one is a real guru, a *Sat Guru*, and knows how to write on the back of hearts ... The Spiritual Guide does not make conditions; he is like a loving mother. The child can be angry, can run away. The mother does not take it very seriously. She cares for it just the same, and does not love it less. Shishyas can and do leave the guru, but the guru is never supposed to leave the shishya.

"And where can the shishya run away to? The guru and the shishya relationship is forever; if one is pledged to one guru, where can one go? The guru is like an experienced rider: and the experienced rider makes the horse go anywhere he wants. But shishyas are not slaves. They are free. But even when the personality wants to run away, it is difficult for it to do so: the Higher Self knows better. Ours is the system of freedom. But the majority does not like it. People want contortions – Hatha Yoga, Discipline, Mind Control, Meditations. They are not happy otherwise, they think nothing is being done.

"Here, I do not ask you even to pray. Just sit here with me. Even speech is not necessary. Only some things one has to explain; sometimes. We live in the epoch of the mind. Mind – *manas* – is the ruler. Most of the people are not satisfied; they will not accept anything unless at least some kind of explanation is given. Our system has never been widespread; it is for the few. And it is from heart to heart, and the Goal is reached in one life. But how many want the Truth? Are prepared to surrender to the Truth? Not with everyone is it possible. But IT CAN BE DONE."

18 *November*

'Have I understood correctly that in other systems the chakras are awakened one by one, and the life-span of an individual proves to be too short for this process to be accomplished? So it can never be completed in one life? Is it so?'

"In our Yoga System the ultimate result is achieved in one life by dhyana.

34

Only one chakra is awakened; the heart chakra. It is the only Yoga School in existence in which Love is *created* by the spiritual Teacher. It is done with yogic power. The result is that the whole work of the awakening, of quickening, is done by one chakra, which gradually opens up all the others. This chakra is the Leader and the Leader is doing everything. If you want to buy a part of my property, do you go to the property? Certainly not, you come to me. You deal with the proprietor. And in our system we deal only with the Leader. I told you once that we belong to the Raja Yoga system. But when you try to study Raja Yoga from books you will be told: do this, do that, concentrate, meditate, sit in this posture. Today it is obsolete. Times have changed. The world is progressing; these methods have been outgrown. They are dead. But our system is alive; it has preserved its dynamism for it is changing with the times."

19 *November*

Was a bit depressed this morning. Everything seemed to be so difficult, not worthwhile attempting even. At the guru's place this evening I asked many questions for the sake of asking, some of them futile, some silly. I did it just to taunt him. He said I should not do it; it is *sankalpa-vikalpa* [projections, distractions of the mind, restlessness of thought]. It is bad and nothing has ever been solved by the mind. L. told me that I was discourteous and he is far too patient with me.

'Opportunity comes once in a lifetime. If missed, who knows how long you will have to wait for another one ... Lives perhaps; who knows? I feel you are missing an opportunity. Be careful not to miss the boat.' Her eyes, very blue, very serious, had a sad expression. To miss the boat ... A feeling of exasperation seized me. I MUST, I simply MUST ... Somehow, I must stop, must accept ... But how? I did not know ...

22 *November*

Once he said that love is created or produced in the heart of the disciple by the yogic power of the guru.

'How is it done?' I asked L.

'I don't know,' she said simply.

'But how can I be made to love him?' He is a stranger to me! I respect him, he intrigues me, I find him intensely interesting; but love? No, there is none of that and how is it to be understood?

'Well,' she said, 'the disciple progresses through love. Love is the driving force, the greatest power of creation. As the disciple has not enough love in him to have sufficient of the propelling power to reach the Goal, so love is increased, or 'created' simply by activating the heart chakra.'

'But how can I love him just like that?' I was puzzled.

'Are you sure that you will love him?'

I stared at her; 'But,' I began . . .

'Are you quite sure that it is *him* that you will love?'

What did she mean? Could it . . . Could it mean that love is not really for the Teacher, or only apparently so? So, that would mean . . . I understood. And all went very still in me. Very, very still.

"Last week you told me that you wanted a miracle," he said, entering the room. "You said that it would give you faith, will stop your doubts. What was my answer? That you would not have believed it anyhow; besides, miracles are not 'produced' on command, to satisfy a curiosity. But how many miracles did happen to you since you have been here? Whether you sleep or not, it makes no difference; the body is not tired; and, in spite of the very low rhythm of the heart, you feel no tiredness either, but are fit and full of energy."

I said that probably later on my heart will also beat very quickly and I will not sleep at all, or very little, as he does; I was told that after a while the disciple's vibrations are adjusted to those of the Teacher, even on the physical plane. He nodded.

'If I understood you correctly the other day, the teaching is given according to the stage of evolution of the shishya and according to his temperament. Truth is only partially revealed, more and more as the progress goes on. So if I believe in karma and reincarnation, you will talk to me accordingly; to L. who does not believe in either, you do not mention them at all.'

"It is of no importance if one believes in these things, and if one believes or not in the Great Hierarchy; karma *is*; evolution *is*. Humanity is taken along in progress; if they believe in certain things or not, it makes no difference. I never mention those things to Miss L.; what's the use? It is not at all important what one believes in our system of Freedom."

In a sudden glow of affection, I told him how glad I was that I came to him; that it was the most wonderful thing that could happen to me, and whom have I to thank for it?

"Thank your Higher Self!" he said. Somebody came at that moment and we were interrupted.

When L. came this evening we went for a walk, the three of us, the guru, L. and I.

'Recently you have said that we are not even asked to pray; but can we pray?' He said one can if one wants to. Told him that I would write down the prayer I said for years and show it to him; but he answered that prayer is not with words; NEVER.

When asked again he maintained that prayer is perfect Unity with God. Only this is real prayer. When going home, told him that I felt hopelessly discouraged; even do not know how to pray, so it seems. And it would mean that the state of dhyana is a *sine qua non* as to what the spiritual progress is about and I feel like a child left outside the fence when a circus performance is going on inside. Dhyana seems to be a ring-pass-not which one has to go through on the way to God.

⤟ 6 ⤞

23 *November*

I lay down on my bed for a short rest this afternoon. Listening within I noticed a vibration. It was like a motor going inside me, vibrating in the whole of the body; or rather, perhaps, like a soundless, supersonic 'sound', or like the feeling one gets after a row; a strong tension, an excitement without excitement. Parallel with it was a tremendous longing for IT, for that which is nameless. And in this longing was peace; only infinite peace. I know it sounds rather complicated, but it is the best I can do when trying to describe it.

When L. came back from the post office, she told me that it is the famous Mystical Sound and it is called *Dzikr*. It is the preliminary step to dhyana. I was fascinated. Was watching it going inside me; such a new experience.

In the evening a man was sitting opposite the guru telling him his troubles of which he had many. When he left, the guru began to sing. I was sitting there, the 'sound' going on inside me, with a tremendous longing; but for what? I was not quite sure . . . Waited for an opportunity to ask. He sang in Urdu and translated it:

> I will come to you in the shape of a nightingale,
> Many branches are on a tree, on each branch I will Be,
> The nightingale is here, there, everywhere,
> When you will hear it, you will know that I am here,
> The nightingale who at all times is everywhere . . .

The room was dark, full of peace, filled with his voice. It seemed to me that he was singing it for me. I have to love him, I thought. The shishya has to love the guru; one can only progress through love. And love for the guru is love for God. He began another song:

> I am here and I am there and I show myself in different shapes.
> And you may wonder what or who am I and you will not understand.
> But in time the answer is given.
> I am here and I am there and it is all the same,
> Everywhere all the time, am I alone . . .

This one I did not understand and was pondering over it when he began another song:

There must be a complete surrender, even physically,
Surrender of everything without reserve and without regret,
If you want to see the Real Shape of the Guru.
Either the Guru has to come down to you,
Or you must go to him, but a complete surrender is needed,
If you want to see the Real Shape of the Guru!

"Did you get the idea?" he asked. Perhaps it was the answer to my request the other day, to let me see him as he really is, I ventured.

"Yes; either you are a guest on my plane, or I am on yours; but at first a complete surrender is essential, complete surrender, beginning from the physical body and on all the levels."

Told him that I understood, and even told L. a few days ago, that my physical body was going to be subjected to much strain, and I was quite prepared for it, ready for everything which might be necessary to be 'taken in gallop' (his own expression).

"Don't say that you are ready for it; rather say that you are trying to do it; it is better."

'Yes, Bhai Sahib,' I answered, and my heart was so full of gratitude.

"If one is pledged, pledged for spiritual life and work, there is no reserve, a complete surrender on all the planes, when one enters the arena. What is a pledge? It is a promise; never to be broken, never."

'It lasts for ever and ever and ever,' I said softly.

24 November

It was like a burning fire inside my heart today. The longing for God.

"Do you think I speak just for the sake of talking?" he said to L. concerning some matter between them. "Oh no! Every word is said on purpose with meaning! And speaking of love: love can never be hidden: NEVER! It is something which cannot help but shine!"

I asked L. how it is that guru's premises are full of most objectionable people? She answered that this is the Sufi way. All those who are without work, who are rejected by society, the awkward, the too loud, too weak in mind, too sick in body, to these he will give refuge and hospitality. So many people live in his courtyard, and one or two thatched huts are even in the garden.

'Poor wife of his! She must be a saint herself to put up with such conditions!'

'Yes,' said L. 'It cannot be easy to be the wife of a Sufi Saint!'

We had a brief walk in the park in the evening. He was completely 'unconscious', walking swiftly with long strides. L. told me that when we are with him we should try to remain on the outside, to protect him from the traffic, for he is quite unconscious of his physical body.

I dreamed my overcoat was stolen. A man came to me and said: 'It is not stolen, come with me and you will get it.'

"You must know how to interpret this one," he said. He spoke with a stony, severe expression. His eyes were half-closed, cold, looking far off.

'But I can't!' I exclaimed; 'How can I?'

"What could it mean that an overcoat is taken from you? Was it an old coat?" he asked, not changing his severe expression.

'No, a new one, of good material, and I was sorry because I thought that it was stolen and I needed it.' He made a grimace of disgust.

"How can you be so dense? What is a coat? A cover, something to cover your body. The cover has been taken away from you." His face was as stony and as stern as ever. I said that I still couldn't understand.

"Do not insist; it is as I say. You believe in karma. When you are on the path earnestly and seriously, your karmas are taken away from you. Either you have to suffer them, as I have already told you the other day, in your physical life, or they will come to you in dreams. One second of dream suffering is like three years of real suffering in life. When you are on the path you are speeded up, and you pay for it in your dreams. If you stay away from the path, once decided, all the karmas you will pay for in full in your daily life. But once on the path, the Grace of God reaches you, catches up with you and the mental karma will go away in dreams. Emotional sufferings are cleared up by the suffering love causes, but the physical karmas one has to suffer in the physical body. We are not supposed to have another one, if we are with the Teacher. So, clearly, all has to be resolved in the present one. There is a place where karmas cannot reach, if it so pleases God. His Grace is infinite, and karmas fall away from you. Every dream has a different interpretation according to whether the dreamer is a man or a woman. For instance: if a man dreams that the roof of his house is falling in and the house is roofless, it means that he is going to be without work. If a woman dreams the same thing it means that she is going to be a widow.

"One day when I was still young, my Revered Guru Maharaj asked me: 'How much money have you got?' Thinking that he meant how much money I had on me, I said: '200 rupees! Everything has been stolen from me except those 200 rupees!' He laughed merrily; why was I such a fool as to think that he meant the money I had at that moment?"

'Oh, but it is unjust!' I exclaimed. 'If he is a saint and knows everything, why didn't he know that you misunderstood him? He took advantage of the situation, I think it is most unjust!'

"This is a silly remark," he said, this time really annoyed, and went out.

'Don't argue so much,' L. said. 'It is a wrong attitude, try to understand.'

But I was furious and I told him so as soon as he came back. It is so difficult to understand him, he expresses himself in such an obscure way; it is most frustrating!

'I express my thoughts clearly enough but, more ofter than not, you pretend to misunderstand me and, as for me, it is sheer agony to try to understand you! You speak in mysterious parables and often you contradict your own statements!'

"I contradict myself," he said ironically. "I really do not know what I am talking about! What a pity!"

L. told me impatiently that my attitude is wrong and I will achieve nothing by it.

He sent me away soon afterwards because he wanted to give her some explanations on kundalini. I left feeling really angry. And what is this mystery about? Why can't I hear it? Felt humiliated.

25 November

Was disturbed and unhappy. I knew that I had displeased him and it made me worry. Also I couldn't see, for a long stretch, how I can accept the squalid surroundings and sit there for hours, accepting his injustice, the dirty beggars, the smelly, noisy crowd which, as L. told me, assembles during the *Bandhara* [a public ceremony; 'the opening of the gates of grace'].

My heart was very heavy. When L. came that evening, I was already sitting outside, brooding on my unhappy thoughts and watching the delicate sunset in greys and soft pinks, fading gradually in the sky.

"You are here? Come inside please!" I heard his voice.

I went in. He was talking to his wife and baby grandchild. Then he took his blanket and we sat outside. Curled up in his chair, his feet stretched out on the opposite one, huddled in his white blanket, he began to speak.

"When my Revered Guru Maharaj was alive so many people came to him only to hear him speak. He had such a beautiful voice, and he could explain so well that nobody ever misunderstood him; no doubt was left in the heart of anybody." He turned to me, "I realize that my English is not perfect," he continued, "I do not pretend that I never blunder; I am not a master of your language."

I told him that his English was very good; it is his obscure way of expressing himself which confuses me; English is not my own language either.* It is difficult for me to accept anything unless I understand it. But here, I not only don't understand most of the time, but he misunderstands me and accuses me of deceiving him; it becomes a hopeless situation. 'You ask me a question, I give you a straight answer, and you get annoyed with me!' I concluded.

"I am not a god. Only if I concentrate on a thing, I know it; but this is not always possible."

'But in this case it is completely hopeless, for I cannot reach you, neither on the mental nor intuitional level.' I felt dejected. He fell silent.

'The thing which keeps worrying me, and I absolutely cannot understand, is how to love the spiritual Teacher. One cannot say to a human being 'LOVE!' or 'LOVE NOT!' just like that. How can one order such a thing! It simply cannot be done! Love just IS or IS NOT. I respect you immensely; I am fascinated by you; but love? Certainly not, I surely don't love you at this moment.'

"Love is produced; is produced ALWAYS," he repeated. "The shishya cannot love like this by himself. For here is not a question of human love. It is some-

* The author is Russian by birth.

40

thing entirely different, and the relationship with the Teacher is a very difficult one. Love is produced and it continues."

27 *November*

He told us how one must have trouble in order to progress.

"In our system we live in the world, have worries about money, family, and the like. How do you progress without worries? If you are worried you make an effort, you make a leap."

I said that if people have no worries, he will create them for his disciples.

"Well I will not make it so that you should break your arm or leg; but the greatest worry will be when one begins to love the Spiritual Guide. At the beginning there are no worries; the Teacher wants the disciple to remain but as soon as the disciple loves him, as soon as there are no doubts, the troubles commence for the disciple. He will feel like crying 'Why does the Master not notice me, does not speak to me? Is he angry? Why is he here and I there?' and so on. Before this time comes one should run away quickly," he added, looking at me.

"What do you feel exactly?" he said suddenly, sharply, looking at me.

'Well, all the oceans and all the seas of the world seem to be concentrated in my head. Walking down the street I had just enough consciousness left to keep to the right side of the road and not to be run over by the traffic. Crossing the road I could not see where I was going. I thought it was dangerous. I could see only when I looked straight ahead; right and left seemed obliterated as in a mist.

'If I see an object, for instance this chair in front of me, between the image of the chair and the realization that it is a chair and not something else, there is an interval of a fraction of a second. I have to concentrate on each particular sensory object to be able to name it. Indeed Krishnamurti mentions in one of his works that we should abstain from naming the things around us so that the interval between seeing an object and naming it may become longer and longer and it may happen that one day, in that moment, illumination may come.' He nodded.

"You spoke of a miracle a few days ago," he said slowly. "Have you still the courage to speak of miracles? The roar of all the oceans is in your head, or the mind is not there at all, or you don't sleep without being tired, while at my home your thinking process is slowed down so much that you 'sleep'; there is a peace not of this world in you which you cannot explain; or a longing so strong that life is not worth while living; upheavals; premonitions; tell me, are these not miracles? Great and important miracles?"

His voice was soft and very gentle as if full of deep compassion. I lowered my eyes and felt small. Smaller than a grain of sand.

In the evening I went there and was first as usual. When he asked me how I felt, I told him my mind was still not working properly but, during the afternoon, while I was writing my diary, it was not too bad. He asked me when I was going to Benares. Checking on the calendar hanging on the wall near the door, I suggested that perhaps I could go on the 4th of December, which is a Monday. He said that he had to go to Allahabad, and he never travels alone; he will come with me, will be met at Allahabad, and I could proceed to Benares. "I will let you know by tomorrow."

I asked him if my brain will continue to be so numb and inefficient while having to travel, because if so, it may prove to be very uncomfortable.

"It will be noted down in my diary."

'Do you mean to say that you will note down in your diary when you have to give me back my wits?' I laughed and he only nodded. That made me laugh even more, at which he joined in. He was grinning into his beard while writing something on a piece of paper which later he gave to his son, with some added instructions in Hindi. I asked some questions:

'Why does the memory not work well at all? Does the memory belong to the mind?'

"The memory does not work well because manas (mind) has been suspended, and though the memory does not belong to the mind, strictly speaking, for it has a different centre, still it has to work *through* the mind. This path of our system is not at all troublesome; it is the easiest path. It seems difficult only when there is confusion."

Well, it seems clear that there has been plenty of confusion in my mind for the last few weeks . . .

"TO ENTER THE ARENA IS TO ACCEPT THE PATH OF THE MASTER."

"The world is for us as we create it: if you say there is a *bhut* [ghost] in the tree, then there will be a bhut for you. This is all manas.* But what is manas? Nothing. Manas is *maya* [illusion]. You want everything but are not prepared to make sacrifices, to pay the price. Here they sit and say: 'I was intelligent, now I cannot even think, where is my memory, what happened to me?'

"People are not prepared to give anything up. If you want to go anywhere you will have to take the train or the plane, you are expected to pay the fare, is it not so? Be always a friend of the Almighty and you *will never die*. Prayer should be done always, even in ordinary prayer; but of course the only *real* prayer is merging, *oneness* with God. Only this is a true prayer. Once we have reached this point within us, we do not need any more factional support."

I keep wondering what will be done, what will happen about this question of love . . . Love will be produced. So he said. Produced? How, I wonder?

29 *November*

"Why are you here?" he asked turning to me. "You have stayed here for the last two months; you did not receive anything. I gave you nothing and still you are here, why?"

* According to the Sufi System there are three activities of the brain: *manas* (mind); *memory*, working through manas; *unconscious*, where all the memories of the heart are kept.

'Because I think that it is the right thing to do,' I answered.

"No!" he retorted. "You stay here because your heart wants you to do so. There is something in the heart, a substance which makes you do so."

'You are right; that's why from the very beginning I could not go away and was so disturbed by discovering this fact. I value freedom so much and hate to be forced to do anything. There is a mystery hidden somewhere and my mind was much frightened. I suspect that the mind was afraid as it knows that it will be the loser. The mind is strong and it will give trouble. Only it looks to me as if you are knocking it out altogether.' I smiled doubtfully. But he only laughed his kindly laugh.

Later he said to L. speaking of somebody:

"Your attitude has to force the Master. Your life has to be lived in such a way that he sees that you are in earnest and is forced to accept you."

1 December

"Do Christians believe in evolution?" he asked.

'Some do,' answered L.

"Does science believe in evolution?"

'Yes,' said L., 'science does; but for plants, animals, etc; many scientists even believe that man has been created through evolution.'

"How does one prove to an atheist the existence of God? By letting him experience it?"

'Yes, I suppose this will be the only way to make him believe in God.'

This for me, I thought. He speaks to L. but it is meant for me. He knows that I believe in evolution and that I don't really believe in God . . .

2 December

Sitting in the darkness after sunset in my usual place, I prayed. How easy is prayer now! Never could pray like this before! The mind is still, transparent, as though paralysed, and the heart flies away like a trembling bird . . . Flies away into the peace of . . . God? Or just peace?

3 December

I dreamed that the storm was approaching from the sea. Huge black clouds rolling on and on, nearer and nearer. I began to close the windows on the side of the approaching storm but left open those on the other side of the house, thinking they were safe because facing the sun; the sky was still blue and clear on this side of the horizon.

"The dream is incomplete. Not much use telling you what it could mean, because it will only mislead you. I have told you that the past will come up in dreams now, as the time goes on. Ninety nine and a half per cent of the karmas

43

will be dealt with in dreams; the remaining half per cent, of course ..." He fell silent looking into the far distance. Into my past or into my future? I wondered, observing his calm, serene brow – the perfect stillness.

The sky was so blue, so beautiful this morning, so fragrant the air. Winter is so lovely in the Indian plains. Deep is my love for you, beautiful India. So manifold, so incomprehensible, darkly mysterious for us from the West.

'Bhai Sahib, what is being done to my heart? It goes completely mad. Stops beating, races, stops again, goes slow, and is fluttering like a bird caught in a cage.'

We were sitting outside, he had his mala sliding slowly through his fingers, lips hardly moving in silent prayer. 'Please do remember that I have to travel. I would not like anything to happen while I am away. If it does I leave everything and take the first train to you!' He smiled.

"Of course when you go away things can happen. A disciple came to a Sufi Saint and said to him: 'I wish this night will never end and there shall be no morning for me tomorrow!' The Saint touched by so much love did not pray for it, but for days there was no morning for the disciple, no sun rose for him."

'But I do not understand what it has to do with me being afraid of something happening when I am away; though it certainly is a lovely story.'

I said, after a while, 'The mind seems not at its best just now.' He smiled again. "All I wanted to say is that many things could happen if one loves. When L. had left here for the first time years ago, such currents of love were flowing that even the people here used to ask me about her and how she was."

But do I love? It does not seem so.

Later on I referred to prayer, and the answer he gave me some time ago that prayer with words is of no use at all, which discouraged me.

He said that he does not explain well enough sometimes; perhaps it has to do with the language. Prayer with words is all right if it is accompanied by the prayer of the heart.

"If the heart is praying, it is all right. 'If your heart has heard your prayer, God has heard it,' says a Persian song! Mohammedans pray five times a day, but many repeat words only mechanically. What is the use of that? Try to understand me, what I really mean; do not stick to the words, then we will overcome the language barrier."

'It may come later, Bhai Sahib; for the moment it seems to me you are asking the impossible. But since the mind does not work at its full speed prayer goes wonderfully well, as never before.' Again the smile, so very still. He closed his eyes. Looking at him, I kept wondering why his eyes were full of tears when he was telling me the story of the Saint and the disciple who did not see the morning. Perhaps it was his own experience with his beloved Guru Maharaj, as he reverently calls him.

My sleep these days is full of colourful dreams which I forget immediately. The only thing I know is that he is present in all my dreams. Never have I dreamt of anybody to such an obsessive extent. He is in all my dreams, as naturally as if he belonged there, as if he were always part of my dream life, in the very depth of myself. Told him last week about it. He said nothing, only smiled as he so often does of late.

⚔ 7 ⚔

6 *December*

Benares was lovely, full of shimmering light, bustle and sunshine.

Have found a marked difference in myself. I seem to have lost all interest in everything. When taking part in conversation, I have to make an effort to fol-low, because it interests me so little and the mind is not flexible, not very sharp. Have neither the desire to go back nor to remain; have much peace though. When looking at the trees, the flowers, the lovely transparent sky, had moments as if suddenly thought was completely suspended in nothingness; just looking, just feeling. The same dream quality which I had so often as a child alone with nature, and which I had lost completely after my school days, re-turned sharp and clear, only deeper, clearer; almost frightening to the mind. It comes without warning in fleeting moments, and every time it happens for a second or more, who knows? I am lost in it; but then it is immediately drowned in a kind of fear. The mind panics in this state of blissful non-being and I caught myself making desperate efforts to remember where I was and to link this state to memory which has disappeared somewhere for the time being. Naturally I succeeded in remembering quickly, but the blissful state was gone.

11 *December*

Back in Kanpur saw Bhai Sahib only twice for a short time. Quite out of the blue got a flat. Two tiny rooms, whitewashed, clean, in a house belonging to some Indian Christians. I took it in a flash, had no choice. And from the 1st of January I can move in. When I told the Guru about it, he approved. He had seen it with L. last evening. Now, when I return, there will be no worry about accommodation. One obstacle for my stay here has been removed.

"No, no," he said quickly, "no obstacles whatsoever!"

Once more he told me not to make any engagements after coming back from Madras.

"The flat is good for the moment. We will do a lot of work there," he said; and that was enough for me.

13 *December*

And so it came ... it slipped itself into my heart, silently, imperceptibly, and I looked at it with wonder. It was still, small; a light-blue flame trembling softly, and it had the infinite sweetness of first love, like an offering of fragrant

45

flowers made with gentle hands, the heart full of stillness and wonder and peace.

"Love will be produced," you had said. And since then I kept wondering how it will come to me. Will it be like the Voice from the Burning Bush, the Voice of God as Moses heard it? Will it be like a flash of lightning out of a blue sky making the world about me a blaze of glory? Or will it be, as L. suggested, that you will produce Love in general, Love for everything, and the Teacher will be included in it? But I told her that it could not be so for me; to be able to surrender completely, to sweep away all resistance, it must be big, tremendous, complete; without reserve; without limit; the conditionless, absolute, forgetting oneself.

But what I felt was not so. It was just a tender longing, so gentle, so full of infinite sweetness.

Like all laws governing this universe, love will follow the way of least resistance. In all my life I never knew the feeling of love flashing suddenly into my heart. It always came softly, timidly, like a small flower at the side of the road, so easily crushed by the boots of those who may pass by; growing slowly, steadily, increasing until it became vast, sweeping like a tidal wave, engulfing everything that stood in its way and at last filling all my life. So it was in the past and this time too; it is coming to me in the same way. I suppose because our hearts are made in a certain way we cannot help being what we are.

16 December

Adyar was as lovely as ever, and so fragrant with many flowering shrubs and trees. Looking up to the deep blue sky, as was my habit, I saw your face, my Guruji, clearly outlined against the azure of the sky. Perhaps not exactly your face – but the expression of it. As I have seen it when you smile; first with your eyes and then it deepens to vanish into the beard; or the faraway look and the blank expression, when, still and composed, you slide the beads of the mala through your fingers; or the face as if cut out of stone, hard, severe, as old as the hills, as ancient as humanity.

When I came to you a little more than two months ago, I knew nothing about Sufism. Nothing of its glory, its tradition, its boundless freedom, its never-ending love! It was like a revelation and I realized how much I had missed by not knowing it before. Even the little I have learned about it fills me with enthusiasm. Once more I thanked my good star (or my destiny) for guiding me to you.

18 December

"Light will come to thee from longing."* I don't know anything about the Light, but I certainly have longing. It is strong and even, constantly going on like a call from far away.

In Adyar, everywhere one is within the sound of the sea. The sandy beach is

* Quotation from a Sufi poet from Sind.

46

very shallow; one can walk far out and the water is still only to the knees. The long, tall waves roll on majestically from afar in steady succession. Just before they curve over when breaking downwards, crested with white foam on the top edge right inside the curve, it is green, translucent with the light of the rising sun behind. And right there in the curve, in the liquid green, there was your face.

Your face looked at me from every lotus flower; it was inside the hibiscus flowers, in every one of them; in the dark water of the pond itself, it was quietly looking at me. Then I knew that there was no escape; that I had reached the end of my road and where I will be going from now on there will be no return for me.

"To make a Saint takes no time," you had said. "But who is prepared to sacrifice everything? That this world should be nothing, non-existent for you anymore; who is prepared to accept it?"

I think I do. For the process had already slowly begun before I met you. Gradually I seem to lose interest in everything. Nothing pleases me. Not the beautiful surroundings, nor interesting people, lectures, friends. Lectures are only words and so many of them meaningless anyhow. People have so little love, are encased in themselves, and even the loveliness of the landscape is nothing if I have to be separated from you.

You said to us that complete surrender is necessary, but now I read that more than that is required. The condition of self-annihilation is demanded from the disciple in your system. Self-annihilation in the Master.

'The latter ascertains by his own powers whether the Union is perfected. If this is so, the disciple is passed to his Teacher's Master, the Spiritual Influence of the original Founder of the Path, or System, to which they belong. This Founder, of course, is long since deceased and for a time the disciple can only come into conscious relationship with him by the aid of his first Teacher. In time the consciousness of the disciple becomes so absorbed in this great Master as to possess all his Spiritual Powers.

'He is then passed still higher up his chain until he reaches "self-annihilation" in the Prophet. By the Prophet is here understood, not Mohammed as man, but as the Primal Element, the First Intelligence, the Word. Beyond lies only the last, the final stage – "Union with God, Truth," what you will. Words are meaningless; it is beyond all telling and the Sufi says: "From him who has made the journey, no news returns." '*

So, this is the Goal of Sufism. How could you say, as you told us again and again, that it is an effortless path? Why do you choose to deceive your disciples? But you will not deceive me. I never believed such a thing and I told you so. Maybe it is effortless for those who are content to sit with you for years, get a bit of dhyana because they are not prepared to pay the whole price, are afraid to go further. But if one goes out for the Whole Thing and is prepared to give up everything for it, to stake everything on one card without reserve; how can that be effortless?

* From the text of J. M. Watkins on Sufism.

Like birth, creation is a painful process. To be able to create, one has to destroy first, and destruction is synonymous with pain. I have seen people who have been with you for the last forty years and they are still petty, still full of the small self. I do not want that. To reach the goal you have to be turned inside out, burned with the fire of love so that nothing shall remain but ashes and from the ashes will resurrect the new being, very unlike the previous one. Only then can there be real creation. For this process *is* destruction, creation *and* love. Another name for Love is Pain and Effort.

⊰ 8 ⊱

24 *December*

I don't sleep well. The roar of the sea is obsessive and I know that from now on the sound of the waves will be synonymous with longing in my memory. Like longing this sound goes on and on, like an obsession, never-ending, all night, all day. While walking alone was thinking of my discovery that in the whole of the Universe there is nothing else but the Lover and the Beloved. This is the Truth; they are the only two, the only reality is this. God and His Creation and the Creation loves God and God loves his Creation. Nothing else has a meaning but that alone. The more I think of it and turn it over in my mind, the more I discover how true it is and how everything absolutely is of this quality, which ultimately will be resolved in Unity. When this day comes then I will be born again . . .

2 *January* 1962

When back in Kanpur felt disappointed for he did not speak to me, actually ignored me completely. He went out with his wife and L. for a walk, returning with a rickshaw. I sat alone in the garden while they all went inside. It begins to be rather cold in the evenings; the air felt damp. After a while I approached the door of his room asking if I could come inside. He did not answer. He was lying on his tachat, hands crossed under his head, looking at the ceiling. I sat down. Then all his family came in and began a never-ending chatter, children making such a noise; it was very trying. This pandemonium went on and on; the wife began to massage his feet; then a young man took over. Poor L. was trying very hard to be in dhyana. I got more and more restless. To make things even worse the boys put the radio on. A female voice, harsh and vulgar, began to howl a song from a film. Then Bhai Sahib began to sing. It was too much for both of us. I saw L. cringe but she said nothing. The voice of a Saint and a 'prostitute' competing with each other. I got up wanting to leave but he said, in general, not really talking to me directly, that *prasad* [food which has been blessed] will be distributed so I understood that I had to stay. The noise of the radio grew louder and louder, everybody talking their heads off, especially the wife and the young man who was a police officer, discussing some local event which amused everybody. I got up and left abruptly; could not bear it a moment longer.

I was already in bed when L. came. She told me he was annoyed. I behaved discourteously.

3 *January*

He ignored me completely. When I come in and salute him there is no response, as if I did not exist. Well . . . here I am; I was prepared to be accepted as his disciple, hoped to get teaching, and he does not even notice me.

4 *January*

I must do something about it . . . Must speak to him. He must know that I returned to become his disciple and yet he behaves in such an irritating way.

But he is not well. Coughing much and he is weak; one can see it very plainly. I had better tell him my intentions as I should have done as soon as I returned. Better to tell him exactly what I want – that is to get some tuition and to be accepted by him. I arrived here with a notebook, prepared to take some notes, but he speaks mostly in Hindi, so it is not much use . . .

About midday, L. left with his grandchild to buy a toy. He got up at once in order to go inside. Just managed to catch him:

'Bhai Sahib, I would like to speak to you!'

He reluctantly sat down again. It was clear that he was irritated, though he tried to look polite. But I too was annoyed; I simply had to speak to him, so I really did not care. We were in the garden, he seated near the wall beside the door of the large room; I was opposite to him seated on a chair.

'Bhai Sahib,' I began, 'I came back to await your orders.'

"Yes, yes," he interrupted me, hurriedly, "I know, I know."

In this moment my heart stopped, my head began to spin, my breath came out in gasps; this time I was even more annoyed with myself, to be such a fool, to behave like a stupid girl in his presence; also I saw that he wanted to go; anger rose in me.

'You who are a maker of Saints and know how to write on the back of human hearts; write on the back of my heart one letter; one letter only: that of *Alif*! Write it with living fire, to be consumed at your feet with eternal longing!'

I stopped, looking at him. I thought it was a good speech; I quoted his own words, and I said my own bit; it should have made at least some impression on him . . .

"Yes, yes," he repeated impatiently. His face was expressionless, stony and cold.

I really got angry now. I leaned forward: 'I challenge you to produce love,' I said, and I laughed. It must have sounded defiant for I was angry.

49

He kept looking right ahead, his face still with no expression. And then, with a voice which seemed not to be his own, but sounded as if coming from very far – from across eternities, flashed suddenly through my mind:

"Many people have challenged me, about many things, many people did . . ."

'And so? Do you accept the challenge?' I insisted; I was still laughing. I saw him stiffen. He looked suddenly as old as humanity, as ancient as the hills; when, with this very empty, far away look of his, the face hollow as if dessicated with age, very slowly, very softly, with a small, thin voice he said in a kind of sing-song:

"I accept the challenge . . ."

'Khanna [food]!' called out his wife, appearing at the door. He got up. "You can go; I am going to have my lunch." His voice was his usual again. He went in and closed the door behind him. He had tears in his eyes.

I sat alone for a while. Felt the cool wind on my cheeks. Fresh January day in the plains, I thought mechanically. Had a poignant feeling of great meaning. Felt uneasy for some reason. Something was set in motion. Could it be a milestone, a turning point? Then I too got up and went home to cook myself something to eat.

5 *January*

In the morning he did not speak to us at all, only in Hindi. Many people were present, mostly from the province. My small notebook was hidden in my handbag – just in case . . .

"What do you know about the Sufi Tradition?" he asked in the afternoon.

'Not much,' I answered. 'Only what I have read in a few books when in Adyar.' And as far as I understood, in the Sufi literature, surrender, as he used to emphasize, is not the end: a complete self-annihilation in the Master is required. The Master will ascertain, by means of his powers, if the Union is complete, and then will pass the disciple to his Master who is not in the physical body anymore. At the beginning the disciple cannot communicate with the Master's Master, but later he will learn how to do it by himself, and at the last stage the pupil is passed on to the Prophet, not as Mohammed, as man, but as God, the Supreme Essence.

He listened attentively, nodding his assent from time to time and murmuring: "Yes, yes, correct."

'But this is such a tremendous goal. It will require a supreme effort of the whole being; how can you say that is effortless? Why do you deceive your disciples by telling them that it is effortless? How can such a thing be effortless when it is beyond even any possibility of imagination?'

"You will see later how effortless it is," he said softly, and his face had infinite compassion, and I felt disturbed; for I instinctively knew that it was I who was the object of his compassion.

"You were explaining to me your idea of merging into the Master," he said later, sitting himself beside me on the tachat. I said that I did not know if this was *the* merging; only the Sufi book speaks of the complete annihilation into the Teacher.

"Yes, I know," he continued, "that is difficult. It takes time and for that purpose you must completely change your attitude Your attitude is wrong! Completely wrong! I never criticized my superiors."

'What is meant exactly by attitude? The right attitude of the mind?' I ventured, hoping to get some clear definition.

"No, of the heart. The right attitude of the heart! Mind is nothing!"

'Then help me; give me longing, intense longing, and sorrow, and fear and love. The other name for longing is love,' I said.

"Yes," he said slowly, "yes, love and longing are one and the same thing; they are synonymous." He kept nodding, with his vacant, far away look, as if seeing something very far in the distant future.

Somebody came in and he began to talk in Hindi. I sat there puzzled. He turned to me: "You will know later what I mean."

All the while, sitting near L., I kept wondering what he meant exactly by the wrong attitude. Suddenly I understood. It was like a flash.

"Yes?" he enquired turning towards me as if I had said something.

'I have got it!' I said.

"And what have you understood?"

'What I seem to have understood is that if I want the whole thing I must behave accordingly. To follow the Tradition the pupil has to obey implicitly.' I smiled at him.

"Yes, this is good enough; it is a beginning," he smiled back. He sent me away earlier than L. and, when I was leaving, I saw this beautiful smile I loved so much and had missed all those days ...

6 *January*

Did not sleep last night, was thinking and thinking. I must change radically.

"Please don't think that I am displeased with you," he said, "if I speak to you like this. If I am really displeased you can sit here for years and you will get nothing."

I got nothing in those last few days and my heart was so full of longing, full of desire to go on. I really must try to swallow everything; must change completely. This morning decided to behave as everybody else. I got up when he came in; I will do that from now on. I saw that his best disciples do it. It seemed to me that he gave me an ironic smile; but perhaps I was mistaken and it was not ironic after all!

In the evening, having spoken all the time in Hindi, he suddenly turned to me:

"Mrs Tweedie, how are you?"

'Thank you, I am well.'

"Did you sleep well?" he enquired. I said that I had not slept since midnight at all.

"And why?" he wanted to know.

'Thinking,' I said.

"Thinking what?" Told him that I was reflecting on his words about me changing my attitude. He kept nodding.

"Yes," he said slowly, "Plenty to think about, isn't it?" He did not speak to me anymore but when I was leaving there was again this lovely smile.

7 *January*

Mr Chowdhary and another disciple were already in the room when I came in. They are usually both in dhyana. I sit quietly in my corner and begin to wait. Listening to hear his step. He sweeps in quickly, seating himself on the low tachat, but does not speak to me. It is like a secret bond, a feeling of unity, a kind of complicity in something that only he and I know. Like a tuning of the whole of my being into him. Nothing is said. A smile and a nod when I leave. That is all.

He told us that he is leaving for Lucknow. Before he left in the afternoon, he told us to come as usual every day the same as when he is here.

"If you only come when I am here it means you are selfish, wanting to get something. Service is an attitude of the heart." I told him that it will be difficult to sit here without him, because of the boys throwing stones at us. He will tell his wife he said. Would he please not disturb his wife with such trivial matters I said, hoping to get out of the unpleasant duty to sit here alone.

"My wife will not mind," he said, "we like guests. Guests for us are sacred. We always have guests having food with us; five or six people every day. No, you are welcome; why should my wife mind? Our culture is different, we are never disturbed."

So I came and sat there amongst fighting, dirty children . . .

8 *January*

His brother was sitting with us in the morning in deep dhyana. Suddenly I noticed that my heartbeat changed. It was quite noticeable and quite sudden. It went powerfully, very rapidly like a big powerful pump, on and on and I listened to it thoughtfully. It was an ordeal to sit in the garden exposed to the curiosity of the urchins playing deliberately around my chair, urinating and excreting and smelling dreadfully. Had to complain to his brother but could not complain constantly. As soon as he left, they did it all over again.

9 *January*

In the late afternoon, the guru came back. Tried to tune in to his thought process. One simple thought is not too hard, but to catch the complete thought process is very difficult. Today I tuned into him for a fraction of a second in longing. This longing has been in me for the last few days. It goes with the more rapid heartbeat, powerful, strong like a pull, and sometimes it is as if the whole body is being drained away in the intense longing, leaving a kind of languor behind. I just sat there as usual praying to him to give me more of it, of this longing, for I can stand a lot more. More longing, more fear, strong and endless, and it should be like a liquid fire in my veins instead of blood ... It was then that for a split-second I reached him in longing somewhere. He was in deep samadhi and I was with him in infinite bliss, infinite pain of non-ending longing ...

11 *January*

'Can you make this longing stronger?' I asked, bending forward. He shook his head.

"No, this is not my method of training. I do it by and by; gradually. An exception was made for my elder brother by my Revered Guru Maharaj. I do it differently. One cannot give food intended for six months at one go. Little by little."

Later he said: "Never worry; leave the worry to me!" He laughed kindly.

"Bodies are different. Need different kinds of nourishment; some need laughter, then they shall go where there is laughter; some need solitude."

I knew that he meant L. and me. She needs laughter and reproached me because, according to her, I have no sense of humour. I know I need solitude.

12 *January*

Day after day to sit in these squalid surroundings. Amongst the screaming, noisy horde of the dirtiest children, all running about the place, roaming freely everywhere, is at times beyond endurance. Twice I cried in sheer despair. But the most frustrating fact is that I do not get a single question answered. As soon as I ask a question, everybody present begins to discuss it expressing their opinion, in which I am not the least interested, for I want *his* answer. But he will sit there listening to everybody, smiling politely, until in utter despair I say that it was I after all who had asked the question and wanted his answer and as I do not get it, only a lot of useless arguing from everybody else, I won't say anything anymore. He just turns to me and smiles in the most maddening way.

It is of no use to be resentful and fight against the circumstances and create a barrier. I will not change India, nor the people, nor his environment. It is much better to make up my mind to bear them patiently. So much more, because I had ample proof that in no matter what beautiful surroundings I am, I don't see them; I long instead to be in his presence. I saw it happen in Adyar.

"Criticize yourself, criticize yourself constantly and you will get somewhere."

13 *January*

He came in with his light step, blanket under his arm. He was smartly dressed because his daughter who lived somewhere in the north was expected sometime about mid-morning. He chatted with his disciples and seemed to

53

sparkle. I saw his profile, his beard, the lively expression when speaking and laughing, and for the first time I noticed a special light around him. A kind of luminosity; I kept staring at it. Durghesh, his daughter, who is pregnant, arrived with some members of his family who had met her at the station and they all went inside.

He came out after a while and sat with us for a long time, talked a lot and was very kind. The feeling of power was tremendous, I felt as tense as a spring.

But in the evening he was not well. From what he said it seems that it was not his own fever, but somebody else's, which he had taken upon himself.

14 *January*

This morning he looked wonderfully well again, the bluish light from the window on his bronze skin made his face look noble, even regal. I prayed for him.

Later, when we were all sitting outside, he told me not to go to bed immediately after a meal, but to walk up and down in the room, or pray, or meditate for a while.

"As soon as you lie down sleep comes; this is not good. Try to meditate and fall asleep while meditating."

⋇ 9 ⋇

15 *January*

Meditated last night as ordered. It went like fire and never before could I pray as I did. Now, prayer seems to come from the heart, without effort seemingly and it is pouring out of the soul to God . . .

Could not sleep well; was awake from 2 a.m. Each time I pray I see his face clearly before me; it is as if I would pray to him. Is it because my God has no attributes? Infinity of Life, the Eternal Immutable Law? Is it because he is the mediator between IT and me that I see his face and seem to pray to him?

16 *January*

I am reduced to the state that I mentally see his picture everywhere . . . not for one second am I alone. Strange . . . a fire is burning somewhere deep inside the body, but I cannot locate it. There is a feeling of heat and wherever I look I see him in everything; it is as if he were all-present and the whole world is he.

54

This morning between sleep and waking I saw his face in blinding light, the beard standing out like living flames, the eyes unseeing, terrible . . . the eyes of deep samadhi. The face is smiling at me; it is like an irresistible call this smile and I throw myself into it like a swallow diving in flight. For a split-second there was a moment of the most perfect, unbelievable bliss, hard to bear. As if the utmost bliss and the utmost pain were one, the very same thing, not separated, and I knew clearly that there is no difference between absolute happiness and absolute pain. It is only our reactions to it. My heart was still beating wildly when I became completely conscious and the vision was gone.

19 *January*

He came out this morning, dressed in white, and as though lit with eternal light. He seemed to sparkle even though his health is not good. He is weak and has not been eating for days. I just look and look. This light; where is it coming from? Radiating from his skin it seems, and is all around him as well. My mind became blank with the suddenness of a switch turned off. Nobody spoke. His lips pressed tightly, he looked far away.

"What happened last night?" He asked suddenly looking me straight in the eyes. He startled me.

'I don't remember,' I stammered, 'no memory at all; but please do tell *me*!' I said it timidly for his face was so cold and severe. He shook his head.

"Such things are not told, if you don't remember. But manas helps sometimes," he added thoughtfully. And then closed his eyes.

And sometimes it doesn't, I thought. Felt completely dazed; could not keep my thoughts together. Like frightened mice they seemed to dash about. Manas . . . How right he is: manas is nothing! For there *is* something else; so tremendous, so wonderful, and manas is helpless; it knows nothing about it.

Then he proceeded to tell us how one merges into one's Teacher, when two Souls become one.

"When I was young with my first wife, I rarely had intercourse with her. Every night I merged into my Revered Guru Maharaj. There can be no greater bliss imaginable than when two Souls are merging into one with love. Sometimes the body is also merged. How is it done? The body partakes of it, is included in it, by reflection, so to say. And no bliss in the world is greater than this: when you are one with your Teacher."

20 *January*

There is this question of surrender. I wanted to know more about the merging; it was not at all clear to me. How can one achieve the physical surrender on higher planes of consciousness? He always said that physical surrender is essential as well. I cannot imagine how it can be done? How can one understand the possibility of reconciliation of the dense physical and of the atomic level?

'Please help me I feel so confused,' I pleaded. I was lost and discouraged, thinking and thinking, getting nowhere trying to understand something which seemed completely beyond understanding. He listened smilingly, lightly fingering his mala.

"I did not want to mention it to you before," he said quietly, "some things one should not mention freely until the time comes. As you have said it yourself, the surrender of the body can be achieved much deeper, more intimately and more completely than in the sexual union. In sexual union there will always be two. How can there be oneness? But it is done and it can be done. I told you yesterday, the Atman, or the Soul, pervades the body, is present in every cell, every atom of the body; so you see, spirit merges into spirit; there are not two bodies as on the physical level – but one. That's why it is so complete. Physically, naturally there will always be two in union; but not so in spirit. There is nothing to understand really ... so simple." He smiled.

'But how will the mind reconcile it? To understand it seems impossible.'

"Manas will be able to reconcile it, by and by. Let time come." I had to be content with that.

He looked so well today, no tiredness, his face shining with golden glow, the eyes full of light, difficult to look into, and difficult to bear his gaze.

People began to arrive. Plenty of people. Much talk and laughter. Some were sitting as usual in deep dhyana. He was full of fun and sparkle, laughing and joking. He had a great sense of humour; he could laugh at himself and at others but in such a way that it never did hurt; he never hurt anybody's feelings.

It was a windy day. White clouds were chasing each other. He sat on his chair, legs drawn up, chin resting on his knees, the conversation was mostly in Hindi. Suddenly he turned to me:

"Supposing there are four doors leading into the Spiritual Life: one of gambling, one of drink, one of theft and one of sex. And supposing you are told that you have to pass through one of them in order to reach spirituality; what would you do?" He looked at me with a radiant smile. I had to avert my eyes: he was surrounded by blinding light; even his white garment seemed to emanate light. My heart made a jump against the ribs. I caught my breath. The mind became completely empty. I looked at him helplessly.

'He asked you a question about the doors and you have not answered it!' said L. He looked at me expectantly, I felt all eyes on me.

'I don't know the answer, my dear,' I answered, trying to control my wild breathing. He repeated it again:

"Well, what will you do, tell me, if it is only through these doors that you can reach your God?" He laughed now outright, looking straight at me.

It always creates a difficult situation; I cannot even think when he looks at me; and to speak – well, I am conscious that I make a muddle of it ... This time the effort to be coherent seemed superhuman.

'Well,' I hesitated, 'well, I suppose that if I have to take the door of gambling I will have to gamble first, in order to pass through it; if it is the door of drink, I suppose I have to get drunk; if of theft, I have to steal something, and if ...' and here I stopped. There were many people sitting, looking at me, mostly men, listening to every word.

"And if it is the door of sex?" he asked with a wicked twinkle in his eyes and just a suggestion of a smile.

'Well I suppose I will have to do that too,' I said quickly. I was really perplexed, not knowing what he was driving at. He threw his head back and laughed heartily, greatly amused. I don't know why but I had a sudden feeling of a foreboding. His laughter ... Why? Somehow it made me shiver ... Then he told us that we are all going to a concert tonight.

"Dress smartly," he addressed L. and me. So will I.

"We Sufis are lovers of beauty. Because we have renounced the world, it does not mean that we should look miserable. But neither do we want to stand out and attract undue attention. We do not wear special robes, because that might create a barrier between other people and us. We behave like others, we dress like others. We are ordinary people, living ordinary lives. We are smart with smart people, simple with simple ones; but we never give a bad example; we will always lead a life of highest morality. We will always obey the law of the land in which we live; but in reality we are beyond the laws of men for we obey only the law of God. We surrendered somewhere: we are completely free!"

The concert was lovely. Never, oh never, have I enjoyed music so much in all my life! I became the sound, the music itself.

With my head full of lovely Indian music I went to bed. It was then at this moment, just when I stretched out comfortably, pulling the blankets over me, that to my surprise I felt a vibration, a sound in the lower part of my abdomen. I sat up in surprise. No, I was not mistaken; it was a sound and I listened to it; never felt anything like it before ... It sounded like a soft hiss, and felt like a gentle tickling as if of butterfly wings; a kind of flutter, or rather a spinning sound like of a wheel. Very strange. A suspicion flashed through my mind that perhaps it was leading to some kind of trouble, but what? There was a deep, dark fear, but where? It was so foreign to my body, so unusual, so out of the blue ...

It did not take me long to discover. Without the slightest indication that it may be coming, I was flooded with a powerful sexual desire. It was just the desire, for no object in particular, just the desire, *per se*, uncontrollable, a kind of wild, cosmic force ... I sat there helpless, shaking with fear ... Good heavens, what was happening? Tried to listen, to *feel* from where this vibration came, where it was exactly. Then I knew; it was at the base of the spine, just above the anus. I could feel it there distinctly. It must be the *muladhara chakra* [psychic centre at the base of the spine]. I went ice-cold with terror ... This was the *coup de grace*!, I thought; he has activated the chakra at the base of the spine and left the kundalini there to ... to what?

57

The most terrifying night of my life began. Never, not even in its young days had this body known anything even faintly comparable, or similar to this! This was not just desire; it was madness in its lowest, animal form; a paroxysm of sex-craving. A wild howling of everything female in me, for a male. The whole body was SEX ONLY; every cell, every particle, was shouting for it; even the skin, the hands, the nails, every atom . . .

Waves of wild goose-flesh ran over my whole body making all the hair stand stiff, as if filled with electricity. The sensation was painful, but the inexplicable thing was that the idea of intercourse did not even occur to me . . . The body was shaking, I was biting the pillow so as not to howl like a wild animal. I was beside myself; the craziest, the maddest thing one could imagine, so sudden, so violent.

The body seemed to break under this force; all I could do was to hold it stiff, still and completely stretched out. I felt the over-stretched muscles full of pain as in a kind of cramp. I was rigid, I could not move. The mind was absolutely void, emptied of its content. There was no imagery; only an uncontrollable fear, primitive, animal fear and it went on for hours. I was shaking like a leaf . . . a mute, trembling jelly carried away by forces completely beyond any human control. A fire was burning inside my bowels and the sensation of heat increased and decreased in waves. I could do nothing. I was in complete psychological turmoil.

I don't know how long it lasted, don't know if I slept out of sheer exhaustion or if I fainted . . .

The whole body was shaking and trembling in the morning. The cup of tea tasted bitter. Felt like vomiting.

21 *January*

When at his place, kept looking at him full of fear. I seemed to be all right now. The horrible vibration was gone. The body seemed normal, only very weak. He was mostly in a deep state. I sat down and looked around; everything was as usual. If the body were not so weak and feeling as if wounded, it would be difficult even impossible to believe that the happenings in the night were real.

'Who are you?' I was thinking, looking at his still face, so serene, so far away, obviously not in this world. Who are you? Who can do such a thing with the body of another human being?

He did not seem to take any notice of me. But I observed that each time he answered somebody's question, before drifting back into the deep state, he gave a look in my direction with a kind of a cruel half-smile, his eyes unseeing; or seeing, perhaps, something beyond the physical world? And every time he did it, a swift, piercing pain was felt in the lower part of my abdomen. It was like a stab of a dagger at the base of the spine. The vibration began, at first very gently, then quite noticeably. No other sensation except of a low humming noise. It was so mysterious, so terrifying. This will be the end of me I thought.

I am not young; this body will not bear it, will go to pieces. Even the strongest constitution will not be able to bear this sort of thing for any length of time.

Felt very tired. Tried to rest in the afternoon, but the body was as taut as a string and something deep inside kept burning, burning, and I could even *hear* the soft, hissing sound . . . It was dreadful.

In the evening he told us the story from the *Mahabharata*: when Draupadi was going to be burned alive together with her dead husband, as was the custom in ancient India, Bhima killed all those who wanted to do it. Arjuna lived in disguise as an eunuch at the King's court. He was teaching the ladies to sing and to play flute.

'Oh Arjuna,' said Draupadi, 'what are you doing here? Why are you in disguise doing nothing? Look at your brother, at his deeds, he is so strong and powerful!'

'Oh Draupadi,' said Arjuna, 'yes, I am in disguise. But soon the time will come, is coming now, when you will not recognise me any longer and you shall see how strong I am again!'

At first neither L. nor myself understood the meaning, and he said that it was meant for me. I gathered that, but still could not get it. But looking in between his eyebrows and quickly down again, as he told me to do when I want to know his thought, the meaning flashed into my mind:

"You see me like this, unwell, weak; I am in disguise. Soon you will see the real me, soon you will see my power!"

He only nodded.

22 *January*

Last night was even worse than the first, if such a thing is possible at all. It was unbearable. Beyond myself with desire, half unconscious, I suddenly noticed in the dark room around me, some kind of whirling, dark, grey mist. Trying to focus on it, I detected that there were strange shapes moving about and soon I could distinguish most hideous things, or beings; leering, obscene, all coupled in sexual intercourse, elemental creatures, animal-like, performing wild sexual orgies. I was sure that I was going mad. Cold terror gripped me; hallucinations, madness; no hope for me – insanity – this was the end . . . Buried my face into the pillow not to see; perhaps it will go, will vanish; but the aroused desire in my body forced me to look. I did not even know, not in this life at least, that such disgusting practices are possible; with dogs, men, women and horses, the most ghastly spiderlike creatures obscenely moving around, all leering at me, dancing, grey shadows . . .

Things I never knew could be done, or could exist; the most lecherous filth, I had to witness this night. Never knew? If I did not know it, how could I see it? It must have been somewhere in my depths, or else how, how could I see it? It must have been in me. One thing I was sure of was that I was going mad. I never suspected that anything like this darkest vice could be experienced by a human mind, for it was *not within* human experience. Such helplessness, such black depression came over me; I was a prey to some terrible, cosmic forces unknown to me.

After a completely sleepless night, the body shaky, I was so weak in the morning and full of shame.

Went early to his place and sat in the garden, thinking nothing, just being so weak that I could hardly lift my head. He came out unusually early, shortly after 9 a.m. Without looking at me, he sat down and began his prayers. All was still. It was a lovely, sunny morning. The sounds seemed to come muted to my ears; the click of the beads sliding through his fingers, the traffic outside the gate; the sudden chattering of a chipmunk. My heart was beating madly, my head spinning. I got up; my legs were trembling. I stepped forward, fell at his feet, clasping them with both hands, pressing my forehead into the dusty soil.

"Why? Why? What is happening to you?" As if he did not know. Got up. Went back to my chair and sat down with head bent. My heart seemed to want to jump out of my chest. He did not seem to understand. Or *did not want to understand*. It was a silent cry for help; for how could I tell him? Could not even look at him, could not speak to him. What could I have said? What can be said in such circumstances?

At his place I saw nothing, no shadowy shapes grinning devilishly in derision, but I knew as soon as I got home that in the night it would be another matter . . . Oh God help me! I just sat there, half-dead.

Once more the night was perfect hell. The creatures were nearer now, all round my bed. So near that I was forced at times to dive under the sheet in sheer terror. The room seemed to be full of them in constant movement, in absolute silence. Not the slightest sound, just the ghostly dance of obscene shapes and activities. Was this what is called the 'Dweller on the Threshold'? All those evils must have been in me! Merciful God help me! There is no escape for me but an Indian mental asylum; a padded cell!

23 *January*

Body was trembling, head empty, felt very sick. Went to his place late. He was not well this morning. It was obvious. He came out late and sat with us in the sun. It was chilly. Looking so frail, his face was full of inner light. He is not very dark. North Indians are much fairer than the southerners.

He sat cross-legged in his chair dressed in his dark-brown overcoat. After a while he sent L. away to get some rusks, for he couldn't digest anything else for the moment.

Took advantage of her absence. Thought that it was better to tell him; it cannot go on like this. Perhaps he will know how bad it is; he will help me . . . Only one man was sitting with us, but I knew he did not understand English. I told him.

"Yes, yes," he kept repeating, as if full of uneasiness. "Is it very bad?"

'Terrible!' I said, 'Unbearable!'

"It will be better," he said. "Be patient." That was all. And he went inside.

24 January

It was better. The night was not too bad. Each time I woke up, I was conscious of some vague presences but was too tired to bother.

He came out that morning still looking very weak, but said that he felt a bit better. He is coughing much but he said that the vomiting has stopped and he could eat a little.

I asked if it is fair to him that I should sit not further than five feet away from him with this *shakti* [power] in my body; will it not disturb him?

"You are still not quite there if you think that you can disturb me." He shook his head in disapproval. "To stay away will be worse; the imagination will work."

I was glad. To stay away would be hell. I am terrified to be alone by myself.

25 January

"Bear it;" he said, "control it. If you cannot, you have to confess it to me."
I felt like sinking into the earth.

26 January

This morning the first thing he had said when he came out was that his daughter Durghesh was delivered of a little girl.

"She is so beautiful," he said, with a radiantly happy smile. We all congratulated him. He must have been in a very deep state last night, the atmosphere in the room was beyond words. I told him so and he confirmed that he was in a very deep state and did not sleep at all.

"And how are you? Any trouble?"

'Plenty! I try to cope with it. I think that I will not go mad after all.'

"No, no danger of that," he said and his face was very still. "No, I am here."

My heart went out to him. I was in good hands; there is no need to fear.

"Is there any fire without smoke?" he asked in the afternoon. He sat in the big chair, the light of the sunset through the open door on his face.

'No,' I said.

"And what is smoke?"

'The impurities which are expelled because they cannot be consumed by the fire.'

"Correct." He nodded briefly.

27 January

The nights are a potential nightmare. I dread to go home every evening. Lying still for hours trying to control this body of mine, shaken by forces almost too powerful to be controlled. In the morning I am shaky, my knees give way, can hardly walk; there is a strong feeling of nausea. I eat very little and often wonder how it is that all the other functions of the body go on seemingly normally. A wonderful resilience and strength has the human frame. But how can it last without any ill effects?

He looked so tired this morning and as weak as a kitten. Looking far away, his face dark, as if full of pain.

"Yes, yes," he said distractedly, in answer to my thoughts. "You can ask."

'Is there a difference between the souls of men and women? It seems to me that on the spiritual level there can be no difference.'

"Yes, a Soul is a Soul, Atman is Atman. Only on the physical plane is there a difference." He fell silent; I too was silent. Felt very weak, could hardly think, and had a sickly, fainting feeling in the pit of the stomach when he happened to look at me. I think it is caused by fear.

Everybody present was in deep dhyana. The Indian disciples seated cross-legged on a few tachats or on chairs. He began to speak quietly.

"If guests come to you, you will entertain them, even lavishly if you can afford it; but do you give your property to them? Certainly not. Your property is for your sons and heirs. A guru can have many shishyas. Not all of the shishyas are expected to reach the high level. Human beings are at different stages of evolution. Not every shishya comes here for the highest state. The guru is duty bound; he gives what is demanded, according to the need. The guru always makes a selection."

I sat very still. My heart was melting with gratitude.

"Something was done to you which I usually don't do so easily." He fell silent for a while.

"But you came from so far away, so I did it. The relationship with a Master is once and forever and there is no divorce." He was silent once more. All was still, so peaceful. Even the garden seemed to listen. The poignant feeling of meaning, of some lost, forgotten bliss . . .

I *must* bear everything. I *must*. Even if it should break me. He knows what he is doing. I must not fear, must hold out, not be a disappointment to him . . .

30 *January*

I lie for hours trying to control the mind not to run away with imaginings; controlling the body, pulling in the muscles of the lower abdomen to bring some relief. Burning currents of fire inside; cold shivers running outside, along the spine, wave after wave, over legs, arms, abdomen, making all the hair rise. It is as if the whole frame were full of electricity. Gradually all the muscles of the thighs and the stomach begin to ache with tension, but this pain gradually increasing through prolonged effort somehow helps to relieve the desire.

The ghastly shapes are here, sometimes clearly visible, sometimes indistinct. Strangely, I am getting used to them. Usually out of sheer exhaustion I manage to fall into a heavy sleep, at least for some hours. Waking up with a dry mouth and a head as heavy as lead. Strong coffee and aspirins help after a bath.

I woke up about 2 a.m. with a mental picture receding into the background. A clear picture of him seated cross-legged, the white blanket which I gave him some weeks ago wrapped around him, the brown woollen cap on his head. It covered half of his forehead, only the shining eyes were seen. He was smiling at me.

Woke up with this picture vividly in my mind and as soon as my thoughts became clear I realised with surprise that my body seemed to be singing. Literally so. Singing softly and resting in Him, in the deepest pool of peace ... It seemed to me that I never felt such a tranquil bliss in all my life. Stretched out comfortably with a sigh of relief; no torture; no tension; just stillness and a kind of sound in all the tissues as if the whole frame of the body was vibrating in gladness to its own inner music; every cell, every particle, happy in its own right. All my being seemed to be streaming forth in a steady flow, but softly, gently, full of unearthly peace. It lasted for quite a while. Tried to think, tried to grasp, to analyse what was happening. Was that the feeling of Perfect Love of Surrender? I could not know and it did not matter. Not really. All that mattered was that the dreadful tension was gone: but can I be sure that it will not come back?

As soon as I saw him he asked me how I was. I said that I was much, oh much, better! The trouble seemed to have gone away. He gave me a quick look and continued to walk up and down, mala in hand. He looked very ill. L. told me later that he did not eat at all for days. Suffers from vomiting. His skin seemed grey and he looked old and worn out.

What a difference there was between that world which had been mine not so long ago and the world of the Master – obscure, disturbing, still unknown to me, a dark *terra incognita*, full of enigmas, disquieting mystery and God knows what secret suffering. This was my world from now on. I myself have chosen it. More than ever before, the life of the world as I knew it seemed empty, devoid of all meaning and I understood why, once on the Spiritual Path, one can never go back; not because there are such secrets which cannot be revealed, but simply because there remains nothing to go back to ...

☆ 10 ☆

1 *February*

"You must write down all the wrongs and evil deeds you have committed since your childhood. It will serve as a confession. A kind of *curriculum vitae* of your sins. Otherwise you may be called by God one day to account for it; but when the culprit confesses he becomes free. Everybody had to do it. L. had to do it too. You must do it if you want to be taken into the Arena.

There is no other way. Confession must be; there must be no secrets before your Teacher."

I went cold. That was an unexpected blow. How can I remember all the wrongs of my life? What a dreadful task! But I understood the value of it.

He was sitting on the tachat, knees drawn up to his chin, the woollen cap covering nearly the whole of his face. He looked so stern; his voice was tired.

Went home and cried for a long time without being able to stop. It is a kind of traumatic state, crying sometimes even without apparent reason; forgetting things, being assailed by dark, terrible fears. All abnormal reactions, obviously magnifying certain happenings which are insignificant and neglecting important duties. It does not look good; let's hope it will end well without permanent damage to my mental state.

2 February

We had a lovely, brisk walk in the park. Again he was saying that only the Will of the Beloved mattered. The Lover is a dead thing in the hands of the Beloved.

In the evening many people came and L. and I sat in silence. An Urdu conversation was going on. After a while he asked me why I was thinking that he was displeased, for he was not. I tried to explain.

"I am really never displeased; the disciple gets a chance again and again, hundreds of times; a good Teacher is never displeased, never."

But I could not quite believe that and was very depressed.

3 February

In spite of my worries I slept very well. Am not bothered much lately. He took it away in His Mercy, to give me a breathing space I presume. L. was saying that *Bandhara* is approaching and he will be transfigured and full of light. I see much light around him anyhow, but I said nothing to her. Tonight when walking in the park he told me that he wanted me to buy some electric bulbs which will be needed for the Bandhara. I felt annoyed. Told him that he has so many young men and boys sitting around and doing nothing, his sons for instance. I am an elderly woman; to be sent on errands like that is not right. Not only that, but he knows well that being European I am always cheated and have to pay more. He said curtly that one must never refuse anything to the Teacher. And it was such a small futile thing, it was petty of me ... His face was sad. I felt bad. He asked for a thing of little importance and was clearly testing me to see how I reacted.

5 February

In the afternoon he gave us a long and interesting explanation on the relationship between the Teacher and the disciple.

"Love cannot be more or less for the Teacher. For him the very beginning and the end are the same; it is a closed circle. His love for the disciple does not go on increasing. For the disciple of course it is very different, he has to complete the whole circle." He traced an imaginary circle on the blanket with his mala. "As the disciple progresses he feels the Master nearer and nearer as the time goes on. But the Master is not nearer; he was always near, only the disciple did not know it."

L. said that her love remained the same from the beginning, but I said that love must grow, become deeper.

"Yes, it is according to the temperament and the character of the people concerned. The Master must be strict, he has to be hard, because he wants the disciple to reach the high state. Absolute faith and obedience are essential, without that progress is impossible."

He demonstrated to L. the exercise which he had had to do when he was young, in which one remains for one hour and twenty minutes without breathing.

"But you cannot do it now," he said to us. "I would have had to have you here with me before you were eighteen and before being married. This exercise is a quick way to take up all the sex power to *Brahmarandhra* [crown chakra], by singing certain sentences in a certain way. My Revered Guru Maharaj knew so many things which I don't know. But on the other hand I know so many things nobody knows nowadays. There are people who have been coming to me for the last sixty years and they know nothing. This man who was here a few days ago and whom you thought to be so nice," he said, turning to me, "he has been coming here for the past thirty-five years. Once he asked me why I don't teach him anything, or accept him as a disciple. Why should I? I select my disciples. Absolute faith and obedience are required before one is taken into the Arena. If you have no faith and no absolute obedience, you will not progress, that's all. Law is law. One cannot cheat God. When we have reached a certain degree of progress we acquire certain capacities and powers. Some come to us naturally, as we progress, and some are offered to us. My Revered Guru Maharaj offered to teach me a *mantra* [word of power] to heal the bite of all the poisonous snakes: I refused." I looked at him in amazement:

'But why, Bhai Sahib? It is such a service to humanity!'

"Yes, and because it is Service, when I have this Power, I have no right to refuse. Never. So I have here a procession of people day and night and will have neither peace nor time to do my own work. This is not very high *siddhi* [spiritual power]; many *fakirs* [miracle workers] can do it. We are trained to do more important work, which they cannot do. I would be wasting my time. We are free. If I had wished it particularly, I would have done it, but we do not wish anything. We are not after powers. We have no desires. Our will becomes One with the Will of God. We are instruments in His Hands. We are called 'Slaves of the One and Servants of the People.' God has also a title, a Name. It is His favourite Name which He likes very much: 'The Servant of the Servants'.

"The Goal of every Path of Yoga is to lead a Guided Life. Guided by that which is Eternal. To be able to listen to this Guidance is the whole purpose of the Spiritual Training. That's why we insist on surrender, and on absolute obedience; and this is the meaning of the sentence of Christ: 'I and my Father are One,' and 'Thy Will be done on earth as it is in Heaven.'"

He fell silent. A cool breeze sprang up, and brought with it a whiff of a delicate fragrance; the lime tree behind the corner of the house was flowering. I took a deep breath . . . It was heaven . . . He suddenly threw his head back and laughed his young, slightly metallic laughter:

"If I smell the fragrance of a rose," he translated from the Persian, "I say how sweetly fragrant art Thou my Lord! If I taste a sweet thing, I say how sweet art Thou my Lord!" And turning to me, "Thank; thank; go on thanking Him always, for everything; for good things, for difficulties, for everything. That's how you will progress!"

6 *February*

I noticed that my mind is only working in so far as my spiritual duties are concerned. For instance, I can write my diary; I remember fairly well all that he tells us; but I cannot do more than that; the brain is not good for anything else. And, what's more, nothing seems to matter any longer. Neither reading nor letter writing, nothing at all. All I want is to sit at his place, and even the silly, irritating chit-chat of the crowd around him seems to matter less and less. Everything seems to fall away from me as in a crazy dream when all the objects are crooked, vacillating and empty of content.

7 *February*

This morning the workman came to erect a large marquee for the Bandhara. There was a lot of dust and hurried activity. The guru was going to and fro; I was sitting alone outside. Saw him speaking to the half-blind man; suddenly he came to me and pushing a medical certificate into my hand told me to copy it with three carbon copies. I objected because I could not read the diagnosis and told him that it is not of much use to copy it if the most important part cannot even be read correctly; besides, it is a confidential document for the doctor and not for the patient to have it copied.

"This man wants a copy," Bhai Sahib said sharply. "If the man wants it he has a right to it!"

I felt irritated; and what about my rights? Every peasant has precedence, everybody has 'rights', I seem to have only duties . . . Am asked to do obviously useless things, wasting my time. The fellow wants several copies just for the satisfaction of having them! My small typewriter can take only one copy, so I have to type it three times! I am not a good typist at any time but now, with the mind not working properly, I constantly make mistakes and have to retype again and again.

Bhai Sahib turned again to the man, who said that he wants three copies for himself because he has to give the original to the doctor. Well ... I was really angry. This is a test again. I have to be really careful. He will keep asking me to do silly, irrational things just to see how I react.

I was annoyed with myself and resolved to be more careful than usual, just now during the Bandhara. He was sure to test me as he warned L. and myself some days ago. There could be false accusations, or something of the sort, and it will be done publicly. God help me with my character! I must not be resentful. One cannot cheat God, so he said. Obedience. Difficult ... All day long I was sitting there alone, nobody taking the slightest notice of me.

8 *February*

Every morning, about half an hour before coming to his place, something happens to my mind. It feels like a tight iron circle closing tighter and tighter around the head. I get giddy and a bit unsteady on my feet; the brain slows down considerably and for a few moments I see his face clearly before me. And my only desire is to go to his place as quickly as possible. Everything else is forgotten. More than ever the world about me becomes an empty dream, a maya, unreal, silly, devoid of meaning. And the heart feels as though wounded. I can actually hear the heart chakra spin round and round at a terrific speed; the physical heart responds by beating madly, missing out beats and behaving as if trying to jump out of the thorax.

The large courtyard and the verandas around it were full of people all seated on the ground. I found a place and a small mat. He came out and sat cross-legged in the middle of the courtyard on a carpet prepared for him. He was dressed with care, looked very elegant in white, woollen garments Already when he came in he was in deep samadhi, looking like a statue of Buddha. I mean the expression; for Buddha is always represented without a beard. Nobody got up when he entered; nearly everybody was in deep dhyana. No one stirred. The stillness was such that even the noises from the street and the nearby bazaar were non-existent. The peace was difficult to bear.

9 *February*

I don't remember much of the Bandhara. Everybody was fed, seated on the floor in the courtyard and on the verandas. Somebody said that there were hundreds of people. L. told me that three thousand meals were distributed in three days. Calculating three meals per day, that would make more than three hundred persons.

When people speak to me I answer, but I do not remember what I say. We all went with rickshaws to the Samadhi of the parents of Bhai Sahib. It was crowded, noisy, too many children all running about and being restless, and disturbing everybody. He was transfigured; a different person. I could not take my eyes away from his face. The light about him; the stillness and infinite peace expressed in his features were indescribable.

67

11 *February*

All day there was much coming and going. Many disciples from the provinces are still here. He did not even look once in my direction. Left earlier in the evening; was tired and depressed; only Hindi was spoken.

12 *February*

The power inside my body did not abate all night and I could not sleep. I noticed something completely new. My blood was getting luminous and I saw its circulation throughout the body. I soon then became aware that it was not the blood; a light, a bluish-white light was running along another system. But of course! It was running along the nervous system which was clearly visible, the light circulating in it as the blood does in the blood-vessels. Only there was a substantial difference; the circulation of the blood stops at the skin and this light did not; it penetrated through it, radiating out from it for about nine inches. The light came out of the body and re-entered it again at different points. Observing closely I could see that there were countless points of light like a luminous web encircling the body inside and out. It was very beautiful. No bones existed; the body was built on the web of light.

Soon however I became aware that the body seemed to be on fire. This liquid light was cold but it was burning me, as if currents of hot lava were flowing through every nerve and every fibre, more and more unbearable and luminous, faster and faster. Shimmering, fluctuating, expanding and contracting, I could do nothing but lie there watching helplessly as the suffering and intense heat increased with every second ... Burned alive. Surely this time I will die? It became more and more unbearable, the whole body on fire. When I concentrated on some part of my body the light and heat increased there to an intense degree. How long it lasted I do not know. When it happens it is in a kind of in-between state, a muddled consciousness, unaware of time, neither sleeping nor waking.

It was all gone in the morning, leaving a great tiredness behind but nothing else.

14 *February*

Sat in the garden. I feel rather sad, for it is noticeable that I have not been invited to go inside lately. Everybody else is asked in or just goes in as soon as they arrive. I have to wait, and I can sneak in only if someone else comes, otherwise I sit alone outside for hours on end.

I gave him the confession. It had been agony for days compiling it and trying to remember all my failing and mistakes since my youth, my childhood even. It was most humiliating. I had an awful struggle with it, dragging out the old skeletons from the dusty corners of my memory; to dig out things I thought I had forgotten, of which I was ashamed. Felt dirty and small and very miserable. Written down on paper it was a crude, revolting and squalid document.

L. warned me not to give it to him before the Bandhara for he was very busy and capable of forgetting it in his kurta pocket and his children could get hold of it. A chilling thought ... I had seen his children reading letters from his disciples.

He took the folded sheet of paper.

"Hmm; rather a lot," he remarked. I felt like shrinking into a speck of dust. There were several foolscap sheets.

'Will you give it back to me after you have read it?' I asked. He shook his head. 'You will not forget it in your pocket; your children could get hold of it,' I ventured with a sinking heart.

"This is an impertinent remark." His face was sombre. I was so crushed and in my anxiety did not know what to say. After a while he said, not unkindly:

"I don't need to read it; I take it in my hand and the meaning comes to me word by word."

'And then you destroy it?' I asked hopefully. Felt like a drowning man clasping at a straw. He shook his head again.

"No, that would not be enough; it is made to go."

'Made to go?' I echoed, absolutely at a loss as to the meaning.

"Yes, it is taken away; the sins once confessed are taken away."

I did not press further. I knew, of course, that if one knows how to manipulate the laws of nature, the paper can easily be made to disintegrate. No great power even is needed for that.

His face is grey and he looks very weak. And I cried silently, much worried; my heart was aching seeing him like that.

15 *February*

I was alone sitting in the garden for a long time. He came out only when L. and her friend Filibert arrived. He looked very weak which worried me. But he was telling us that the Saint is usually ill all the time; his Guru Maharaj also was.

"When I am ill, I am really more healthy, for I am spiritually very powerful. When the body is very weak, the Soul is very strong." Later he said to me: "You were here shortly after 4 p.m."

I nodded. I already knew that he always knows when I arrive. Several times in the past he would say to me: "You came at such and such a time," or "I saw you sitting there under the mango tree," etc. And I knew that he was resting in the courtyard and could not have seen me coming in; at least not with his physical eyes. He also said once that the guru is supposed to know what the shishyas are doing all the time. But if he sees them doing something wrong, he never says so to them. So, it means that he can look at us at any time wherever we are and whatever we are doing. Since I have known that, somehow I never feel alone, and try to behave in such a way that I could be seen at any time of the day without being ashamed of anything.

16 February

He told us about the qualities and attributes of a Sat Guru. A guru is not a guru if he has desires left. The real guru can be recognised because he is without desires. The shishya must still have desires, but not the guru; he has none. The same is with a Saint. But a Saint need not be a guru. The guru will not do anything to damage the shishya's reputation; he will never give a bad example or take advantage of a situation. A *sannyasi* [a wandering Hindu monk] can have only a few real disciples, but a Saint, if he is also a Teacher, and lives in the world and has his sexual vitality well transmuted, can have thousands of disciples; it matters not how many. The vital energy in human beings is the most precious thing. It makes a Saint fly; it takes him directly to God. The vital energy must be transmuted, so that it will function from the navel upwards and not below. Only then are high states possible. To expand, to flow out without any destination, this is the Path.

We must live within the very turmoil of life but not be influenced by it. We must get rid of likes and dislikes. We must return to the very core of our primitive being in order to become whole. This will naturally produce conflicts for we have to accept ourselves as we are and not as we *think* we are. If you suffer from fear or some sadness, it means there are still attachments to get rid of.

Every guru has only a very few 'seed ideas' which represent the fundamental note or chord of his teaching – only those ideas which he has absorbed and which led him to Realization. He cannot give more. He will constantly manipulate those ideas for it is they which took him to the Truth, through his personal effort, and which represent a living Truth for him. Consequently no Teacher ever conveys the whole amount of the teaching, only what he himself has assimilated. Besides, no teaching can be transmitted until the disciple has reached the stage of comprehension; one cannot teach a small child the principles of higher mathematics. We have to grow up to the Truth, only then is it communicable. And it is the task of the guru to help the disciple to grow. How is it done? One has to merge into the Teacher. Only then the little self will go. It is like a voluntary death in the guru's essence. It is called *fana*. A complete surrender to the Teacher is the first step leading to complete surrender to the Will of God. Only little by little can we get used to this idea. It must be absorbed, become part of the blood. Just as food is absorbed into the body and becomes part of it. I must be integrated as a Wholeness into the mind. And this is the Goal of the Spiritual Training.

He was also saying that one does not need to ask questions; those of immediate urgency will be answered automatically, almost immediately; and the others, which are at the back of the mind, will be answered by and by as time goes on.

17 February

It was raining this morning. I went at 9 a.m. The room was open. I hesitated but went inside because it was too cold and draughty to sit in the doorway leading into the inner courtyard. Through the open door I saw him having his breakfast in the next room. I timidly asked if I could sit here in the meantime because it was too cold to sit outside. He grunted something and I understood that I was not welcome. So I went out and sat in the doorway. It was raining steadily and a cold wind was blowing in gusts. I was cold and my feet were wet. I hoped that he would soon call me inside. But he did not. Sat for many hours, and I must confess that I was resentful. Everybody else was allowed to go in. As soon as they arrived they went in. And everybody else had precedence. Always the last and least and the shabbiest dog; that's me, I thought bitterly. If I wanted something of importance, there was never time for me. As soon as I opened my mouth a procession of people would start; crying babies to be blessed, servants, people in and out, children fighting, or howling, or quarrelling; and so it went on. I was always the last.

Felt like crying; my feet became colder and colder. When L. came I stood up and went inside also.

18 February

When I came in the afternoon, somebody told me that the door was open and I could go in. He was with an old Hindi woman who was telling him her troubles. He nodded when I entered, his face stern.

I was very depressed. Began to cry silently. Nobody saw it, for no one took any notice of me; they were all too busy talking. Only his son Satendra asked me if I was not well. I lied that I had a cold. Saw the guru glancing several times in my direction. Then he sang a Persian song which he translated:

> Give me the pain of Love, the Pain for Thee!
> Not the joy of Love, just the pain of Love,
> And I will pay the price, any price you ask!
> All myself I offer for it, and the price you will ask on top of it.
> Keep the joy for others, give me the pain,
> And gladly I will pay for the pain of love!

This was the song his father had composed, and he used to sing it often. Again I was sure that it was meant for me. He thinks that I am crying because of the pain of love and I am just resentful, I thought. And when at home I cried my eyes out. Just cried and cried. It brought a kind of relief.

19 February

This morning he was giving a special sitting. L. told me quite simply to wait in the doorway. I would have preferred if he himself had told me to stay out. I confess I cried bitterly. Honestly, this is the limit! Special sitting indeed! I

71

never got a special sitting and never was anybody asked to leave the room because of me! Everybody can speak to him, ask the most irrelevant questions, even those who come in from the street! And he is polite and full of consideration for everybody, but at me he snaps at the least provocation! I am left sitting in the rain, and if I have a question to ask, even a vital, an important one, I am interrupted constantly . . . These things do hurt! Oh how they hurt, Bhai Sahib! After a long while, he came out into the doorway, just when I was thinking of going home, for I was stiff with cold and my feet were like icicles!

Later I told him that if he persists in telling people that it is an effortless way, he is deceiving them! Love is the most peaceless state imaginable; and it takes the greatest effort of the whole being to be able to bear it, to go on. He seemed sincerely astounded:

"Deceiving?" he repeated. "But I would never deceive anyone! Would never do such a thing! *It is* an effortless way!"

'I will invest in a drum and if you persist in saying that it is effortless, I am going to proclaim by the beat of the drum outside your gate, to keep away from this place! For I know how effortless it is!'

"It will look nice, you standing in the street with a drum," he remarked coolly.

Later he told us that according to the System one does not need even to be acquainted with the Teacher or Spiritual Guide personally. One still gets the same amount of Grace.

"Many of my disciples have never seen me in their lives and they never come here. They are treated just the same and get the same as everybody else."

'In this case,' I said. 'I need not be here at all; I can go away; it will be the same.' He shook his head.

"If one attends the *satsang* [being in the presence of the spiritual teacher], one has the chance of becoming the Master, because the body is included."

I asked how this is to be understood but he said it is not to be explained.

"All I can say is that at the later stages the teaching must be communicated from heart to heart; the physical presence of the Teacher helps very much. If you need to be the Master of the System, the body is taken into it. What it means is that the body is getting used to the vibrations gradually; it is 'quickened' as well. But it cannot be done rapidly. It takes time. The physical frame of the individual is dense. But not everybody needs to be the Master of the System, so all get the same; bliss, peace, everything the same."

Here could be the explanation for the treatment I am being subjected to, I thought . . .

I sat there suffering intensely. And from time to time when I didn't look directly at him, I noticed he was watching me.

"If there is love there is great uneasiness," he was saying. "The greater the love, the more uneasiness. Love is not the same all the time. It cannot be. Love at times is intense suffering."

72

Was it because I complained yesterday, or because he was watching me and saw my depression? At any rate, I have deep peace today. And how good it feels after so much turmoil and torment. Just peace. It is like a rest. For how long? God knows ... I am bound to get the lot; I have no illusions about that ...

He was telling us about a woman in France who wrote telling how she was merging in him.

"Of course, I knew that she was in great trouble, so I thought that it was my duty to help her," he was saying. I listened with interest. Would it mean that the Master must do his part in order that the disciple should succeed? If I only knew what it all meant ... heard so much about it since I've been here. How is it done? So I asked him.

"Why do you want to know? IT IS DONE, that's all."

'It cannot be explained!' exclaimed L.

'If one wants to, surely it can be explained?' I said. 'I never get a question answered; that's the plain truth!'

"Why do you want to know?" He spoke sharply. "Why do you want to understand how it is done? Try to grasp it; try to do it!"

I felt a mounting exasperation. 'But how? Is it not natural for me to want to know? I have been hearing so much about it since I have been here. Don't we all want to try to understand? Is it not the purpose of us being here, of the whole of life, especially Spiritual Life? How can one merge into someone else?' I felt completely nonplussed.

'But it really cannot be explained,' said L. again. He kept an irritated silence.

'Never mind, Bhai Sahib,' I said. I was irritated too. Good heavens! Everybody else is free to ask as much as they like, anything and at any time, and he always answers, but I cannot ask the most simple question! True, it is probably not the most simple question, but perhaps the most esoteric part of the whole System. Still, he could at least make some effort to help me understand, at least partially.

During Kirtan I kept thinking that I am a fool to be irritated. I know well that he will treat me badly, and he will wipe the floor with me. So, just as well; I had better try to get used to it ...

In the afternoon he came out late. It was already dark. He proceeded to tell us how his Revered Guru Maharaj never spoke to him in thirty-six years. It was difficult to believe that it was exactly like this. But he said that it was to cure him from his hardness, because being Hindu he did not like Muslims. I wondered if he intends to do that with me too, to cure me of my hardness?

"When one is a victim of Love, one is taken into the System sooner or later.

As a mango fruit is plucked when it is ripe. In our hearts can be only room for One."

He came out late. We were alone, for everyone else went to see Dr Aslam, a famous herbalist. I did not say anything, saluted him only when he came out and sat down. Noticed that once or twice he looked at me and smiled into his beard, but averted his eyes when I happened to look in his direction.

23 *February*

We were sitting in the garden under the trees. It was a lovely, clear day, as it is so often at this time of year. It is getting warmer now, day by day. Such clear, sparkling sunshine. He began to tell us how the shishyas are trained.

A Saint has no desires, he never indulges in anything because he becomes universal, belonging to the people. It is a law that what can be done by simple means should be so done; no spiritual power should be wasted. One must never waste spiritual energy. No two shishyas are treated alike; human beings are unique, and the guru, if he is a Sat Guru and knows his job, will treat them according to their possibilities, their character, and their past conditioning.

The teaching is given according to the time, to the place and the state of evolution of the shishya. A Saint will never give a bad example. He is free; he obeys only the law of the Spirit, not human Law; but he will always conform to the law of the land. He will never go against any religion, for all religions for him are alike; they are only different roads to the One Truth.

"For the Roads to God are as many as there are human beings; and as many as the breaths of the children of men," says a Sufi poet.

I asked him about the sheaths of maya that I had dreamed about the previous night. He listened, his eyes far away, as if covered with a bluish mist.

"There are five sheaths which cover the Atman: the sheath of the physical body, *annamayakosha*; the sheath of etheric energy, *prānamayakosha*; the sheath of the mind, *manamayakosha*; the sheath of *buddhi*, or knowledge, *gnamayakosha*; the sheath of the soul, or bliss: *anandamayakosha*. All these sheaths still belong to the illusion maya which covers the Atman. They have to be got rid of, ultimately, when one merges into the Reality. In other words, you have to renounce even the fruits which you have attained in the state of samadhi; nothing must remain, if you want the Truth; nothing but the Ultimate Truth."

I told him how wonderful it is to be given teachings in a dream.

"It is done so in our System," he said thoughtfully. Told him that I will try to refrain from asking too many questions, in spite of my impatient eagerness to understand, for I begin to see that he will give explanations when necessary.

"Yes; do not run after explanations, some things will be told in words, some

74

have been told already, some are infused, no speech is necessary. They are reflected from heart to heart. Your mind knows nothing of it; but it will come up when you need it."

Went home as in a dream. The bliss was such that I did not dare to fall asleep for fear of losing it. But finally fell asleep. And in the morning it was gone.

⊰ 11 ⊱

25 February

In the evening we were in the room; he sat cross-legged on the tachat. He was telling us that if the devil comes we should make him our friend. If he is our enemy how will we be able to fight him? We will never be able to get rid of our vices. But if he is our friend he is harmless. I did not understand. Neither did L. So he said:

"If the devil will come; what will he do to you? Devil is evil and he will do evils with you. He can take the shape of anything; of a man or of a child, or of an old man with a beard; he will be clean and pleasant to look at, he will be nice; he can take the shape of a dog, an elephant, a tiger, a lion – anything."

He asked L. in which shape she would prefer the devil and she said in the shape of a camel. He laughed.

"Good memory; camel, animal of the desert."

I still did not understand and said so.

"If you want to steal, why not steal? Learn to steal well, to deceive well."

'If you order me to do it I will obey,' I said.

"Why should I ask you to be a thief or a deceiver?" he asked. "The devil is the manas in you; why say I will not do such and such a thing because I have a strong character? Why not say: 'I am nothing!'?"

I still did not know what he meant and he added:

"It will be for the next time!" and changed the subject.

26 February

"You cannot say to your Beloved: 'I love you only so much and not further.' If you love you have to give a blank cheque. Even before you know that you will get anything ... A blank cheque of everything you possess, but above all of yourself, in utter, complete surrender ..."

"Of course," he continued, speaking very slowly, narrowing his eyes to slits, as if looking into distances of which the mind knows nothing, "Of course, there will be a blank cheque on the Master's part also. It is like a bond and it is never broken, *can never be broken*."

He fell silent. I never saw such an expression on his face; a personification of destiny itself, if such a thing is possible. So infinitely mysterious, it evoked an echo in me somewhere, and I was profoundly disturbed.

Again I had that feeling of being at a cross-road; was it a milestone? A turning point? As if answering a dimly formulated question in my mind, he said softly:

"There is only one Teacher; only one Spiritual Guide in the whole world for each of us. For only he alone is allowed to subject a free human being to sufferings and conditions; only he, and nobody else."

1 *March*

Bhai Sahib was telling us how one must trust God and never think of tomorrow.

"We are not allowed to make plans for the future. If we make plans it means we lack faith. We obey orders. We lead guided lives. And this is the meaning of living in the ETERNAL NOW. We do not think of yesterday; we do not think of tomorrow; we listen within and act accordingly. The result is that we can only live in the present.

"I do not save money for the future, with one hand I receive, and with the other I spend. There are four kinds of people: *pamer* – he is like an animal, he wanders here and there and he gets; *vishar* – he is a beggar, debauchee, with great difficulty he gets; *giaggiasa* – whenever he demands he gets; *mokt-purush* – he remains sitting, not engaged anywhere; he gets from people serving him.

"Only the love of the guru and shishya is not *moha* [attachment]: every other love is moha. The shishya can never know if he is progressing; only the Teacher knows."

6 *March*

He does not speak to me at all. Speaks only in Hindi with others. I come and go unnoticed. He ignores my greeting.

He snubbed me because I plucked a small wild flower to show its beauty to L. Later he was kind again, talked to us and explained that the group-soul theory is false. Animals can never become men, nor can the devas. But it is true that the soul passes through the devic plane before it manifests on the physical.

There is nothing but ONE BEING experiencing through everything created. His Light is in everything. His Light is not only in men but in every atom of His universe.

We went for a walk in the evening as far as the water reservoirs. It was a beautiful evening. A sunset of fire and crimson and the most luminous gold. I said how I loved the deep, red sky, the dramatic sunsets of India, the graceful silhouette of the temple, the palm trees against the glowing sky.

"How many things do you love?"

We sat down for a short while on a bench near the edge of the reservoir, the colours of the sky reflected in the water.

'Oh, so many,' I replied. 'The song of the birds at dawn, the flowers, mountains and sky, India, England, the forests burning with the colours of autumn, and people and ...'

"Your heart is like a hotel," he interrupted darkly. "One can love only One, You cannot love two masters; either you love the world or you love its Creator."

'Oh, Bhai Sahib,' I sighed.

When I mentioned in conversation that pride is considered to be a great impurity, he said:

"Yes, but also a great thing; it is like the two opposite ends of the same stick; the pride of the personality and the pride of the Atman. 'The Garment of God is Pride,' says a Persian poet. Sometimes somebody would say to my Revered Guru Maharaj: 'It cannot be done!' And he would say: 'Oh it cannot be done? It can. I will do it!' And it was done. He had the right to speak like that. He worked from the Atmic level. Certain people when they have reached a high state cannot be measured by our measure, nor can they be judged. They are beyond it."

9 March

"First one learns how to catch the hint of the guru, and afterwards, when one is well merged, the Divine Hint, which is faster than lightning. The guru will hint first; if the hint is not understood, then he orders. An order is easy to understand, but the guru trains the disciple to catch the Divine Hint rather. The guru can give orders again and again if the disciple does not understand; but God does not do so and the Hint is lost, and one may wait for a long time to get it again. To grasp it one must be deeply merged, so merged that one even looks for a place to stand upon, but there seems to be none.

"To grasp a Hint is to act accordingly, and not even try to understand it. Acting accordingly is necessary, rather than understanding. The Grace of God cannot be seized; it descends. The actions of the guru are nothing in themselves; they are to be seen in connection with the disciple. They are only for the good of the disciple. First one is loved by the guru, afterwards the disciple loves the guru; but this situation is rare. It does not happen often. Usually it happens that the disciple loves the guru first and is loved afterwards by him. One must not even think 'I love you,' because the 'I' remains. But 'I want you to love me,' he wants only the Master and not what the Master possesses. Here lies the difference between the *bhakta* [devotee] and the disciple. The disciple is after knowledge; but if you ask the devotee what he wants, he will answer 'Nothing!'

"To say 'I love you' is easy but to realize it is difficult. Here is hidden the mystery of the Realization of God or Truth. Because you have to realize one fact: 'You are in my heart, you are everything, I am nothing.' If you begin to

77

realize that, then you really love, and your own self diminishes, the external things begin to lose all importance. The self, and everything else, remains with the Beloved from then on, and the Beloved remains with you permanently when there is no self anymore. The guru will never put conditions, but the shishya does; but it is the nature of things, it cannot be helped. When the whole life of the disciple is always according to the ideas or wishes of the Master, the training is terminated.

"Saints are like rivers; they flow where they are directed. A river never flows uphill. Small rivers join the large ones and they all flow to the ocean. We do not need to carry the burden when we let it flow. If a Hint is there, I have to do it; and if I don't, I am *made* to do it. A Divine Hint is an order. Sometimes Saints have to do things people will misjudge, and which from the worldly point of view could be condemned. Because the world judges from appearances. One important quality required on the Path is never to judge by appearances. More often than not things look different from what they really are. There is no good or evil for the Creator. Only human society makes it so. A Saint is beyond good and evil. But Saints are people of highest morality and will never give a bad example."

In answer to L.'s question: "A man who is impotent can never be a Saint or a Yogi. Women too can be impotent. The Creative Energy of God which manifests itself in its lowest aspect as procreative instinct is the most powerful thing in human beings, men and women alike."

L. said that according to some scriptures women reach the state of wholeness through the 'innate capacity' which is inborn in their essence, but man must make voluntary sacrifice and undergo definite discipline.

"It is correct. The training in each case is different.

"The possible relationships between guru and shishyas are: firstly, Lover and Beloved (lovers in fact). This is mostly practised in Tantra Yoga. In our System such a relationship would be considered an obstacle; secondly, father and child; thirdly, master and obedient disciple; fourthly, friends."

L. commented that my relationship with the guru was that of an obedient disciple whilst her own was that of a daughter. 'I never need to get up when he enters or touch his feet; I am treated like his children.'

He said that the Divine Hint is a subtle desire or a prompting, the Will of God which flashes into a still mind. The Saint has no desires of his own, but the Will of God which he executes. It becomes a Hint when the human will is not quite merged, not completely at one with the Divine Will. Where there is a Hint some duality still remains; otherwise the Hint would not be needed.

12 *March*

I asked if I could speak to him alone. He nodded. Told him that I had taken out all the money from my account as I understood that he wants me to give it away. Does he want me to go away in the summer as L. does? He said that if I wanted to stay, of course I can do so.

78

"I know other Europeans who do stay, I don't know how they do it. It is difficult even for us although we are born here. If you are courageous enough, then you can do it. You would come early in the morning, go home before 11 a.m. and come here again in the evening."

I laughed and said there is no question of courage. I have no choice . . .

Later I said that it is frightening that all my money should go. 'What will become of me?'

"If you are afraid, keep it," he shrugged. "I don't want it for myself at any rate."

Does he mean perhaps that after all I do not have to give it away? Something tells me this is not so.

13 March

'If the shishya cannot love by himself and love has to be produced, can it be taken away?'

"What is given can be taken away at any time, but the teacher does not take it away. The love ceases by itself if one has not got the faith in the Master, or obedience. But the teacher who has planted the love in the heart of the disciple will look after it, as the gardener looks after a plant; he does not want it to die. The disciple must surrender completely; only then the teacher will judge if he is ready for more."

15 March

The last two nights have been almost unbearable. The terrible creatures were with me again; could not hide from them anywhere. My physical condition is deteriorating. This state has been going on for already two months with short intervals of peace from time to time. I feel so weak. I am burning. The spectacle of the flow of light is fantastic and frightening. An old woman at the mercy of some cosmic force.

Went at 4 p.m. He was walking up and down in the garden as if waiting for me, his grandchild in his arms. Went directly to him as soon as I came in and began to tell him that I cannot go on any more, that I am going mad, that it is he, with his powers, who is responsible for the weird changes in me. I went on accusing him, attacking him, desperate with frustration and anger. As soon as I opened my mouth, the child took a look at me and began to wriggle and howl. He could hardly hold it. I was in hysterics, practically breaking down; the child banging his face with his little fists, howling in a mad fury and slipping from his arms. He was trying to control the child and could not hear what I was saying. I was nearly shouting in a vain attempt to be heard but realized that it was useless to try to compete with a baby screaming literally into his ears. I slumped down in helpless sobbing. He got firmly hold of the struggling child and with quick steps went inside and closed the door. I realized afterwards what a blessing it was that nobody was present. Such a scene ... and how was it that the noise did not attract the mother of the boy to see what was happening? But I knew already that conditions were always suited to his requirements.

I kept sobbing and could not stop for a long time. Then the servant came and looked at me with curiosity. Realized that soon people will come; I had better control myself ... But nobody came. Sat alone in the darkening garden.

17 *March*

He kept being difficult, telling me off for one thing or another. He would ask something, then pull my answer to pieces. Could not do one thing right. At last could bear it no longer, burst out crying, took my chair and went to sit under the mango tree near the fence, far away from all of them. There I cried; it must have been for more than an hour. He kept talking and laughing with L. ... perhaps they were laughing at me, God knows. I did not care; my heart was aching so much. I had had enough. But apart from that there was such a longing. Please a little, just a little peace and kindness and compassion ... A little encouragement ... A little warmth. I was lonely, my heart cried out for Truth.

It hurts so much! He hardly speaks to me for days, and when he does it is only to increase my confusion, to hurt, or to create a doubt, a mental torture. Yesterday he accused me of something I have not done; it was an insignificant thing but it was very hurtful and he was so angry; oh, it was so painful!

18 *March*

It was a clear, luminous Sunday. Many people came in the morning and in the evening. L. left for Paris. I was glad. Although she means well, she was constantly giving me advice without the slightest idea what it was all about.

I felt even more alone. To be in the hands of a man who will do anything, absolutely anything, for the sake of training is a chilling thought.

In the evening it happened that everybody left early and we were alone. This is always so when he wants to speak to me. He began by saying softly, with great kindness, that he did not understand why I was so upset the day before. "The whole day my heart was with you. I felt it so much."

I tried to tell him that I was upset because he deliberately seemed to misunderstand everything I had said and was accusing me and was angry. He ignored this remark.

After a while he said, "If you knew what I have in mind for you, for your future, you never would cry, never would be upset. About the end of April a flat will be available for you, a more suitable one. Do not tell people that I told you to remain here; they will not understand, for they all think that you Europeans cannot stand the heat."

19 *March*

"There are three *lokas* [repetitive thought-desire causing reincarnation]," he said, "*mirt loka* – the loka of the physical plane where we are born and we die; *kama loka* – the loka of the desire of the physical body, even of desire by itself; *swarga loka* – heaven, the world of effects where the good deeds done in the physical body reap their rewards. From these three lokas one comes back into incarnation again.

"When we are in the mirt loka, if we are attached to the Spiritual Guide or Master, and if the Master is spiritually powerful, he will leave no desire with the disciple at the time of death, the desire which would lead to another incarnation. The Master serves as a focus of attention for the mind, for the mind needs something to hold on to.

"The love to the Master is also a *vasana* [locality], but it is this vasana which will lead you beyond the lokas of change. It will carry you right through. There are four other lokas in which there is neither birth nor death. According to desire or necessity one goes from one to another in a glorious body made of light."

'Could you tell me the names of the other four lokas?' I asked. He shrugged.

"I could I suppose; but what for? The names are not to be told because, if they are, an explanation is needed. Then it will be the same as when an experience is described in a book. If one comes to know the same experience as described, the value of the experience is partly lost, for the simple reason that one knows about it. Knowledge without experience is a hindrance. Those lokas have to be experienced by the disciple. So for the moment let us just say that there are four other lokas making seven in all."

20 *March*

Too much talk was going on. Everybody seemed to talk at once. He was doing his mala; he did not listen. It is surprising how he never seems to be disturbed by anything.

I left soon; this constant droning makes me tired.

21 *March*

I told him that I had dreamed: I was looking at myself in the mirror and saw that I was very thin, very pale, my hair in disorder.

"It is a very good dream," he replied. "Thinner and thinner; until nothing remains."

22 *March*

"There comes a time in every Saint's life when Yama, the King of Death, becomes his friend. It is when the Saint reaches the point on the *Nirodika Path* [the Path of No Return (into incarnation)] where the devas cannot go further, only humans can."

"When you have received the wealth and want to drink the Wine of Love, do it silently so that nobody should know about it." Thus he translated a Persian couplet. Bhai Sahib then went on to explain the meaning: "People can be an obstacle; they can shake your faith before you are firmly established in virtue; but once you are established everybody can know."

He spoke of Mogul emperors; some of them were very cruel.

'Some Saints are cruel too,' I said. He looked at me seriously.

"Yes, Saints are very cruel. It is because they want only the good of the disciple. That nothing should remain, no impurity, no obstacle; no defects to hinder them. Is the doctor not cruel when he takes the knife and cuts the abscess?" He had his searching, unsmiling look.

For the last ten days I seem to have been completely alone.

26 *March*

We were alone nearly all the time in the room this morning. He had his mala. It was very hot. I saw him give me a quick look and I knew that he had seen that I was full of peace. He will take it away from me I thought. We went inside under the fan. When in the room he was very kind; talked to me on all sorts of topics. Told him in conversation that Babu and Satendra, his sons, wanted to come and see where I lived. I said 'I don't mind that, but Babu is so curious that he constantly asks me where I am going and what I am doing. I find it annoying. I don't need to give an account of my life to a boy. It is not his business.' He took the opportunity to tell me off; how hard I am still; he is trying to change me but without success. I was wincing under his words.

"I am not going to waste my powers," he was saying. "I am not going to help you now. You must help yourself. I gave you such a big place in my heart and you are still nowhere! You do not know what respect is. There are people who are so afraid of me that they do not dare to speak to me and you, you are disrespectful to the family of the guru!" And so he went on for a while.

He made me cry desperately; could not stop crying. Told him that he was right. What harm was there after all if the boy was curious. What did it matter? It is all pride again. So I cried and he went outside closing the door.

❧ 12 ❧

27 *March*

Had to ask him for help this morning. The whole night fire was flowing through my body. Liquid fire in the veins instead of blood; it felt like that. All the chakras seemed in turmoil. Did not sleep at all; but there were no 'creatures' around me. Nevertheless the physical body was suffering acutely; the pain was unbearable.

The head is light this morning. Have an airy feeling of the complete unreality of all around me.

Tonight he was talking to me from 6.30 to almost 8.30.

"Each of us has a work to perform in the world. Some of us work on the inner planes; some are training people; some are in the midst of worldly events guiding human beings aright."

'Also in politics?' I asked.

"Yes;" he nodded, "it was so in the past, it is so now, and it always will be. Humanity needs guidance. Where would the world be without Great Souls appointed to watch over the destinies of men? The goal of men is to realize the Truth. This is the purpose of the whole of Creation. But what can you say after you have realized it? How can you describe things which cannot be described in human language? People run after the world and after worldly things – phenomena, sensations, illusions. They know that they will remain 'in the cave' forever. (An allusion to the cave of Plato.)

"First you realize who you are; then from where you came, and where you are going. After that no desire remains, everything is gone. One becomes silent, one has nothing more to say. You won't be able to lecture, but people will come to you and you will take them one step nearer to the Truth. At the beginning and in the middle one has a great desire to work, but at the end even this desire goes; nothing will remain. You cannot realize God or Atman through books or lectures. Never! How can we realize Truth through the intellect? Where is intellect? Nowhere!

"In our system we never lecture, never write books. If one day you will see me go on a platform and lecture, then you will know that I came down!"

'I remember you said that you are training me according to your System and still you want me to lecture in the future. And you also told me to keep a diary which will be a book one day?'

"This is quite another matter. Orders are orders. I have just told you that each of us has a certain work to perform in the world. For a while this will be your work. Later, further orders will be given. We must all reach the stage when we are guided from within."

'If you are training me according to the Ancient Tradition, then the time must come when you will send me away to go and do some work. For as far as I know this is the Tradition; is it correct?'

He nodded. "I send my people away, as soon as the training is finished; 'Now go and work,' I say; and they go. My people are tested with fire and Spirit and then sent out into the world, and never, never do they go wrong."

And so it was that from his own mouth I came to know for sure that one day I will have to go, broken hearted, leaving my teacher behind ... May this day be far away, may it never come ... But after all, His Will ultimately will have to be done ... Only please, may it still be in the far distant future!

83

It was a glorious night. The stars seemed so near, so large. Venus was low and pale blue, huge against the sky already dark.

29 March

Just sat in the room alone. The rhythm of the Indian household was all around me. The servants were quarrelling, the wife cleaning the jars for the pickles at the fountain, water being filled into the earthenware jars, the crackling of the firewood, the smell of food being cooked. A child cried somewhere nearby. A woman's voice was singing softly – a monotonous, sad melody. It was hot; it was good. How I loved India.

In the evening we had a talk on the doctrine of karma which he said was a childish belief. I was more puzzled than ever. I retaliated with arguments of the logic of karma, how it explains so many things which otherwise would be incomprehensible. But point by point he kept defeating every argument most brilliantly with clear, sharp insight. His ability for discussion is devastating; he leaves one mute, speechless . . .

"It is difficult to become one with the Teacher," he said. His eyes were incredibly bright, shining, looking right through me. The light of the street lamps moving through the foliage of the trees was catching them and they were shimmering with brilliant, cold, green light. A cat's eyes in the dark, or the eyes of animals caught in the headlights of a car, shine with this brilliance. I never saw such a phenomenon in any other human being, or any creature. Especially when he was gay or laughing, small sparks seemed to fly from his eyes.

"It is difficult to become one. Manas will fret and work on it and ask questions, until it happens. Then of course, you will know. But on the physical plane there will always be differences; this is natural."

30 March

All the morning sitting there alone I kept worrying about the doctrine of karma. If karma does not exist, how can one account for the order of the universe? One can see everywhere the law of action and reaction, the cause producing its effects. He himself admits the existence of karma by his statement that the attachment for the Master produces such strong vasana that it remains forever. And what is vasana? Are not vasanas subtle desires arising from samskaras* which remain as impressions of actions in chitta?†

'This is part of the System,' said Professor Batnagar when we were discussing it. 'To destroy all the preconceived ideas, all your beliefs which come from book knowledge and learning. Perhaps some of the ideas will get confirmation later, but by then they will be a living experience; not book knowledge any longer. As far as I understand, as soon as a Saint wishes to give you something,

* Impressions of actions in Universal Mind which lead to the wheel of rebirth.
† Universal intelligence.

84

from the moment he sets eyes on you, karma cannot reach you any more. He does as he likes. He can give to anybody his property, just as he wishes. Karmas are for ordinary people still under the influence of the law of cause and effect, but no more for you if you are with a Saint. People do not surrender; they are *made* to surrender. If I may give you some advice; put all your doubts and worries into cold storage and leave them there. They will all be solved one day; then they will be seen in a new light for you. Do not ask questions any more.'

1 *April*

Every day it becomes hotter and hotter. A scorching wind springs up, pushing the temperature well over 100°. Nights too are very hot and airless. Slept only from 11 p.m. to 12.45 a.m. The rest of the night I was lying awake, thinking and listening, and watching the currents chasing each other in my body. The pain was tolerable. It is a very well-known fact that when one cannot sleep, the mind begins to work feverishly; every problem becomes magnified and if there is pain in the heart, that can become unbearable. Lately, I notice that the longing from which I have been suffering so much becomes more and more difficult to bear. Something in me is full of sorrow, so deep that I cannot reach it, cannot analyse it; only the claws of pain are tearing my heart apart ... Something in me is crying desperately.

Today he reprimanded me for not sitting properly in the presence of a Teacher.

"To sit in a chair crossing your legs is rude. To stretch your legs out is even more rude. You have to sit modestly, knees and feet together; never mind the heat." His face was hard as stone and he went on like this for a while, finding fault with my behaviour.

I burst out crying and could not stop. Had such a helpless feeling of despair. Must be a kind of hysteria. My nervous system is shaken. Cannot bear seeing him angry or even to think that he is displeased.

"Keep walking," he said. So I got up and began to walk up and down in front of the house. But it did not help.

"Keep walking," he repeated. He was sitting in his usual place in the big chair, mala in his hand. "When my heart is melting you feel it and you cannot bear it."

Strange how the telling off and the melting of the heart can go together. So I continued for a while. The trees smelt of greenery, the garden was dusty. He went inside. Like most men, I think, he cannot bear to see a woman cry, so he always disappears.

While I was still crying, he came out silently and sat down near me on a chair. He began translating in a low, monotonous voice a passage from the *Tulsi Ramayana*:

"A sweet smell has the dust at the feet of my guru; never have I cried before but now there is no end of sorrow for me ...

85

"Do you remember that I came out to meet you when you came for the first time? When you came from the station and Mrs Ghose brought you here? Usually I never go and meet anybody."

I was still occupied with trying to dry, at least partly, my cheeks. My skin was burning and painful from salty tears mixed with perspiration.

'It was an act of courtesy towards an elderly lady,' I mumbled feebly.

"Yes, yes, maybe," he smiled. "Maybe it was, but perhaps there was another reason." His smile deepened ... This expression again; this strange, luminous expression. As though I always knew it so far, so deep in me, that the memory of it could not be pinned down clearly ... This expression always profoundly disturbs me, haunts me like a dream of long ago.

"The bird of manas flies here and there until the hawk of love catches it. Where the King is, how can anything else remain?"

3 April

So much sorrow is in me that there is no speech left to express it. Have no desire to speak to him. Go there in the morning and sit. About 10 a.m. he sends me home. I am sort of empty. Everything seems to be dead. No desires are left, only one; only this terrible, deadly longing. But there seems to be no hope. It is a sort of peace made of darkness.

4 April

He did not speak to me all day and I did not attempt to say anything. There is nothing to say, nothing to ask. All is dead inside me. Such hopeless feeling. And the most amazing thing is that something in me does not mind this sorrow. More and more of it ... As if I was interested to see how far it can go? Where is the very depth of it? Or is it like a bottomless pit into which I will sink forever? The natural thing for a human being is to seek pleasure and to shrink from pain. But for reasons which are beyond my understanding, I want more and more of this sorrow, though I have no idea why I am in such a dreadful state. Pleasure and pain are the two poles on which the world of samsara [the wheel of birth and death caused by illusion] is revolving, the two opposites – attraction and repulsion. But I don't shrink from sorrow; why? It seems as if the whole of my desire would be to dissolve, to be submerged by it ...

Told him that my body is defeating me because of the vomiting condition, and I can hardly eat. I also have reasons to think that my eyesight is deteriorating because I am weeping so much. I happen to know a case of someone who cried so much after the death of her husband that her eyesight became weak and the colour of her eyes watery blue.

"It was because she cried about worldly things. If one cries for love, it never happens. I cried for years for my Revered Guru Maharaj, and my eyesight is all right. My father cried until the last moment before he died, and I myself ... well, I still cry. You will not cry for a few weeks, but for months, for years."

All seems to be still inside me. As if something has died in me. Do not want to ask questions; do not want to speak; and if he does not talk to me it does not matter either. Even the mind seems to be still.

"Keep being flooded with love for the next few years," he said. What did he mean by that? I was not sure . . .

5 *April*

He was chanting the *Ramayana*. It was already dark; and I was watching his luminous eyes in the darkness.

6 *April*

Something happened last night. I cannot find myself. This morning I experienced the nearest state of non-being since I am alive . . . Mind does not work at all.

Tried to read a journal forwarded to me from Adyar and could not comprehend a thing.

He was praying silently. Every time I looked up, I saw his radiant face shining with a new light. Great was the pain inside me. And the world around was a crazy, mad dream; and the brain refused to function.

7 *April*

This morning I was complaining publicly that I was unjustly treated; for hours they talk in Hindi. Bhai Sahib explains interesting things I cannot follow; nothing is ever translated to me. I sit there like a cucumber and miss the benefit of his explanations. The night was full of stars. So near, so large. Could not sleep at all. The fire in the body was terrible.

9 *April*

Stronger than before seems my love. And the nearness to Him was great. When I use the word 'Him' and write it with the capital 'H', I don't mean the guru. I mean the Great Beloved Himself, God.

Sitting near Guruji this morning, my heart was beating so loudly that I thought he would hear it too. For hours on end it was beating like that, stopping, missing out beats.

11 *April*

In the evening, by questioning him, I was given to understand that the sex urge was not awakened by him, by his power, as I had assumed, but that it was already there, latent, a sort of powerful vasana.

"Ancient karmas form part and parcel of the blood.* It was in you. It would have dragged you back again and again into the womb, but from now on it will burn itself out. From time to time this fire will burn in your body. This is purifying fire, this suffering, and you will need a lot more."

Well, I thought, not a very bright prospect to put it mildly.

"When you meet your Spiritual Guide, this is supposed to be your last karma-bound life. After that one is supposed to be free to go where the Teacher directs you. There are many planes, besides the Earth plane, where Service can be rendered. Disciples must be free. And if the Teacher is powerful he will take them through all three planes. But surrender and absolute obedience are needed."

When at home, could not help wondering how many evils I must have had in me to be burned to such an extent.

⋨ 13 ⋩

21 *April*

We all went in a truck to the Samadhi of his father. A lovely place, seven miles outside the town amongst the plains. It was like a lovely dream. The day was cloudy and it was not at all hot. How fragrant are the Indian plains, the wind coming from afar smelling of wood smoke, cow dung and dust and sun-drenched distances. To me it represents the smell of freedom, if freedom could have a smell . . . Peace was in me. Such peace.

Told him that I notice that things first happen on the inner planes before they come to manifest on the physical plane. Many things are already happening somewhere; soon they will be here. He nodded with a serious expression.

"The stages of love.

"One can see women carrying jars full of water on their heads, on their shoulder, in their hands. They do not spill the water, nor do they break the jars. But even if a jar is broken, there is but a small loss; another can be purchased and filled with water again. Those people are still far off from the Lane of Love.

"One can see acrobats performing on the rope and in the air. They can fall, have bones fractured and even die, but they are still using tricks to safeguard themselves as much as possible. These people just begin to come into the Lane of Love.

"Switch on a lamp and you will see insects attracted to the light, and there is great competition amongst them to come nearer and nearer. They throw them-

* Unconscious memories are stored in the blood stream. C. G. Jung, *Memories, Dreams, Reflections.*

selves into the light without reserve, without condition, and burn to death. Only this is the Great Love."

'Why am I in such a depressed state periodically? This fear of you? Such a fear of you that it is sometimes like panic.'

"It is the mind again," he said softly. "And it will come again and again; it will come and go, until the mind merges somewhere."

'But no wonder that I am afraid of you, Bhai Sahib. I feel so helpless, and the feeling of utter helplessness is frightening. Human beings are afraid of the dark, afraid of sufferings. I am afraid of new sufferings you may give me; it seems I had enough of them until now.'

"Sufferings?" he asked. "You have not begun yet!"

I looked at him in amazement. 'Are you joking or do you mean it seriously? Do you mean to say that the horrors I suffered until now are nothing?'

"Nothing. Nothing at all. It has still to come. On our line such suffering is given that there are no words for it."

'No wonder I am afraid of you,' I said, hardly audibly, looking at his serene face.

"But what's the use of repeating how much you suffered? What's the use of being sorry for oneself? Why not say courageously 'It is nothing, I will bear more.' The river has to be crossed, so let's go on."

'Thank you. It will be a help to think like this; you are right. It will help me in the future.'

He smiled. "Up and down it goes; full of love and empty again. In our System in one second things are done and in a moment the tables are turned."

'Does it mean that I don't love enough?'

"No, it is because you love deeply that it happens. Would the mind bother if there would not be the great disturbance of deep love? No, certainly it wouldn't. And the fact that the pain is sharper and deeper each time is a good sign. Pray that you should love more and more."

He got up and asked me to come into the room. There he took off his kurta and Panditji began to massage him. The whole scene was so Indian – the devoted disciple massaging his guru with reverence, with so much love.

"This body is perishable, yes. But it is extremely important. Why? Because Atman is in this body. We evolve through this physical body. That's why we have to surrender the physical body as well. When the body is surrendered, the progress is quicker. The Master can do with the body what needs to be done to train it according to necessity."

'Even to kill it?' I asked.

"Yes, even to kill it," he repeated. "And sometimes it is done in a certain way. But not always is it necessary. At any rate it is much better to be in the Teacher's presence. Remember the Atman pervades the physical body from head to foot, every atom of it. If adverse thoughts are in your mind, if the suffering is great, why don't you ask yourself what is in my heart?" He looked kindly at me. Panditji's hands went on kneading his shoulders. Like a bronze statue he was, shining with oil, and his face was all light.

'Why are cranks attracted to all spiritual organisations?'

"The question was put wrongly. Try to put it right, then ask."

'How can I put it rightly? If it is wrong, I ask you as my teacher to tell me how I should ask. Please tell me.'

"But you put it wrongly," he said impatiently. "Are they not human beings? Those people whom you call cranks are attracted to places where they instinctively hope for help. But who is a crank and who is not? If you speak to a madman he will say that you are mad and he is normal."

15 *April*

This morning the old man who comes every day was obviously in distress. When the guru came out he looked at him with those eyes of his which see beyond the physical and went into samadhi. The old man kept groaning softly, half conscious. I suddenly felt the guru quite near. He was somewhere and I was with him. I just rested in him and in Love and it was wonderful. I was so happy resting in deepest bliss ... Where was the mind? For minutes – or was it much longer? – I had no sense of time; there was practically no mind left.

In all the Yoga systems one has to make an effort to still the mind and what an effort it is! But here it represents an effortless state and I have not only *not* to bother to try to still the mind, but have to search to find it!

'Where is the mind?' I asked later. No answer. 'Guru Maharaj, where is this *shaitan* [devil] of the mind?' It is quite an effortless state – just no mind – when I am resting in Him in infinite Love. '*Namaskar* ['I greet you.' (Bengali)]' I added, walking away.

"Namaskar, namaskar," I heard him say. And from the tone of his voice I knew that he was laughing. God knows from how many human beings and how often he had heard this question, 'Where is mind, Guru Maharaj?' Please do not cause a separation any more – I cannot bear it! It becomes more and more difficult as the time goes on ...

16 *April*

I asked Mr Chowdhary and he explained that this stillness of the mind is the fifth state of the mind as described in the Yogic treatises and the outcome of it would be samadhi.

"You are in the higher state," Bhai Sahib said.

So, he proceeds to take me to his God after all. It is not frightening at all; it is very peaceful. All the time sitting near him I was resting in Him; in God; and was so ideally happy. Told him that all the worries about money matters and all else were useless, non-existent. The only thing which mattered was His Will and His Will only.

He smiled. "A very nice state, very nice indeed."

Then I told him that the state of separation becomes a problem. My eyes are red and sore from continuous crying for someone who is so far away ... If it is His Will, nothing can be done about it, but if it is my fault, could it be corrected?

"It is not your fault," he said softly, "not at all." His face was full of tenderness. "It will be like this for many years."

'For years? How will I survive if it is so bad already now?'

"You will." He smiled.

17 *April*

"If for instance I say, 'This is my chair,' how do I know that I am not proud of possessing it? If I don't care about it, if I am not attached to it, then I am not proud of it. Can the pride hide itself? Certainly not. It will always put itself in evidence. If you don't care about possessions, then it does not matter even if you have them. Inwardly we are free of them. You must forget everything."

'It will take time!' I answered doubtfully.

"You are at a turning point; at any moment it can happen, the state of dhyana. The mind must take a dip before it can go to a higher state."

Had a night full of currents of love. Last evening, sitting near him, the body was full of an unusually peaceful feeling, a kind of indifference to the surroundings and when he did send me home I thought it was only 7.30 but when at home I saw that it was after 9. The time went so quickly ... So that is dhyana ... Very peaceful. But not much consciousness. Some kind of state of being.

18 *April*

"In the whole of the Universe there are only two, the Lover and the Beloved. God loves His Creation and the Soul loves God. In order to be able to create, the One Being had to become Two and logically there had to be a difference between the Two. The creation was only possible because of the two opposites; everything in creation responds either to positive or to negative forces, or vibrations. There is the Sound and the Echo, the Call and the Response to it, Light and Darkness. Without the opposing forces how could the world exist? Even in the Angelic Kingdom there are Angels of Power and Angels of Beauty. As soon as the Creative Ray of God touches the plane of Manifestation those two forces come into play inevitably.

"On the physical plane those two forces will manifest either as masculine or feminine, as male or female. Both forces are inherent in everything and either one or the other will predominate. Upon the predominance of the one or the other, sex is determind. Even some plants are either male or female. Every living thing has this procreative, or sexual, energy in its make-up, for it is the Creative Energy of God manifesting on the dense, physical plane of creation."

91

⋇ 14 ⋇

19 *April*

This morning I witnessed something unusually interesting: Bhai Sahib has driven an evil spirit out of a young man.

Arrived early, about 7 a.m., for it was very hot. Everybody had already left except for Happy Babu who was in deep dhyana. Bhai Sahib asked us inside the room, where it was cooler under the fan. It was very quiet. He was making entries in his diary. Both doors were open, but the *chiks* [a kind of blind made of bamboo sticks] were down.

It must have been about 11 a.m. when I saw two men coming through the gate. One was old, the other very young. They were dressed poorly; Muslim villagers, I thought. Satendra, who was outside, went to meet them, then came into the room and gave a slip of paper to his father. Bhai Sahib read it and said to them to return on Tuesday and continued to write. A conversation followed between Satendra and the men standing outside. Then the boy came back and said they came from a far-off village and could not come back.

Bhai Sahib put down his writing material, got up, went to the door and I was a bit surprised to see him remaining inside the room behind the chik talking to the men who were outside. It was unusual because he always asked everybody to come inside the room when he was in. The young man sat down on the step before the door and the guru, holding one corner of the chik slightly raised with his left hand, just stood there looking at him. Nobody spoke.

The young man, clad in a chequered cotton dhoti, had a rather simple and primitive look about him. Suddenly he uttered a loud cry and then began to howl like an animal, with his mouth wide open, his eyes glassy and spent, like the eyes of a dead man. The expression of his face was terrible to see; it was like a contorted mask.

'What goes on?' I asked Happy Babu, for I couldn't see clearly what was going on, the guru's back nearly filling the frame of the door, and the chik partly hiding the scene from me.

'I don't know,' murmured Happy Babu. So I ran quickly into the next room and through the inner courtyard into the front garden.

When I approached, the guru gave me a quick warning glance. I stopped. Bhai Sahib was still standing in the room behind the raised blind. The young man was now lying on the ground having convulsions, froth streaming from his mouth, his face contorted and terrible.

'Don't touch me, don't touch me, I will destroy you!' he was shouting. The voice had nothing human in it; it was like a desperate wailing.

Bhai Sahib continued to look steadily at this unfortunate creature; he was in

92

deep samadhi, his eyes like bottomless pits of still, dark water, unseeing, veiled.

The young man was shouting louder and louder; his convulsions increased to a paroxysm. His father was squatting near the wall of the bungalow, trembling like a leaf with fear.

Then, with a pointed finger, very slowly, as if describing a circle around this demented body, "Go away!" Bhai Sahib ordered sternly. He repeated it twice; then the voice which came out of the young man's throat, and which had nothing human in it, shouted three times:

'I am going; leave me, leave me, leave!'

"Go!" said the guru, making a stabbing movement at him with his raised forefinger. All of a sudden there was silence. The tormented, frenzied body became motionless, as if emptied, devoid of any spark of life. He is dead, I thought; how dreadful! But I knew it couldn't be.

Bhai Sahib let the chik drop,* still standing behind it. A few long moments passed. A small bird whistled in the treetop; somewhere a car passed by. Slowly the young man sat up shakily. His nice, simple face had a perfectly human expression again. And with a lovely smile, lifting one corner of the chik, he silently touched the feet of the guru and so did his father who until now had been crouching in the shade near the wall.

"Go, my son," said Bhai Sahib gently. "Go both of you, in peace." They went, dazed. Not a word more was spoken. He let the chik fall back and went into the room and I followed him. He stood in the middle, motionless; he was still in samadhi.

'Well,' I said, 'that was something!' He fixed me with the eyes that see other worlds.

"*If he comes back, I will burn him,*" he said darkly. "Sometimes they are rogues and then they come back. Then I will burn him and all his relations!"

I went home most impressed and, I confess, rather shaken.

When I came back after 5 p.m., he was sitting outside in the garden; a few people were already there.

I asked him what he had meant when he said "If he comes back I will burn him and all his relations?"

"Oh, that," he said. "It is quite simple; those kinds of spirits are rather powerful elementals. If they want an experience on the physical level, then they attach themselves to a human being. In other words, they obsess him. They are really most horrible things, most ugly to look at. More often they attach themselves to women. In Rajasthan I had to do some of this work," he added thoughtfully.

'Why women?' I asked.

* Later I asked his eldest son why his father was standing behind the chik, invisible from the street. It was because the father did not want to create a sensation. Seeing a young man having a fit in India, no passer-by would bother; but if a tall, white-robed figure pointing a finger at a boy was seen, a crowd would be sure to assemble.

"It is because a woman is weaker and easier to obsess.* We all have good and evil spirits in us – the good and evil in us – and who wins is the master."

'I thought it is in the mind,' I said.

"Yes, the mind also. But spirits too. And is the mind not an elemental as well? Everything in Nature is the bitter enemy of the human being. Why? Because he is the King. Everybody hates those who command. The human being is the Master of Creation, the Ruler. And also, if I say 'I will burn him,' it is not so easily done. One does not destroy so easily. They also have the right to live; they are a parallel evolution to man. They have no notion of good or evil. If they have a desire, they fulfil it. But I have to protect my race, the human being, so, I will help him and get the spirit out. If he should come back, I will drive him out again and give him a stiff warning. If he still comes back I will destroy him then, and with him all his relations. Shaitans are many; a whole race of them usually. But when the Saint is powerful, they are afraid to come back!"

And he laughed his ringing laughter which made him look so young and so free.

Professor Batnagar came and much talk was going on about Masters and the training. So very few people come for the sake of spiritual life; mostly they come for worldly matters; they waste the Teacher's time. They come for a bit of dhyana or bliss, or they want children, or some other blessing. But few, very few, come because they want the Truth.

Then he asked us all inside and was massaged by Panditji.

21 April

"According to the System, the shishya is constantly kept between the opposite ups and downs; it creates the friction necessary to cause suffering which will defeat the mind. The greatest obstacle on the Spiritual Path is to make people understand that they have to give up everything. If I give an order, and they obey the order, there is no merit. They must understand it by themselves. Sometimes the Master will say, 'Bring your wife to me,' or 'Bring your child to me.' Out of a thousand, out of a hundred thousand, only one will obey such an order. For he will think, 'Why does he want my wife, or my child?' The mind will give trouble; there will be doubt; they will lose faith.

"There is a secret behind it; if it is not obeyed they will not survive. This is one of the supreme tests. Only a Sat Guru knows when to give such a test. That's why the Teacher will hesitate to give such an order. The shishya is attached to wife and children; he has to give them up. And attachment is the greatest obstacle. *What is dearest to us must go.* This is the Law. One cannot serve two Masters. Either the world or the guru. Everything has to be given up, absolutely, nothing should remain, nothing at all. Even self-respect has to go. Only then, and then only, can I take them into my heart."

* The personality of woman, having been subdued for millennia, is more likely to be influenced than man's.

He was full of light. So full of dynamism that even those few simple men who were sitting there were staring at him as if not believing their eyes.

Later he said; "Mental sufferings are Dwellers on the Threshold. Bear them." He spoke very quietly. I suddenly was flooded with nameless sorrow and began to cry.

"Go home; may God help you."

26 April

This morning there was such a crowd of horrid, smelly men, I was really in despair ... Dust, heat, smells, yelling children ... How am I going to stand it for years and years to come? Sitting here for hours and no hope, no change ... Being ground down to a powder, every day the same, every day hotter, every day more disagreeable ...

And so, during a pause, I followed him when he went into the room and told him how difficult it is to sit for hours amongst a smelly, shouting crowd.

"I know, I know, my dear. I understand," he said quickly. "I know. But the satsang must be; it is essential, and what can I do if it is my life? These conditions are part of my life too."

'But you can escape by going into deep samadhi. L. could too; she did not suffer much from it, she told me herself. One simply goes away, but I cannot do it! I sit here fully conscious of the surroundings. It is an acute discomfort! I will go mad!'

"No," he said softly. "Never will you go mad. There are things from heart to heart; this is the only real language. All else is nonsense."

His expression was so kind when, with slightly bent head, he was listening to what I was telling him, while others in the meantime were shouting at each other in banal conversation.

'I seem to cry all the time now,' I was saying, 'either because I feel so alone and full of longing, or because my heart is full of sorrow, or because ... I just don't know why ... A great loneliness, an emptiness which fills me with despair. And it is not my mind giving me trouble this time; the mind is still, as still as a candle on a windless day. I will need much help. To sit here amongst evil-smelling men is such an ordeal and it will be my destiny for years to come ... Please, help me to cross the bridge, to be able to reconcile it all within myself.'

He nodded gently.

"Love should grow; try. Try to do it yourself. If you cannot, then the ladder will be there for you."

'But do you mean to say that I am failing?' He shook his head and just smiled.

But he is right. It is the lack of love for other people; I really cannot stand them. If I could have more compassion I would not object so much to the smell and dirt and noise and ignorance ...

This morning I learned that he left for Allahabad. It means that he will be away for at least three days or perhaps even more. And I am expected to be there as usual. His brother is laughing and talking in Hindi all the time. Just now there seems to be an especially mad crowd, shouting all together, and laughing; such a din ... Elaci Baba was rubbing his shaved head with a *loki* [a variety of marrow] to refresh his brain, so he was saying. But the sticky juice dried on his head giving out a sour smell. And I have to sit. And to sit. Trying to bear it as well as I can ...

⊀ 15 ⊁

9 *May*

Moved to a new flat on the 1st May. It is comfortable. Only, oh, so hot! The small courtyard paved with red bricks gets as hot as a baker's oven. All around is a high brick wall making the whole unit very private.

Went to the park to see the trees called 'The Flame of the Forest', now in flower. A magnificent sight they are; rows and rows of them, feathery foliage of deep green, and covered with large clusters of blossoms ranging from deep orange-gold to flame and even crimson. It seemed that the glory of the scarlet, crimson and orange flowers, as though painted on the deep blue sky and my strange, terrible longing are, for some inexplicable reason, one and the same thing.

I remember L. telling me that the disciple is subjected to such states of loneliness and longing that it could be almost suicidal. A great Master is needed to get the disciple through this state of separation.

Guruji came back on Thursday looking very tired. Told him about the complete separation and darkness and that for the last few days the mind has not been working at all. He only nodded.

"Love is a gift," he was saying to a man who came for the first time. "Love is a gift and it remains forever, once it is given; only sometimes, like embers. it is covered by ashes and it is not evident."

I wondered what those ashes were ... our little self, the 'I'? Or is it the world closing tightly around us?

Have no money at all. A few rupees are all I possess. It is surprising how little it matters. I have to learn how to be a beggar; to trust Him and Him only. Whatever arrives from abroad from now on is not mine any more; it will go into his account to be distributed to all those who are in need. I will receive sufficient to buy food.

To be a mindless creature; how strange it is and quite painless. I can still do my daily chores, whatever is necessary for daily life. My brain is no good any more.

'I am nowhere, I cannot think,' I said to him and he nodded gravely. To be nowhere is also a strange feeling. I sit here, so clearly I must be somewhere in space. But certainly not in this world . . . Everything seems to be just a funny, crazy dream; a maya of some kind. The heat and the glare, and the vomiting condition, and the people, and the feelings of fear and loneliness and the simple necessities of life . . . Just crazy . . . Difficult to reconcile all this; impossible to understand.

The silly talk of the noisy crowd did not seem to matter at all today. It simply did not exist. The mind is in such stillness, it seems to be permanently fixed on him, in fear and apprehension. What will he do next? Only this concentration on him is effortless, easy and natural; all else is an effort. It appears that the only effortless state is thinking about him; for it is quite automatic.

I suppose that this is the reason why in this system of Yoga a teacher is considered essential; he becomes the focus of attention for the mind. By this method the one-pointed concentration is easily achieved; whereas in all other schools of Yoga it is difficult. The effort lies somewhere else; in the power of endurance, the capacity for sacrifice, the will to go on, to hold out at any cost. And also the eagerness, the perseverance; this is the shishya's part to play. And it is here where the greatest effort is needed. A very great effort indeed . . .

14 *May*

Fasted for two days. No food at all. When I went to him, I had a palpitation and pain in the heart. Probably brought on by the emptiness in the bowels, due to the empty stomach.

He had not been to the bank; said that an employee of the bank will bring some money. I doubted it. His expression was severe, hardly looking at me, speaking abruptly. He looked remote and ruthless; his face was like a stone. In my heart there is much fear when he is in this mood.

He stood at the gate waiting for the bank employee to arrive. And I went home to take some medicine to stop the palpitations. When I came back, he was talking to two young men at the gate. They were from the bank, he later told me. The money arrived; I was relieved.

"You were perplexed," he said to me. I explained it was because there was something wrong with my heart; my body seems to be well in spite of the heat. I did not expect to get such a reaction after only a short fast. He said that he will give me some money for food tomorrow.

15 *May*

His face was stony. He was talking to two men already sitting there when I arrived. He did not acknowledge my greeting. How much fear there is in me when he is like this . . . I am terrified of him and speaking becomes difficult. I asked him timidly if I could have some money.

"Wait," he said. When the two men had left, he got up, went inside, and then gave me some money. That will see me through until the end of the month, I thought.

"How is the new flat?"

I said that it is very private, very pleasant.

He did not come out in the evening. After giving Babu, his son, his English lesson, I sat alone. Lately he takes every opportunity to make my life as uncomfortable as possible. He decided that Babu needs his English improved. The boy hates it and does not hide his feelings. I have to come at 4 p.m., when the heat is simply suffocating. After he has had his lesson, I sit alone. It is all so difficult, for the mind is not working and the heat does the rest. Furthermore, I have to type continually, with several copies, job applications for his son, or medical certificates for the half-blind man who is coming daily. Needless to say, the certificates have to have several copies as well ... Much later the usual crowd arrives. Lately, his brother is always present, talking and talking ...

Now the temperature is 108°–110° in the shade and every day the *Loo* is blowing from 9 a.m. to 6 p.m. The Loo is a hot wind coming from the deserts of West Pakistan which pushes the temperature up to 120° in the shade at times, so I have been told.

17 *May*

In the evening a few people were sitting and talking to his brother. He came out and began by telling me that one should not sit on the same level as the guru. I said that I never thought that I did, but he ignored my remark. Many people seem to object to me and I asked why.

"Yes," he said. "People are free to object and it satisfies them. Look at my devotees, how they behave when they come here; I personally don't mind; it is not for me, but for the people who come here and object." I said that I respected him so much that I never thought that at any time I behaved badly.

"You must become part of our culture; I took on the culture of my Revered Guru Maharaj; you must take on mine. You will be changed."

I was perplexed. 'But, Bhai Sahib, I have been in your hands for such a short time, how can you expect me to change so quickly? I know I have to change and I am prepared to do it as quickly as possible; I will co-operate in every way, but give me time!'

"You see," he laughed, "it took you more than ten minutes to understand what I want. Look how dense you are!"

'Yes. When you speak to me, my mind goes blank. You speak in a manner difficult to grasp for the Western mind. Your mind works in a different way from ours. Your way of expressing your thought is different.'

"First one must learn how to obey; then how to understand the Hint."

'I will try, Bhai Sahib.'

He nodded, smiled and went inside.

18 *May*

'What is *ahimsa*?' the Frenchman had asked the other day.

"Real ahimsa cannot really be practised on the physical level; not completely at least, and not by everybody. What about regions in which nothing
grows and one has to eat meat or fish? What about insects we crush unknow-
ingly under our feet? The germs we swallow or destroy; they are life also. It is
the mental ahimsa which has to be practised and by everybody and completely
so.

"Non-killing is only a crude conception of ahimsa; for it is much more than
that. The real ahimsa is not to injure the feelings of others, nor to injure oneself. That is, not to harm others, and not to harm oneself."

'How can we injure our own feelings or harm ourselves?' the Frenchman
wanted to know.

"You injure your own feelings by creating habits. If, for instance, you are
addicted to drinking tea, and you cannot get it, you suffer, don't you? So your
feelings are injured by the created habit. Never, never to injure the feelings of
anybody and never to create habits is real ahimsa. By creating habits we imprison ourselves; imprisonment is limitation. And limitation is suffering."

I think that is a very interesting answer; and here would lie the explanation
why the guru has no fixed habits at all. I keep coming here every day; and
every day it is different. One never knows how it is going to be. Sometimes he
is here; sometimes one learns that he is away; and never the day or the time of
return is known. Or he would be gone for a walk, or resting, or having a bath.
He will sit outside or inside, or he will not appear at all. He has no fixed hours
for anything. He might sit in meditation the whole night, or sleep till 9 a.m.,
have his first bath at 4 a.m. or at midday. At any time of the day he may
announce, "I am going to have my bath." I think he has two or three baths
every day. One never knows what he will do or not do.

One day he told us, "Even my wife never knows what I am doing or how
much money I have. Sometimes I go out without money and come back with
a large sum. Sometimes I go out, my pockets full of money, and I come back
without. The only thing I can say for sure is that I don't go out of my premises
without an order."

At that time I did not understand what he meant; now I understand, at
least I think that I do. L. said that all Sufis are like that. They do not try deliberately to be; they become like that by following the System.

20 *May*

At last the ceiling fan has been installed. He made me wait for it until now.
I waited and waited for him to give me the money to buy it. I kept walking up
and down the veranda in the afternoon stark naked, like in a dream, blood
boiling, drinking and drinking from the warm water in the earthenware jar
... indescribable suffering.

Still, windless nights; sleepless because of the heat inside me and all around. Burned alive within and without. A sacrifice to Agni [God of Fire] in the real sense of the word.

24 May

In the evening when I arrived, he was sitting alone in the garden. Lately he avoids sitting with me but to my surprise he began a kindly talk to me. At first he told me about himself and how he became his Revered Guru Maharaj's disciple when he was only fourteen years old.

"You come naked into the world and you go naked. When you come to the Spiritual Teacher, you have to be naked!"

Suddenly it dawned on me! Of course, it was the second birth according to Tradition! Silently I thanked my good star that I was able to offer him all I had, sensing somehow, dimly, that I had to do it. It was not a knowledge, rather a *feeling*; an intuition that it has to be, that it was *expected* of me, that there was no other way to go. I remembered that not long ago he said that the shishya has to give away everything but he must do it by himself. The Master cannot order it; the Teacher cannot say 'do it' for then it will be an order and there is no merit attached to it. Besides, even if the disciple gives everything up out of love or regard for the Teacher, who can say that deep in him no attachment remains? One does not get rid of desires and attachments by ordering them to disappear. It will never work this way. One has to reach the stage that everything begins to fall away from one. Possessions are attachments and can become an obstacle to Spiritual Life. If one understands it and acts accordingly, the way is free.

28 May

I greeted him as usual when I came in. He ignored me completely. He was walking up and down on the brick elevation in front of the house, mala in his hand. Had a premonition of some trouble brewing, but chased this thought away. He gave me a quick look and continued to walk up and down. Then I noticed: the Great Separation was here ... It is useless to try to describe it to someone who has never experienced it. It is a peculiar, special feeling of utter loneliness. I use the word 'special' intentionally, because it cannot be compared to any kind of feeling of loneliness we all experience sometimes in our lives.

All seems dark and lifeless. There is no purpose anywhere or in anything. No God to pray to. No hope. Nothing at all. A deep-seated rebellion fills the mind. Only this time it mattered less than usual. The mind was in such a state, there was so little left of it. No trouble at all to keep it still; it was automatically blank. I just sat there. The thoughts, if any happened to float in, were drifting slowly, lazily, passing by as if on a screen, and then all was blankness once more. This state was not new to me; it had begun to come on periodically for the last few months; increasing gradually in intensity each time it happened.

The nights are still, full of stars and oven-hot. A sheer agony. My eyes are constantly red and inflamed from the perspiration running into them. Men go around with twisted handkerchiefs around their foreheads to prevent this happening, and some wear twisted towels round their necks. I shower three to four times a day but there is no relief as the water tank is on the roof and the water is boiling hot.

Today the Loo was terrible; the temperature yesterday was 117° in the shade. Today it felt even hotter, like the entrance hall of hell . . .

⤝ 16 ⤞

30 *May*

Will I remember those days without peace, days with no mind and of the most exhausting heat? Days of the most terrible longing? One's head like a leaden weight sitting on one's neck, the bones of the skull like an iron ring pressing tighter and tighter around the brain. All the objects in the room so hot that sometimes it burns the fingers to touch them. And it is hot, and it is hot; oh, it is hot!

And the mind does not work. I fail to understand the simplest things and forget what I did only one moment ago . . .

I told him of the experience of having to live practically without mind. What a pity that I won't remember these states in the future; states which are leading one into an unknown dimension. I talked for a while, he listening quietly. We were not interrupted, not even once.

"Where there is intellect, there is no love. Love begins where the mind stops."

In the evening he was standing in the garden when I came, looking at the sky. A dust storm had been gathering on the horizon for the last half hour. As soon as he saw me he went in and closed the door. I went into the doorway not daring to go into the room and sat there in the passage in the whirling dust. He was inside the courtyard not taking the slightest notice of me, talking to his wife and to his brother and I sat there crying bitterly. How hopelessly inadequate I felt; only half understanding and feeling deeply the humiliation of not being asked into the room in these appalling weather conditions. The dust choked me; I had difficulty in breathing.

The storm soon subsided and Panditji began to wet the ground in the garden with a hose. Guruji came out and walked up and down. Panditji always looks so serene, existing in a world of his own, distant, tranquil, living very much his own inward life. Mostly sitting in dhyana, or massaging Guruji's feet. Sometimes one can see him standing and staring with wide open eyes and there is such an expression of bliss, such a tender quality in his face, a happiness unknown to me and probably to the others.

Professor Batnagar came. He said that I do such a *tapas* [penance] by staying here in circumstances to which I am not at all accustomed. Probably get so much bliss and happiness, otherwise I would not do it!

'Oh no, no bliss; such things are for other people; I only have trouble,' I said. Bhai Sahib, who was talking to a group of villagers turned and looked straight at me. His eyes were shining like diamonds in the half-darkness. After a short silence he proceeded to tell me once more how he does not like to hurt people's feelings, but it was necessary sometimes to do his duty. Actually he told me off this morning about something which I don't remember, due to my mind being in such a state.

"My Revered Father and my Uncle were surrendered before my Revered Guru Maharaj in every possible way, and still he often told them 'You understand nothing. You don't know how to pay regard to me!' Professor Batnagar can tell you how my Revered Father paid the greatest regard to him always. Of all his disciples he had only two who did completely surrender; my Revered Father and my Uncle."

'How great is the capacity for love in the human heart?' I asked.

"No limit; there is no limit!" He smiled his radiant smile.

31 May

Mind not working, feeling giddy, all around is maya. Told him that I cannot be a good advertisement for him, for I cannot even walk. This morning I was walking zig-zag like a drunkard. He gave me a kindly smile, fingering his mala.

"Ye-es," he said thoughtfully, "the poets call us drunkards; we are drunk with the Wine of the Eyes of the Beloved . . ."

Then I began to talk non-stop for a long time. It was like an urge, an inner necessity. One moment afterwards I did not remember what I had told him. Though I do remember saying that if I talked too much, he should stop me. But he only smiled gently and said nothing. Plenty of people came in the meantime and towards midday when all had left, he said:

"This morning you were telling me that you were talking too much. Sometimes one is made to talk. The Divine Power wishes it so. One has to talk.

"I am supposed to hear everything, to listen to everything. If the disciple is asleep, the Master is behind; if the disciple is in trouble, the Master is with him. It is a troublesome job to be a guru," he concluded. I asked him if he would know if I was in danger, and he nodded. His face was very still. I asked him what did he mean when he said, "One is made to speak." I felt an inner urge, an irresistible desire to say all that was in my mind. Is it done to let him know things which he perhaps may have overlooked? He nodded absent-mindedly. I was not sure that he was listening.

6 June

This morning at sunrise, about 5 a.m., the sky was covered with the most exquisite, feathery, magenta-pink clouds. Deep in me there was a strange, never-experienced happiness. It was different; different from the glimpses I had had of it before. So ethereal, so elusive. It seems to have nothing to do with me as a person, nor with my environment, nor with my state of mind. It does not belong to me; it is just there. It appears like a state of Grace; I cannot create it at will. It comes when it wishes and goes so silently that I don't even notice that it has gone. I only realize suddenly that it is no more.

During the night, I listened to the currents inside my body. For my body was full of Sound ... A Sound connected with the light circulating in it, with this mysterious web burning my tissues. The outlines of the heart were clearly visible; it was surrounded with a faint, bluish light, beating regularly; a beautiful sight.

7 June

This morning we sat in the garden and we were quite alone. I spoke little, trying to merge into the stillness of non-being. But he began to speak and remained with me for over three hours; something which I think never happened before in all those past months. Not only that, but there were hardly any interruptions. He touched upon many topics, but he began by saying that today on 7 June his Revered Father had expired. It was the anniversary of his death.

I told him that the vibration was at the base of the spine again this morning and I was afraid that the horrible visions would come back. He shook his head. "Forget it. This is in the past. It has been taken away."

I suddenly realized that from the moment in March when I was breaking down almost in hysterics in his garden, I never saw them again.

"I told you, if I remember rightly, that past karmas form part and parcel of the blood."

'But what I saw was so horrible! I did not even know that such things could exist!' I protested. He slowly shook his head.

"Souls are old. How can the Soul remember everything; all the past? It was all there in your blood. It was the worst situation possible. If this room is full of water, all the doors and windows are closed and the water cannot flow out, what will happen? It will get foul. If the patient has to be operated upon and the doctor operates, for a while the patient may even curse the doctor; but the doctor will do his duty just the same. It is not as you have accused me, that I have caused this trouble by using my yogic powers. Why use the powers to do such a thing? If a horse is going slow and another, a quicker one overtakes it, the first horse quite simply gets wakened up. That is all there is to it. Why can't you understand it? Why should it be so difficult to grasp? Why do we insist on satsang? Because it is a quickening. We do not teach; we quicken. I am stronger than you so your currents adjust themselves to mine. This is a simple law of nature. The stronger magnetic current will affect, quicken, the weaker. If you let flow an electric current through two wires, side by side, one a strong one and the other a weak one, the stronger will affect the weaker. It will increase its potency. It is so simple."

⚔ 17 ⚔

8 *June*

'Completely mad!' I laughed. 'Gloriously mad; irresponsible and drunk with joy!' He was standing inside the fountain, his torso bare, clad only in a pale blue longhi. He only glanced briefly at me, occupied as he was in pouring buckets of cold water over his head and blowing like a walrus. I felt fine, so free, so mad. Where was the mind? One is better without it really ...

"Today my Revered Father was taken to Samadhi;" he said, rubbing his shoulders vigorously with a towel. Some prasad was distributed later to a few people who came. Then we remained alone. It seems to me that I accused him of some contradiction.

"No contradictions here; only your mind makes it so. In the morning one says something which belongs to the morning; at midday one says things which belong to this time; in the afternoon and in the evening one will say what is suitable to that particular time. There is no contradiction. We speak according to the time, the place, and the state of progress of the disciple. I will never say anything praiseworthy about you to yourself, but to others I may."

How is it I wondered, that he has changed so much lately? He *is* different, there can be little doubt about it. He seems to have acquired a different quality, a non-human aspect, a kind of transparency, something unearthly about him. A being from another world, so strangely beautiful. A quality of inner beauty becoming more and more visible to me. Cannot explain what is happening. Can only look and wonder. When I told him, he had only boyish and happy laughter in response.

"Only things which you cannot explain are lasting. What can be comprehended with the mind is not a high state. If you cannot express it, cannot put it into words – those are things not of the mind and they will go on forever!"

'Oh, please help me! I am so confused!'

"Why should I?" He looked straight at me. "If I begin to help, you will ask again and again for help: how will you cross the stream? You must do it yourself, I will not help. If I do, you will get used to it and will never be able to do without my help. We all have to cross the stream alone. Don't you realize that this is the way? I am telling you, showing you the way. THE ONLY WAY. Why don't you realize that you are nothing? It means complete surrender. It takes time. It is not done in one day. It takes time to surrender."

'How long?'

"The whole life, twenty to thirty years. If you live a thousand years, it won't be enough. Sometimes you are near, sometimes very far away. I am helping you as a matter of fact, but you cannot be aware of it and I will never say so.

My harsh words help you, my sweetness never will. Now, let us take your case. You have renounced the world, all the material things you have apparently renounced. But the invisible things. Have you renounced them too? Renounced your character, your will, everything? The character one inherits from the parents which together with the will moulds the life of a person. If you have not renounced your will, your character, in your case the surrender has not yet begun. Only the surrender on the physical level has been achieved. But this is the easiest one to achieve!"

I could not conceal my disappointment; how disheartened it made me feel. I doubted that I would ever reach the goal!

"Never, never think like this! These are negative thoughts. Failure should never be contemplated! But you should not lean on me; you must be able to rely on yourself alone. I can only create the conditions. I am helping you and will do so in the future, but will never say so. You will not know when and how you are helped. And whatever you do I will always tell you that IT IS NOTHING and you should do more! Otherwise how will you get rid of the shaitan of pride?

"Surrender is the most difficult thing in the world while you are doing it; and the easiest when it is done. Those people whom you see here they don't know how to sit before the Master, how to speak to the Master. All sorts of silly talk is going on!"

'But those are only outward, exterior attitudes. They cannot mean much,' I said.

"What is in the heart becomes expressed outwardly. The exterior reflects the inner attitude; it cannot be helped. If one feels reverence, it is bound to show itself. It is like love; it cannot be hidden. If I don't speak to you for days, you just sit. If I speak, you speak and never, never must you complain ... This is the door, the *only door* to the *King of the Heart*. What is surrender of the heart? You people do not even imagine. Not only Western people, I mean Indians too ... Learn to be *nothing*, this is the only way."

He looked so gentle. He *is* changing ... or is it I who am going mad? Could not take my eyes away from him. Elegant. All in white. How the bones of the cheeks shone through the bronze-coloured skin! It gave a kind of transparent effect.

'If you understand it, if you can express it, it will not remain, so you have said just now. So what kind of experience is that of which I can know nothing and cannot understand? It is not mine, if I know nothing about it!'

"I have told you so often; try to know my thoughts and wishes. Why for instance, have you always adverse ideas? So many doubts. It is your character. It is rare that anybody surrenders at the first go, very few do it. If the mind goes, where does the character abide? When nothing remains what is left?"

'Only love,' I said.

"Exactly," he answered and his eyes shone like stars. "Look what you were seven months before and look where you stand now."

'I do want to surrender completely, believe me, but how to manage it, how to achieve it? I feel an urgency. Something is telling me that there is not much time left.'

"You will," he said shifting into a different position. He sat now in guru *asana* [posture]; he often sat like that when he was talking to me. No one has the right to sit in this asana in the presence of the Teacher, so the tradition goes.

"You will," he repeated, "you are put on the line and you will."

'Oh, I wish you had told me all that before; so clearly and in detail, I mean. It is such a great help. But you never seem to have time to speak to me even if I sit here for hours every day! Only lately it is different; you speak to me sometimes.'

"Again: why such adverse thoughts come into your mind? I speak to you as I never spoke to anyone before! You must understand that you have to change completely. Everyone says, 'my' character, 'my' intelligence; everybody desires self-expression, to assert his individuality. You, for instance, have been successful with it in the world. Your will, your character, still run after the worldly concepts, as they were used to do for many years. You see, now it must be completely changed." He fell silent. A silence which was almost physically felt, descended in the room. It was deep, so solid, one could hear the ringing sound of absolute silence. He glanced at the clock standing behind him in the recess.

"Are you satisfied? You can go home now," he added casually, and I went. But I touched his feet before I left. My heart was so full of gratitude.

9 *June*

I was silent this morning; I had nothing to say. Neither had he, for he prayed. Was still thinking over what he told me yesterday. All things of importance in my life usually happen on Friday. Felt that yesterday's discussion foretells a change. Some turning point is imminent. But what? I could not know, of course.

Slept little in the night. Thinking of the line of conduct to be taken, the difficulties ahead. The mind was revolving in a kind of slow motion. Was very tired in the morning; the sheets under me were completely wet with perspiration; felt weak. My head was aching as if an iron band was screwed tighter and tighter round it.

10 *June*

When I entered his gate this morning, he was already sitting in the garden with quite a few people around him. It was like a physical blow into my heart to see him so full of light. Had a moment of deepest joy for being able to see it; it was as if his physical body was not a reality; it was submerged in the light surrounding it and only the light was real, not the physical being. He did not seem to have noticed me and did not acknowledge my greeting.

Later, in the room – we could not sit in the garden because of the dust – Durghesh's baby was brought in. Guruji took the child from the mother; such tenderness was in this gesture as he was gently rocking it. When he looked down at the child in his arms he seemed like one of the timeless statues of the Buddha of Compassion. Then I knew what the transformation in him was, the change which caused me constant perplexity. It was the quality of the super-human in him. Whenever there was an opportunity, I kept asking people if they found any change in guru's appearance in the last ten days or so. But everybody said no; he was the same as usual.

11 *June*

In the night could not sleep. All the chakras were humming. Fire was burning inside my belly; blood was liquid fire . . .

'You are the King of Contradictions! Just to give an example; once you said when L. was here that there is no love in your heart for anybody or anything except your Revered Guru Maharaj. A few weeks back when Professor Batnagar was here you said that your heart is so barren that you cannot love anybody at all. But one only needs to see you together with your grandchild or to have noticed the look in your eyes when you were talking to old Gupta yesterday afternoon to see how much love there is in your heart. How can I reconcile all that?'

He suddenly smiled, gaily and boyishly, the smile when he is much amused, but said nothing. And so I talked on, how to reconcile this and that, how he keeps denying what he said only a short while ago, and so forth. Maddening.

16 *June*

Truth is One; learned men call it by different names [*Rg Veda*]

Professor Batnagar quoted it. It was during a conversation in which he was also saying, 'If you want God, you have to sell yourself first. This is the essence, the core of every religion; of every philosophy as far as I have read and understood. Reduce yourself to nil, to nothing, and you will realize the Truth.' I asked him if he can notice the difference in the outward appearance of Bhai Sahib.

'The transformation of the guru is one of the mystical experiences. It is mentioned in the Yogic treatises. It is the developing capacity of the disciple to recognize the divinity of the guru.' I glanced at Bhai Sahib. His face was quite expressionless; he did not seem to listen. His eyes were closed.

Speaking of the Path, I mentioned how depressing it was that all the odds were against me; I have to fight my character as an elderly woman already crystallized in a certain way of behaviour . . .

'And,' he interrupted me, 'the three thousand years of European civilisation as your heredity, your education with the emphasis on competition, on assertion of the individual with all its ramifications, freedom of expression, emphasis on self-respect, and so on.'

'Yes,' I said, 'and also the fact that we are conditioned to consider your civilization somewhat inferior to ours. And also the guru's ideas sometimes seem old-fashioned and out of date. Furthermore he deliberately puts all the appearances against himself. Sum it up together and you will see that I am at a disadvantage; have to overcome many more obstacles than anybody else in this circle. All seems to conspire against me!'

Professor Batnagar was of the opinion that Sufism was Islamic Buddhism, but there was no historic evidence for such a belief as far as it is known. Bhai Sahib was very much against this idea. He said that Sufism is very much older than Islam and even Buddhism. True, it took on the terminology of Islam, but this was due to the customs and religion of the country where it was allowed to flourish. (That is in Arabia and later in Persia.)

Lord Mohammed was once asked to which religion did he belong and it is said that Christ was asked the same question. The fact is that all Saints, all Prophets, belong to the same religion; the religion of the Lovers of God.

18 *June*

The loneliness and depression are terrible again. The heat is slowly grinding my body down. All is dry. The rain is late this year and every evening when I go home I smell the sweet fragrance of flowering shrubs, also tired, thirsty and longing for moisture.

21 *June*

'You used harsh words last time when I said to you that for me the guru and God are one and the same thing.'

"I use the words which seem hard to you because this is sometimes the only way to make the shishya think. We teach according to the stages. There is nothing wrong; nothing right. When the child is in the cradle, he will think that the cradle is the whole world. Later, he will think the room is the whole world. Later still, the veranda, the garden and so on. To think that the guru is God is a very preliminary stage."

'Kabir said, "When two stand in front of me, the guru and God, who is the greater? Surely the guru, because he will take me to God," ' I quoted. 'And if it is good enough for Kabir, should it not be good enough for me?'

"Who is going to listen to Kabir? Kabir was only a poet! If somebody is saying that stealing is a good thing and should be done, am I going to listen to him, only because he says so?"

25 *June*

Great stillness. A kind of inner security. Until now the mind was in the most restless, insecure state. I wonder how long this stillness will last . . .

30 June

The monsoon is still not here. Long, hot days, very often with no movement of air, not even in the mornings or evenings, and the nights are as wind-still and as hot as in Madras. I am steaming with perspiration, giddy, and with headache. My eyes are red and inflamed all the time. Most uncomfortable. The mind works badly. Cannot see the whole aspect. Asked him the meaning of what was happening.

"Sometimes your mind is made to work at only fifty per cent capacity, sometimes at twenty-five per cent, and sometimes it stops working altogether."

What happens if it does not work at all I wondered; where does it vanish to?

'I was so proud of my learning, but when I stand in front of thee, oh my guru, my mind is blank; I have forgotten everything' goes the text of one of the Persian couplets. Well, it could be my case. I was thinking only this morning that I seldom remember anything of my past; never think of it. Thinking has become such a laborious job. Where are my qualifications? Travels I have done, knowledge which I have accumulated during so many years? Gone! Seem never to have existed!

Only I find that there is still much resentment in me. He treats me so badly. "Idiot," "Stupid," he calls me in front of everyone, at the slightest provocation. I complained; I protested. He hissed at me because I said his wife asks sometimes pretty unintelligent questions; what about that? If you say that people are at liberty to criticize me, am I not at liberty to criticize others? He himself says that he is not a god; if so, then he is not infallible. It follows that I am at liberty to find faults with him too. Mistakes can be made and if I notice it, why can't I say so? Why this distinction; one law for others and another one for me? But he glared at me, called me ignorant and impertinent and I don't know how to respect the Teacher and his family, and so forth. Very well, Teacher ... But why should I respect his family? What have they to do with me or I with them?

6 July

"The thinking faculty of the mind, which is called in the *Yoga Sutras* 'the modifications of the mind', with its constant movement, prevents us from perceiving Reality. In order to help the disciple, the Teacher will 'switch off' the current of the mind; will paralyse it temporarily in order that the *buddhi* [intuition] quality can come through. The mind cannot transcend itself, some help is needed. We live within our own mind. How can the mind get out of itself?"

'Do you mean to say that it is the Teacher who, by his Yogic powers, puts the mind out of action?'

"It is done," he said, ignoring the first part of my question. "And it is done very simply by activating the heart chakra. And the more the chakra is activated, the less the mind is able to work. It is quite a painless process."

Oh, I know that all right; it does not hurt at all to be mindless; one cannot think, that's all.

"Even on the worldly platform it works in a similar way. If one is much in love, the lover is forgetful of everything else except the object of his love. He is distraught, people call him mad. The law is the same on all levels of being. Only on the spiritual level the law is more powerful because there are no obstructions caused by the density of matter."

And after a moment's silence he added with one of his flashing smiles, "We are called the fools, the idiots of God, by the Sufi poets."

Tonight he left with Babu for Allahabad. His skin was golden, full of inner light; sparkling eyes; he looked so young.

During his absence I thought much and took stock of my situation. On 2 July I had been here for nine months. Nine months. The time to produce a child. What kind of child have I produced? None at all so it seems . . .

Two days before he left he was explaining a bit about his seeming rudeness.

"If one chooses the way of the System; if it is done according to the System, then it takes a long time. If one chooses the Way of Love, relatively, it does not take long. But it is difficult. Life becomes very sad. No joy. Thorns everywhere. This has to be endured. Then all of a sudden there will be flowers and sunshine. But the hard road has to be crossed first. People will hear one day that you have been turned out; and not only that, but other things too. And it is not the disciple who chooses which road to take; the Teacher decides.

"There are two roads: the road of dhyana, the slow one; and the road of tyaga, of complete renunciation, of surrender. This is the direct road, the path of fire, the path of love."

'But will you not treat a woman differently from a man? A woman is more tender; the psychology of a woman and of a man is different!'

He shook his head. "The training is somewhat different. But it does not mean that because you are a woman you will get preferential treatment."

'But don't you see I am at odds against your Indian disciples?' I exclaimed. Again he shook his head. "No, it is always difficult. For everybody. If it is not one thing, then it is another. Human beings are covered with so much conditioning."

❧ 18 ❧

13 *July*

For the last few days re-orientation has been taking place. At first I had some sort of peace. Not a peace in the real sense of the word: for that there was too much pain in my heart; but a kind of stillness. Is it a lull before the storm? Or simply some numbness due to too great a stress on my physique? This morning I woke up deadly tired and weary. The whole body was aching.

Dragged myself to the kitchen; aspirin and black coffee helped a little. The sky was as serene as ever and still no sign of rain.

When going to Pushpa's for lunch today, I was so acutely aware of the suffering of nature, of so many little things dying in the drought. The air boiling, the soil parched, Guruji's garden withered, leaves hanging from the branches, getting brittle and yellow.

Still, I was aware of a leaden peace; joyless, dark, but none the less, peace. There was much heartache, a permanent feature nowadays. Even the feeling of love is no more. Such is the maya. Nothing remains save the pain in the heart.

Went to the guru's place, but felt awful. Asked Satendra to tell his father that I went home because I was not too well. At home felt even worse. Took my temperature, it was 104°.

14 July

He asked how I felt. I was better. Told him about the feeling of peace.

"Love assumes many forms; sometimes it is peace, sometimes it is happiness, sometimes bliss or joy, restlessness or sorrow. Love is the root and, like a tree, it has many branches spreading around." Later he said, "When we are ill, then we know our body is not us. When we have a headache who is going to help us? If we are amongst the crowd or alone in the forest, who can help us? Nobody! If the mind is not there, if the body is not ours, what remains? Only the soul. Only the experiences are ours. Only those are true. 'Like the wind which carries the perfume of blossoms from bough to bough,' says the Persian poet. This only will remain."

He is also not well. I wonder if he took my feverish condition; but I knew I couldn't very well ask him. I know now to abstain from asking certain questions.

15 July

This morning at sunrise, when I opened my eyes and looked up into the sky – the first thing I always do on awakening, I saw a large, pink cloud, striped with delicate bands. Mackerel sky means water, at least in England. Told Bhai Sahib we might have rain. The rain came in the afternoon. And it became cooler.

18 July

When I admitted that I had not been able to pray for the last few days because it is like a dark curtain between myself and his Revered Guru Maharaj, he answered:

"Yes, sometimes it happens like that. It can be like a dark curtain or sometimes like a curtain of light. One can pray and then one cannot. It is good that it should be so. Otherwise how could one progress? Doubts and fears and anxieties; I myself have them. Now, for instance, I don't pray for over two months; to whom should I pray, I ask myself?"

It took my breath away. 'Bhai Sahib, what a glorious state!'

"Oh no; this is my pride," he said with emphasis.

'But you have no pride! You are surely beyond that?' I exclaimed. He smiled his still smile.

"That is what you say because you are so devoted. But on the physical level some imperfection will remain always."

It made me think. But I still believe how wonderful it must be not to be able to pray, for such is Oneness that no separation remains and one has to ask oneself to whom should one pray.

Yesterday was *Guru Purnama* [the day when the guru receives presents, according to tradition]. I did what he told me to do: brought some sweets, some fruit and a few rupees and in offering it to him touched his feet for the first time in public. I found it easy to do; don't mind at all. It comes naturally and I never cared for the opinion of others.

20 July

'What is this stillness? Could it really be peace? Isn't love the most peaceless state? I don't remember having experienced such deep, uniform state of stillness and lasting so long.'

"I call it the natural state," he answered. "Why should I say that I am giving it to you? It is given; that's all. And it is the natural state. But one does not always realize it. The soul is covered with so many sheaths, veiled by many curtains."

'One curtain has been withdrawn?' I suggested. He nodded. 'But there is so little understanding left, I am puzzled . . .'

But he was in samadhi.

21 July

This morning I realized in a flash that love cannot increase in quantity. It is given from the beginning in the exact measure the Master wants to give, according to the size of the cup the shishya brings with him. If the cup is large, more love can be poured into it; some containers are larger, some smaller. The shishya learns to respond to it better and better, so it seems to him as if it is growing. Love at the beginning and at the end is *the same*. I was astonished at this piece of knowledge, for the mind cannot even think clearly.

The beginning and the end from the point of view of God is the same always; it is a complete circle. I know it from books. But now I experienced it as my very own flash of knowledge into a mind which is sterile . . . Strange, and wonderful. And my work will be the same as before. I had to work with people, trying to help them to come one step nearer to the Truth. When I leave this place, (may the day never come!) I will continue on the same lines as before, though the conditions will necessarily be different (or perhaps not). But the work itself will remain the same. We are given work according to our capacities.

He smiled when I was relating all this to him and when I asked how is it possible that any glimpse of knowledge can come to a brain that can hardly function and with the greatest difficulty can put thoughts together, he said:

"If the cup is empty it can be filled. It is the knowledge of the soul which comes through. It comes to the physical mind and then it becomes the real knowledge, the integral part of you. If I would tell you, and you would have faith enough and believe me, then the faith and the knowledge would be two things, is it not so? But like this nothing is told. You will realize it yourself. It becomes part of you. There is no duality. You see how it is done, how easy?"

Then he began to tell me how men and women are trained; the difference in the practices; the approach to the psychological make-up of the trainee. How forces from the depth of the unconscious are gathered and chanelled. And this is the work of the Teacher and each individual is treated differently. I listened, fascinated, hoping fervently to remember it all.

'From what you have told me just now I have to conclude that you wish me to guide people?' I asked, feeling disturbed. 'It is a great responsibility! Do you realize to what kind of life you are sending me out?'

He did not answer but gently looked down at his feet as if examining his sandals.

'I hope, I hope that I will not go wrong; to have power is a terrible thing,' I said, fear creeping from the very depth of my being into my heart.

"I know," he said, half-audibly, with a still and serious expression.

'Is it not too heavy a burden for the shoulders of an elderly woman? I will be accused of contradictions. If I have to live like you, I will have no habits. I am bound to do and say things which people cannot or will not understand. My words will be twisted, misinterpreted. There might be lawyers in the audience who will twist my words, accuse me of contradictions!'

He suddenly laughed. "Lawyers know of one thing; the transfer of property! The property, the power, the knowledge will be transferred; there is no question of being a woman or not. It makes no difference."

24 July

It is raining. A soft drizzle. And it is hot. I asked if I should remain a vegetarian. I know some of his disciples are and some are not. He said he leaves it to me. Vegetarianism can become a creed, an obstacle, a religion.

"You cannot eat yourself into heaven; do what is best for you."

29 July

'Why did God create flies?' I was disgusted by so many of them.

"Who are you to ask such questions?" He turned to me "Do you know why you have been created? And supposing you do know. Do you fulfil the purpose for which you have been created? You commented on the fact that I am so free, that one day I do one thing, the other day something else. I am outside or inside, I speak or I do not. Now, even if I, in my limited way am so free, what about Him who is the Lord of Freedom? He knows what he is doing."

Later. "He is one only. He has no father, no son or any relations. He is definitely and most emphatically al-one."

Still later he was telling me that I don't follow him as I should because I still love to go to Pushpa's Kirtan. I told him that, lately, more and more I feel like that too. That it is a waste of time; but have not the courage to stop going for fear of hurting her feelings.

"*Tabla* [Indian drum], harmonium, the singing – it pleases you, you like it. You do not realize that it is useless from my point of view."

So I had better tell Pushpa sincerely why I have to stay away and hope that she will understand.

"Human beings are full of errors, and, if it were not for errors, how can they progress? We are the result of our failings and errors; they are a great lesson. I never act myself; I do as I am directed." And he made a graceful gesture with both hands to illustrate the channelling from above.

"Saints are like rivers; they flow as they are directed. Those criticisms – they will go. Never complain, never. If you don't complain they gradually will go completely. Pray for it. Pray to the Higher Ones or to God, or to whom you will. Pray that such feelings should stay away and if they remain the love should be greater. In your case they are not so many as with some other people. You are only six months in training. Look where you are! Are you not much further? Is there not a great difference in you?"

I had to admit that there was.

"Nearly everyone has these doubts and criticisms. I have seen how my father and my Revered Guru Maharaj were training people. This is the way of training, to make you speak as you did. I make you angry and then you speak and I know what is in your mind."

⤺ 19 ⤻

3 *August*

It was stifling, unbearably hot. The rain downpours are few and scarce; the heat humid and sticky. Only Bandhari Sahib was there in the morning at first. And because of the heat we soon went into the room to sit under the fan. Then came the smelly madman who belches so much. He had never come into the room before. He seated himself next to me. And there he sat, belching, speaking loudly, making silly remarks and grunting noises. The smell from his mouth was abominable and sickening. He is about seventy and has black and yellow teeth which must be full of pyorrhoea. Some weeks ago he said to the brother of Bhai Sahib that washing is not necessary for him because he does not perspire!

I was thinking, not without bitterness, why all the most disagreeable people are attracted here, and why on earth will they always sit near me, or be shown to sit next to me? Why must I suffer such additional difficulties when the physical conditions are already difficult enough and hard to bear. And suddenly the cognition came: he is training me to detach my mind at will from all that which I do not wish to notice. To conquer the small irritations. Immediately the full significance of it became clear; here is partly the answer to the fact that he can live with his family without ever being disturbed. He does not need to go into samadhi to escape the physical conditions; and he is teaching me to do the same.

'Help me to build the bridge, to reconcile,' I said to him some months ago, when I was practically in despair because of the smelly crowd of dirty men. 'You can escape to a different level, you need not listen to them or even see them, but I cannot. I have to endure it, here and now; the lot.' He only smiled then, he did not tell me, "I am showing you the way; I am showing you how to do it if only you are able to see it . . ." He did not say so because at that time I would not have understood, or accepted it. He was training me all the time. I must learn to exclude it all in full consciousness. It meant in practice that whatever happened around me, if I chose I need not notice it. I could remain at his feet in stillness, always in peace somewhere.

"I don't look at many things. I don't want to burden my mind. And, if I do look, I don't keep or hold it in my mind; so I simply don't see it and I don't remember it either," he said one day, when I laughingly told him that he does not look at the ladies.

4 August

Guruji joined us at about 11 a.m., looking frail and tired. He was obviously still not well.

"What talk was going on?" he asked. I told him Bhandhari Sahib was discussing whether it was not easier to renounce the world like me, or a sannyasi, than to try to do it while remaining with all the responsibility of a family.

"Only when the discursive manas is disciplined does the real sannyasi-life begin. Sannyasis do not necessarily renounce the world, nor are they without desires because they happen to wear the orange robe. The middle way is the best. On our line we remain in the world and reach Reality in spite of that; or if you like, because of that."

8 August

He asked me last night why didn't I go to the Kirtan. Told him that I will never go again; and that I have talked it over with Pushpa.

"Please tell her," he said, "that I will never ask you not to see her. Friendship is something very different from religious services or Kirtans or the like."

I did so this afternoon and she seemed pleased about it.

Told him about the strange irritation I felt against everything and everybody, himself included.

"It is good and bad." He smiled.

'Good?' I wondered.

"Yes, not bad. But the best would be if you never doubt. This is the ideal condition but it is very rare. I personally don't understand it because I never doubted, or criticized my superiors. Little by little the mind will give in. Then there will be no trouble. The mind is the shadow of shaitan; if this shaitan has yielded, the whole barrier is gone. It takes time."

How wonderful he looked today and I said so. It is not so much the features; it is the expression.

'But this special expression you do not always have. Last winter when I had those big troubles, very often I was so bitter because I was convinced that you had created these conditions with your power. I used to come to you full of resentment and you just sat there and looked like Buddha himself and after a while resentment used to vanish. I just took it; what could I do? Thinking that you could not have known how much I suffered, otherwise how could you have such a wonderful expression? This gentleness and compassion ...' He smiled.

Then he went into samadhi and he looked once more like the Khmer period statues of Buddha; so tender, so still, so remote; just the suspicion of a smile on his lips. The bliss of another world. I gazed entranced.

9 *August*

"This is how it is done in our System," he said. "For the one to whom it happens it is very wonderful because one cannot do it by himself alone. But for the guru it is a very ordinary thing to do and this is what Bhandhari Sahib meant when he was telling you that my brother used to turn the heart of people."

'And it is done through the heart chakra?'

"Yes. And there is the place which is called the Heart of Heart. But to the public we just say, 'It is the heart.' It is good enough."

'But this you do every morning,' I said and he smiled. 'You turn my mind off. In the mornings it is done in a more gentle way; it happens gradually at any rate. I never know the exact moment when it happens; it is just there. Then I know.'

"When you will tell people about those things, they will be impressed. Write down everything. It is such a subject that you can speak of it for months; for years. For instance, what happened yesterday and how it happened. After two or three years, you will say, 'In what a wonderful System have I been trained!' You can speak of how human beings are trained in the simplest and easiest way; how they are put to work according to their attitudes and desires. Then, the desire is taken away and the shishya must do the will of the guru.

But the guru puts him to do exactly what he originally wanted to do, and can do best, of course. But there can be no self, or ego any more now, because the shishya does not do his will any longer, but that of the guru."

10 *August*

Told him about the dancer-like quality of his movements; so oriental, so smooth. No other member of his family has it, neither his brother nor his children. I saw it in India only in the professional dancers and in Hatha Yogis, but only the best ones. They walked like gods and moved with the same feline grace. But they were very much body conscious, very much aware of their movements. But he was not; it was completely unconscious with him. He smiled quietly on hearing all this.

"It is because at the stage I am, I can leave my body at a second's notice – a split-second's notice, I should say; and the body expresses the state as well as it can."

Here lies the explanation of his Christ or Buddha-like quality: the body mirrors, reflects, the higher states of consciousness. That's all.

11 *August*

This morning I felt very bad; vomiting condition and severe headache. Went there about 9 a.m. He was not outside; Babu sat in the room under the fan. Felt miserable. Not a leaf was stirring in the trees and it was very sticky. Exchanged a few words with Babu; then he came in.

I told him how I suffered last night. I must confess I was sorry for myself, could not sleep, so bad was the perspiration and headache.

"You should not sit here for hours," he interrupted me sharply, "it won't help you. The mind is not working, you are apt to criticize, unnecessary questions arise in your mind which you may think are helpful, but they are not; they are of the worst possible kind. You must come here from nine to ten, for one hour in the morning, and then in the evening for a short time."

I began to weep. 'You are sending me away into the heat! How cruel! You know that my flat is as hot as a baker's oven. The coolest place is this room of yours under the fan!'

"You just come here for one hour in the morning," he repeated. "What are you doing here?"

'What am I doing?' I said blankly, the mind not working. 'I suppose I am here to be with you. You insisted that satsang is essential; ten hours a day I spend sitting here. I understood that is how it should be.'

"To be with me," he repeated scornfully. "Others are with me too. My wife, my children are with me also. My wife massages my body for several hours daily; my children serve me! But what are you doing?"

By now I was weeping bitterly. No use asking me what I was doing because the mind refuses to function and I cannot think at all. All I knew was that I was being deprived of his presence. He seemed angry, so I went about 10, still weeping all the way home. It is going to be very hard to stay in the boiling hot flat nearly all day long.

"Go for a walk at eight in the morning." But if it is already so hot at 5, how will I be able to? To drive me out of the only cool place; that one would not do even to one's enemy. It is a shameful thing to refuse hospitality to somebody who is already suffering so much. No, it is not he, it is not in his character; it is done for a purpose, it must be a test ... And the mind went still and did not give me any trouble. A matter of training ...

Went there in the evening as usual. He was sitting outside and asked me how I was. Now I am sure that he is testing me, for he is expecting an act of rebellion and complaint. But I only said that I was all right. He looked very weak and admitted that he did not feel well at all. Told him that if I have to spend so many hours at home from now on, I had better look for another flat for the next hot season in May.

"Who will think of the next year? Who knows what is going to be? ... Never think of tomorrow ..."

12 August

When I arrived he was playing chess with a friend whom I never saw here before.

"You are very late," he remarked.

'I do what you have told me. You ordered me to come from nine to ten.'

He nodded, continuing to play. His torso was bare; he was clad only in his longhi. His opponent was a thin man with a serious face. Both were engrossed in that they were doing.

Listened to the clock ticking away, thinking that soon I will have to go. But when I got up at 10, he asked without looking up, "You want to go?"

'It is ten already; you wanted me to stay only for one hour.'

"No, you can stay here." And I sat down again.

He played with concentration, his opponent seemed to be a good player. I tried to tune in to his thought, as he wants me to do. But I saw soon that it wasn't the right way to proceed. Like this the mind creates a barrier and one does not get anywhere. Those flashes must come from beyond the mind; I cannot force them, they must come by themselves. Finally I decided that he wanted me to go at 11.30 and so I did.

⁕ 20 ⁕

13 August

"You wanted to tell me something?"

He asked, because I mentioned last night that I had an unusual experience

118

which I will tell him about tomorrow. He hardly ever asks me if I want to speak to him. On the contrary, when I have to tell him something he usually avoids me and interruptions begin. Told him about my erratic heart beat and the sleep which did not seem to be a sleep. His smile was tender and strange.

'Do you remember in spring I said it seemed that I had two hearts beating in my breast? Such a strange maya it was.'

"You are right," he interrupted, "we have two hearts."

'One beating rapidly and strongly and the other my own?' I asked, and he nodded. Did not ask further; had the feeling he will not say more ... The one must be the Heart of Hearts which he mentions sometimes. I dimly remember that the Heart of Hearts is the Atmic Heart. I will know one day of course. At least he always says so ... Must not be impatient. Must train myself to wait in stillness.

16 *August*

He did not come out last evening. After sitting alone in the damp garden went home early. Since this morning I have been suffering from intense irritation; it is so unreasonable; against everything and everybody. Sometimes the irritation is even directed against him.

He too seemed to be in a bad mood; he ordered me to plant out some vegetable seedlings which one of his disciples brought, but I argued. 'What's the use of planting such tender things if they haven't got the least chance of survival? First get rid of the goat,' I said, 'which those dirty people living in the shed let loose all the time to roam freely in the garden. And what about so many children and stray dogs coming in from the street? And the cows wandering in, Munshiji running after them, chasing them out?' But it was of no use. He became annoyed. I planted the seeds.

We had an unpleasant discussion and he told me that I have no brain and no understanding and am stupid. And he kept abusing me and I fought back. And then he said:

"Come inside, why should you sit here alone?"

'You mean inside the courtyard?' I asked in astonishment. He nodded. Well, I thought, full of amazement, he was never concerned before if I was sitting alone. I do it for months on end, in the cold, in the dust, unnoticed, forgotten, neglected, resented even by some people.

So, I went inside. They all played cards for hours. For him, no matter what he does on the physical plane, it is all the same. His consciousness is partly somewhere else anyhow. This state is called *sahaj samadhi*; effortless samadhi. And to this state his superiors brought their shishyas effortlessly, so he said once when I commented on this capacity of his to be in two different states at one and the same time. When he was playing cards it was very evident that although he paid attention to the game, he was somewhere else too. One could see by the expression of his eyes.

17 *August*

In the morning there was a new young man whom I never saw before and Bhai Sahib spoke to him in Hindi explaining the System. Several times he used the words 'Self Realization' in English during the course of conversation. An idea arose in my mind: 'Please Master, could you tell us, how does one know that one has realized God? It is something which I find very puzzling. How does one know that it is not an illusion, a maya of some sort? I met so many *sadhus* [holy men] and sannyasis in Rishikesh and elsewhere; they all call themselves "Realized Souls".'

"If one says that one is a Realized Soul, one never is. It is never said. A *wali* [Sufi saint] is a balanced person. He knows that this world is not a bad one, and he has to live in both worlds; the spiritual and the physical, the life on this earth. There is nothing good or bad for him; good or bad are relative concepts."

'But I have often heard you condemn worldly things!'

"Because to ordinary people one has to speak like this," he laughed. "How will they know that gambling or chasing after wordly possessions is wrong? But why bother to understand? To *realize* it is important. Only the things we understand through realization are really ours."

Later: 'I gathered that before one comes to the Master or a wali, the karmas are valid; but as soon as the wali takes you in his hand, no karmas remain.'

"Not immediately; but little by little, as the desire goes, no karmas remain and another set of karmas takes over. One makes other karmas which bind you to the Master and which take you to Realization."

18 *August*

He was sweeping his room when I arrived. I was full of joy because of the heavy, tropical rain. Have never seen such a downpour – sheets of water, no question of drops! It made the air so pure and fragrant.

Told him about the depression I had last night; it had really lasted for the last three days, but yesterday it was very bad. I have had periods of misery in my life; who has not? But I don't think I have ever been so miserable in my whole life. Does he know about it? He nodded.

"There was some depression, and something was done that it should not last long."

Then I proceeded to tell him how I was irritated because of the shed in which Tulsi Ram's family lives. It is painful to see that he uses some of my money to repair the shed of dirty people who give him trouble and annoyance in every way. After all, it was money from selling my house, and the money my husband had left me; it would have served me for my old age. I gladly give it to him for a worthwhile cause but it is hard to understand why he does certain things. After all they ruin his garden, quarrel, make a mess; Tulsi Ram does not want to work, and a shed like this one, they can erect anywhere in the Indian plains. Why should it be in his garden?

He listened silently. Then he told me how L. gave a blanket to his Revered Guru and he was so pleased with it. But a few days later he gave it to somebody else.

"I must admit I hoped he would give it to me, but he gave it to someone who did not matter to him at all. It is done like that. We give things away; our family, our property, it matters little. I never came with empty hands to him, but the things I brought he distributed immediately amongst the people present and they did not mean anything either to him or to us. It is done like that."

20 *August*

The irritation was still with me, more than ever. Like a storm it was blowing inside my soul. My very insides seemed to turn.

In the evening he came out and they played cards again in the courtyard. Had moments of fleeting happiness, like a golden cloud inside my heart . . .

21 *August*

Yes . . . the Longing. The Great, the Endless . . . Let us remember how it was exactly. I was waking up at the usual hour, about 6, and there it was, in between the waking and the sleeping state; the longing, sharply painful and so deep. Longing for what? That was the first thought of the waking consciousness. I really did not know. Sometimes a deep sigh from the bottom of my heart seemed to relieve the tension; so sharp it was and so cruel. From the very beginning I never knew for what I was longing. Confused, tortured, the mind not working, I did not, could not, analyse it. It was just longing from the very depth of the heart, the poignant feeling of some vanished bliss . . .

At first, it seemed just a longing for its own sake, for nothing in particular. At times it was more, at times it was less, but it always remained in the background, throbbing softly. I was never without it and it could grow so terrible at times that I would lose the will to live. There must be a reason for it; didn't he say that there is a reason for everything?

I looked deeper into my self. Deeper and deeper still. And it took me quite some time this morning to discover that it was in reality the same yearning I had had all my life, since childhood. Only now it was increased to the utmost degree. Even when I was quite small, every time I saw golden clouds at sunset, or the sky so blue, or heard lovely music, or saw dancing sparks of sunlight on the trembling surface of the water – each time it came, an endless sadness, something was crying in me.

Often I wondered what this yearning could be. Never understood it, not really. Was it my Slav heredity, the innate sadness of the Russian temperament? This morning I knew: it was the cry of the imprisoned soul for the One. The Lover crying for the Beloved; the prisoner yearning for freedom. For a few seconds it seemed to be breaking my heart apart, so strong it was, causing even

121

bodily pain. Then it ebbed away, leaving the understanding of its very nature behind ... So simple. All the time it was never anything else but *the cry for the real Home*!

We bring it with us into the physical life. We bring it from the other planes of being; it forms part of the very texture of our soul; it is intended to take us home again where we belong. Without this longing, which is a gift not from this world, we, deluded as we are, would never find the way home ...

If you love and you were asked, 'Why do you love?' and you are able to answer, 'I love because of his or her beauty, or position in life, or charm or good character' – in other words, if you can give the reason for your love – then it is not love. But if this question is put to you, and as if in a sudden wonder, you must admit that you don't know, that the WHY never occurred to you; you just love, that's all, so simple ... then, only then, is it REAL LOVE.

He looked weak and slept nearly all the morning. I tried to keep the flies away by closing the shutters and the doors and fanning him while he was turned against the wall. Went home early. In the evening he did not come out. I was glad that he was resting.

22 *August*

When I arrived he was going to have his bath, but he told me not to leave. "You sit here," he said, so I knew that he wanted to speak to me. He came back clad in a white longhi and made himself comfortable in the big chair. Told him about the vibration which disappeared so quickly and he smiled.

"Now is the time," he began, and suddenly I felt that he was about to tell me something very important and I listened carefully to what he had to say.

"Now is the time that you should note down all the experiences."

'I do; everything I note down – what you tell me and my own experiences and all my doubts and comments, everything.'

"Doubts should be noted down," he nodded, "otherwise how will the solution be understood? It will serve for the book you write. The experiences you have, and will have in the future, you can find only in the Persian language, mostly in the form of poetry, and very little of it has been translated until now."

I listened partly with astonishment, partly greatly interested. 'I abandoned the idea of writing a book long ago, because you had said that those who write books are idiots and so are those who read them. But nevertheless I kept a diary; I remember you told me once that the diary will help me.' He nodded.

"Those who write from reading other books and not from proper experience are idiots and idiots are those who read them. But you will write from your own, real experiences, living experiences. We live in the age of knowledge; some knowledge has to be given out to the world. I want you to do it. You will have to take my message to the world. All the doubts, the trouble the mind gives you, do not really interfere with love. Not really. The mind tries, but love is not really affected. Had it not been so, I would never have diverted my attention towards you." And he smiled kindly.

A man came with a worldly request – some help in a court case, or the like. When he had gone I asked: 'How many people come for the sake of spiritual instruction?'

"Very few. And those who come here are not very keen. And if you write a book do not forget to emphasise how love is created. We are the only Yoga System where love is created in this way. My Revered Guru Maharaj was always saying, 'If you can find a better, a quicker way, do go away by all means.' So broad-minded he was. But where will you find a better one? My disciples, if they live as I expect them to live and they follow me in everything, they realize God in this life. Absolutely. And if they are too old, or the progress is too slow, I make them realize on their death bed. God MUST be realized in one life, in this life, and this is the only system which does it."

'Yes, it is a simple and a clever way to get the human being exactly where one wants.'

"True; and I am scolding you because I know that love is greater than everything. My Revered Guru Maharaj was always scolding me, and I just sat there with my head bent. I kept thinking that he is right and I am a fool to rebel all the time. He never scolded anybody else as much as he did me."

⊰ 21 ⊱

23 *August*

When I arrived his wife was massaging him; he was turned against the wall. When she went out, he seemed asleep. Flies were bothering him and I began to chase them with a towel. He does not want the fan because he is coughing and perspiring; currents of air are disagreeable to his condition.

'When this book is going to be written – and it will be written, there is no question about it because I see that it is your wish – it will be for your glory.'

"The books are mostly written when the person in question is deceased." He spoke slowly with closed eyes.

'But can I write it before I have achieved at least something? It is not going to be easy. Many things cannot be expressed. You have said to me that I am the first woman to get the training according to the Ancient Tradition.'

"I told you already that the experiences are not recorded anywhere except in Persian writings. I did the easiest thing; I am giving you experiences and you do with it what you like."

24 *August*

This morning when I arrived the young man was already there listening intently, for again, as last evening, Bhai Sahib was exceptionally kind, explaining so many things.

123

Then he sent Satendra out of the room, ordered the door to be closed and the young man arranged his legs in *siddh-asana* [one of the yogic postures] and it was clear that he was giving a 'sitting' as they call it here. I was interested and watched carefully.

Bhai Sahib seated himself in *guru-asana* [a traditional teaching posture], his hands clasping his toes. The young man sat still, his eyes closed. The guru did the same; his countenance expressed infinite love, his lips had a tender smile. He looked so wonderfully young and full of love. I did not notice the precise moment when the young man went into dhyana. As I happened to glance at him, he was unconscious. The guru sat motionless for about fifteen minutes, the same tender smile on his lips. Then he opened his eyes and looked at the young man; I saw clearly that he did not look at the physical body. I knew this expression by now, when he is observing something non-physical. The young man did not stir; he did not even seem to breathe. The guru closed his eyes again for a while. Then he opened them again, looked at the young man in the same way as before and relaxed. He crossed his arms and looked outside the door through the chik. A fly was crawling on the young man's cheek; he only felt it when it came too near his mouth; he twitched his lips but did not wake up. For another ten minutes or so, the guru sat thinking, looking sometimes through the door or the window. Once he glanced at me; a passing, indifferent glance.

Then: "*Bass beta* ["Enough, my child"]," he said softly in Hindi, and the young man came to his senses immediately. The guru began to talk to him in such a kind way that I could see the young man's heart was melting. After a while he sent him away, because the servant came to tell him that tea was ready. He went out and I remained alone for a while. I began to cry silently. Felt so hurt, so lonely. No interruptions at all. And when I have to talk to him how many interruptions there would be ... And my questions are dismissed as 'vague' or 'irrelevant' and, as for a 'sitting', I never had one ... Stopped crying after a while; what could I do? ...

When he came in his face was stern, hard, without expression, as though carved of stone. He sat down in the big chair.

'How are you feeling today?' I asked.

"Better than yesterday," he answered in a harsh way.

'May I ask a few questions?'

"Yes," he said curtly, his face was stony.

'Was that a "sitting"?'

"Yes, it was."

'You met him for the first time yesterday; Gandhiji brought him to you?'

"Yes."

'You put him in dhyana. I saw that his face was twitching so I knew that something was done and he listened so attentively to what you had to say. You sat in a cross-legged position and with the fingers of both hands you were clasping your toes. From the books I have read in the past, I learned that this is done to close the circuit of the auric force; is it so?'

"Why should I tell you what I was doing?" he replied. "If I do, you will misunderstand and misinterpret it. It is beyond your understanding just now. What I do with others is not your concern."

'I thought it would make an interesting entry in my diary,' I said.

"Write in your diary your own experiences only; other people are not your concern, nor what I do with them."

'You told me in the past that you had said to Mr Chowdhary that he could sit in any position he liked, when for the first time he was put in dhyana. It is many years ago now; but this young man was sitting in siddh-asana. Why so?'

"I did not tell him to sit in any particular asana; he did it himself." He got up and went to lie on the tachat. I felt deeply frustrated. Here we are, I thought with bitterness; there seem to be two laws, one for me and one for the others.

Others can ask the most stupid questions, anything at all; but mine are not answered and I have questions which sometimes torture me for months. But they are considered 'vague' and he can get quite rough and annoyed when I ask.

'Please,' I said. I was so upset. 'Tell me one thing. Is he completely surrendered?'

"How do I know if he will surrender completely?" mumbled the guru, visibly irritated. I was surprised.

'But I understood that one gets dhyana only when one is completely surrendered! I thought that dhyana is the last stage!'

"Dhyana is the first stage; the first thing according to our System, the first step. Before you have reached this stage you have not even begun." Now he was really vexed. "I told you so often, why don't you listen properly? One begins with dhyana, and then goes on from there!"

'But why in my case is it not like this?' I was even more puzzled now. 'Does it mean that I cannot go on?'

"You have said and repeated so often that you don't want dhyana! You will get an experience of dhyana but it is not your path. You are trained in a different way; your way is the other way; in full consciousness."

'But according to your System, dhyana comes first, you told me. You never answer my questions clearly; or they are dismissed as vague and stupid; how can they be if they torture my mind for so long? They are important!'

"They *are* vague and you don't know *how* to ask the right kind of questions and how to listen properly. Don't you see how confused you are? Look at yourself! Your mind turns round and round!"

He turned to the wall. I sat there profoundly puzzled. What on earth does he mean by the right kind of questions? When he turned in my direction after a while I said:

'As far as I understood, I am supposed to be on the Path of Love, which apparently is not your System then? In this case, which System is it? It is all so confusing! L. got dhyana in the first fortnight, so she is trained according to the System, is she not?'

He was lying there on his back, hands crossed behind his head looking more forbidding then ever.

'Please say if I have understood well!'

His face hardened. I began to cry and couldn't stop. His wife came in; and the servant; and the children. Could not care less. It was all of no use. I have to take everything. He is burning me. And when somebody is jealous of me, as I have learned that some of his disciples are, just tell them what you do to me, how you burn me and if they want it, they are welcome to it too . . . I thought bitterly and went home. At home I did not cry. And my heart was aching and aching, endlessly.

28 *August*

It seems to me that love will go away soon; there are small signs pointing to it. Only longing will remain. The dryness and the pain. Oh, God, what a life have I! Oh, Bhai Sahib, my Revered Guru Maharaj, make it that such feelings of criticism should not remain; and if they have to remain for some reason, please let the love increase!

In the evening a new lady was sitting with him.

"She said to me that for the last twenty years she did an *abhyasa* [spiritual practice]. I explained to her that she should not take a guru until she is quite sure. And I told her what the signs of a good guru are."

'And what are the signs?' I asked, hoping to hear more.

"I told it to you often before."

'No, Bhai Sahib, perhaps you said it in Hindi, to somebody else, surely not to me.'

"I did, I remember well," he answered with irritation. "You never know what I say to you."

'I will not contradict you, but really you didn't tell me,' I said, getting confused.

"This is your attitude; always like that," he said, annoyed. "A very wrong attitude it is!" Tears came into my eyes. The way he said it hurt me deeply. Strange how I over-react to what he says to me; the slightest thing hurts so . . . I was annoyed with myself for this lack of control; if the feelings are hurt, then the feelings are stronger than love. If love is the strongest, nothing should hurt . . . He continued to talk in Hindi. I just sat there.

Later he was singing: "If I knew how troublesome it is, I would have proclaimed by the beat of the drums, 'Don't come near to the Lane of Love!' What can I do? Helpless I am . . ."

29 *August*

Yes, the wave of love is slowly ebbing away. He will be friendlier today; he always is when I am in trouble.

As soon as I came in he told me that he is feeling better. We were talking about the gurus and the *ashrams* [places for religious retreat] and that there is not much spirituality to be found in most of them. Admitted that I did not really believe in gurus, but had been to see some for the sake of curiosity. Each time I saw those *swamis* [teachers], I thought, this is not much of a Yogi or Saint! About him I could not think like this; it is something very different. He smiled slowly.

"It must be said that we human beings, we sometimes have links with each other from the past. From other lokas, from where we came. My Revered Guru Maharaj told my Uncle and my Revered Father that we have connections with each other from another loka ¬here we were together. And the connection is improved this time. My Uncle said in the presence of my Revered Guru that his duty was fulfilled because he brought us, my brother and myself, to the System. But my Revered Guru did not train us for the first years."

'Perhaps he did,' I said, 'but you knew nothing about it.' He gave me a quick look with a smile hidden in his beard.

"And he treated my Revered Father and my Uncle until his last years in the same way, roughly, as he treated us, my brother and myself." I understood. It was a 'hint' for me . . .

"Trainings are different," he said after a while. "Some are trained according to the System, and it is a long way. Some are trained according to their liking. Some are trained according to the will of the guru." He fell silent. Then he got up from the big chair and sat himself cross-legged on the tachat and began his correspondence.

'You really feel better,' I laughed, 'when you begin to answer your letters, this is a good sign!' He just smiled broadly without answering.

'I would like to ask you something; I am not expecting an answer, for I suspect that you will not answer this one; I will just take the chance. When I cannot sleep in the night, do you put me to sleep on some occasions? There are many nights when I hardly sleep at all – just watch the stars and think and think. But very often, and it always happens between two and four in the morning, all of a sudden there is like an inner call, a great peace, a sweetness and a deep longing. The body relaxes; it is a lovely feeling of surrender to this peace and I go off like a candle that has been blown out. I keep wondering if it is you, or is it something else perhaps in me, which puts me to sleep? Who knows? As I said, I don't expect an answer; I put it before you and leave it with you.'

His smile was delightful to watch. His head was lowered and he obviously did his best that I should not see it. For a while he continued to write. Some sparrows were quarrelling on the window sill outside. With a great rattle a lorry passed by. All was still in the room. Then:

"Tell me everything," he said slowly, raising his head. "I am not supposed to give an answer to everything. Tell me your troubles, every one of them."

'I try. Only I wish my mind would remember more of the help you are giving me,' I said regretfully. 'Even on the worldly platform, love is a painful thing. But sometimes there are spells of great happiness. But it does not seem to be the case with spiritual love. My love is one-sided. There is no happiness in it, and by now I am quite sure that it is not love for you. Not directly, at least. It looks to me more like love for its own sake, or for God, or something. Difficult, practically impossible to define. It is as if I would love *you*, but when I look at it closer, I see that I seem to love something *beyond* you. Strange, isn't it?'

"Love in the world is not love. It is *moha* [attachment], and moha only. The only real love in this world is between guru and shishya, and it is once and forever, and there is no divorce. The love for the guru takes time to stick firmly. When it does, then the greatest happiness will be felt. People in this world love this and that. There is the greatest purpose that it should be so. But when the real love comes along, everything else loses its value. One cannot love or be interested in anything else . . ."

I was complaining about the strong vibrations. It is wearing my body out.

'Just see how thin and dried up I am. It causes vomiting; I cannot eat; fire flows through my veins as if the outer temperature was not enough.'

So I talked for a while, telling him that he will ruin my body permanently and that the conditions here in the Indian plains are difficult enough without this additional suffering.

He sat up slowly from his lying position and his face bore a hard, cutting expression:

"You have no brain to understand," he began ominously. "Why do you say that I am putting you in this condition? You are a believer in karma; why not say it is your karma which makes you suffer? If you believe in karma, you will suffer from it. Don't you think that all the wrong done in the past must be paid for up to the last farthing with suffering?

"On the other hand, if you don't believe in karma, where is the karma?"

'But didn't you yourself say that this earthly plane is not the worst loka because here we can make karma? So, is there such a thing as karma or is there not?' I asked, much puzzled.

"Do not repeat what I have said," he replied severely. "I myself do not have faith in such a thing as karma; it is all nonsense. You don't follow me if you have beliefs contrary to mine!"

He continued in this tone for a while, breaking down one by one my remonstrations and objections. His angry irony made me cry. His wife came and they talked endlessly in Hindi and I cried silently for two hours.

When at home, I saw that he was right; until I give up all beliefs, there can be no humility. If I believed in karma, I was making samskara. Any belief will make samskara as a corresponding result. Of course, *I am creating it*, and nobody else. But if I could switch over somehow, believe in his God (if he has one), that would be an act of humility.

Then I will be nothing; have no beliefs of my own; accepting Grace or suffering as it comes, in humility . . .

❧ 22 ❧

In essence it boils down to 'Thy Will be done and not mine.' Where is karma then? If one is not the doer any more? . . .

To give up the belief in karma . . . I realised that it was the last belief I was clinging to; it seemed to explain so well the order and justice in the world. But supposing the created Universe is beyond justice, beyond order, as we know it? What then?

Became completely confused. All my beliefs he takes away from me! I seem to have nothing left. This was the best, the last, the most logical belief; all the others I have lost somewhere along the way. . . . Do not know in what kind of God he does believe, or if at all. Nonsense! He speaks like that because of the training. Every Hindu believes in karma, *must* believe in karma. But here apparently lies my mistake; he said that he does not believe in karma, even though he is a Hindu by birth. I also know that if you ask a sadhu about the working of karma, he will answer you, 'Karma will be for you, but it is not for me.'

A great fear seized me. What will remain when all the beliefs are gone? Love alone will remain. This Love which is drying up my body; this terrible 'thing' in my heart. Whom or what do I love? The guru? Yes, in a way; but not quite! HIM – or rather IT, the One? But who is the One to be loved? And didn't he say, some time ago, that even Love will have to go one day? What then?

But I know that one thing will remain – the terrible longing. And so full of terror did this thought fill me that I wept and wept helplessly.

When I arrived at 5, he sat in the courtyard on the tachat. He was not playing cards as usual but seemed to be waiting for me. I went straight to him. Could not wait to tell him as soon as possible, for I was desperate.

"Why?" he smiled, as if nothing had happened.

'The human being *must* believe in something! You take all my beliefs away from me.'

"I try!" He laughed gaily. "I am trying but until now I was not successful. So strong is this belief that you stick to it until now, in spite of everything . . . It will take time. By and by, this will go too . . ."

'But you take a belief away and you don't give another one!' I exclaimed, exasperated. 'You don't even take the trouble to explain anything.'

He got up from the tachat and stood leaning against the column. "If you let the belief go, then after a while you will discover something very different," he said quietly, looking afar with half-closed eyes. He stood very still and again this feeling of *meaning* came over me, so strong, so powerful ...

He went inside and I remained alone in the garden. A yellow sunset dramatically lit the sky; everything around was glowing with gold ... Oh, to merge in all this wonderful gold, the colour of joy! Disappear in it for ever, to forget, not to think, not to doubt, not to suffer any more! The western sky ... liquid azure and aquamarine between the delicate feathers of shining gold, shimmering through the foliage. A feeling of magic as in dimly-remembered dreams ... The air was so pure, the earth so fragrant. All the objects around – the trees, the leaves, the stones, the whole town, seemed to breathe.

Suddenly, crystal-clear, a thought floated into my mind: a belief which is taken up can be given up; after all, you were not born with this idea of karma. You accepted it; what is accepted can be rejected. This is the way the mind is made ...

Well, I thought; that's that. And went home.

Put up my *charpoy* [rope bed] in the courtyard and lay on my back looking at the sky.

Then it happened. It was as if something snapped inside my head, and the whole of me was streaming out ceaselessly, without diminishing, on and on. There was no 'me' – just flowing. Just being. A feeling of unending expansion, just streaming forth. ... But all this I knew only later, when I tried to remember it. When I first came back, the first clear, physical sensation was of intense cold.

It was shattering. But what was it? Was it prayer? Not in the ordinary sense. For a prayer there must be somebody to pray. But I was not. I did not exist.

3 September

Hoped to be able to tell him in the morning. But when I came, he was in deep samadhi.

When he opened his eyes, I stood up and said '*Namaste*', the usual greeting. He hardly answered; had the impression that he did not register it.

To get to bed now; it is a secret joy; an appointment with THAT.

The door was open; the door to what? Whatever it was, it was wonderful. There must be an infinite sea of it. Like a terrific pull of one's whole being. Is this the 'prayer of the heart'; is this 'merging'? I don't know. Because when I am in it, there is no mind. I seem not to exist at all; and when the mind begins to know something about it, it is already past. But even the idea of praying to somebody or something seems pointless now.

Lay for a long time; wondering.

A girl was singing a monotonous lullaby, her soft voice coming from far away in the warm, moonless night; and the breeze and the stars and the sky, and myself, all merged in the one wonderful feeling of completeness ...

This is ABSOLUTE security, I said to myself. But to reach it, one has to traverse the no-man's-land; one has to wade through the morass of insecurity, where there is no foothold of any kind and where one cannot even see the ground under one's feet ...

And with a sigh of relief, I fell asleep, blown out suddenly, like a candle by a gust of wind.

4 *September*

He was still asleep when I came back. He has been having severe stomach pains since Sunday and, when I noticed how much medicine he had left, I knew that he did not take it anymore. I became worried, something was very wrong.

When he woke up he told me that, according to Ramji, the medicine has side-effects and is of no value. He changes his medicine every few days. I think it is the worst possible thing to do. It is like changing gurus I said to him; one does not get anywhere. Hopeless situation and he gets weaker and weaker.

5 *September*

Last night he did not come out into the garden. He is very weak. His face looks transparent and thin. How I prayed, seeing him like this ... He is very ill, no doubt about that. He suffers from amoebic hepatitis and has done so for many years already. In the rainy season it apparently gets worse.

This afternoon he went for a short walk in the park. He seems a bit better.

In the evening he was on the roof and a man went to see him. I sat alone in the darkening garden for hours. It was dreadfully hot; not a breath of air. It is much cooler on the roof, but he did not ask me up. With bitterness I thought, in all these months how many times I have sat alone in the heat and dust, unnoticed, ignored. He is bound to treat me worse now. For when the human being is in despair he turns to God; when he is happy, God is forgotten. He will drive me towards his God now ...

I saw the man coming down and leaving and a few moments later he appeared. We were alone. Trying to describe the experience of the night I asked, 'Is it God?'

Could not see his face in the dark. He silently listened to me; or perhaps he did not. He remained silent until, getting up, he told me to go home.

8 *September*

What happens in the night frightens the mind now. A state of being as though one were thrown Somewhere or in Something. God it cannot be, not after only nine months training. I am satisfied to think that I probably tuned into the Sheath of the Soul; for there is love, unimaginable happiness, and time is not there. But the mind is experiencing great fear. It wants to understand what these states are – for they are nothing, a complete insecurity. The absence of the belief in karma represents an additional insecurity. But spiritual life is the tearing down of all securities. For only then can we reach the Ultimate Security.

It seems to me that if I don't give up all beliefs absolutely, pride will never go. It is of no consequence if the belief is a correct or valid one, it has to go. It has to be an act of faith in the guru, in his wisdom, and it is the only weapon I have to defeat the self.

But what is disconcerting is the fact that the whole of my personality is standing up in front of me, fighting me; everything in me, united against me, so to speak.

It started so simply, from a small irritation . . .

I told him that my mind was troubled because of an ungenerous remark he had made about a woman who had written to him about her difficulties. What he had said was expressed in ungentlemanly terms; one should not speak about a woman in this way. Nobody is free from faults. 'And you have a way of bringing people's faults to light, to bring out the worst in them. Something in you makes people react.'

"But why should I do such a thing?" he asked angrily. "It is the evils in them which come out!"

'But if you know that, then you should be even more generous. If by simple contact with you, people's faults come to light, then to talk as you did in front of everybody was most ungenerous. You yourself are not free from faults; no human being can be. A great Master said somewhere that he is infallible only when he is not functioning in his physical body, using his brain. As a human being he is fallible and liable to make errors. Surely that would be valid for you too? There are many things in your environment, your family and your way of life which I could point out as being far from perfect!'

"I don't want to listen to you!" he hissed at me. "You don't know how to respect people like me; you never learned what respect and reverence mean! You are an ignorant, dense and stupid woman, and you try to preach to me?"

'I am nothing of the sort!' I retorted angrily. 'I have had enough of this treatment. You are an arrogant autocrat. All I was asking for yesterday was to be helped to understand what is happening to me. For nine months now I have been pleading for help but it is of no avail.'

"Did I give you your trouble? It is your own sins which are coming back on you! The evils in your blood!"

'But it is *you* who put me into this state!' I shouted, beyond myself with fury. 'All I ask is do it gently! I understand why it is done, that it is necessary, but have a heart, I am at the end of my strength.'

"Nonsense!" he shouted back, leaning forward and glaring at me. "You idiot!"

'But all the people with whom you are coming into contact cannot be evil. If you see all these evils in them, they must be in you. Look how full of hatred you are! Look into the mirror; is it the face of a good man?'

And all the time there were interruptions – his children, the wife, the servant, popping in and out for one reason or another, bringing with them loud bits of conversation, carried on from one room to another. It made speaking difficult and increased my irritation to a paroxysm.

It was too much; I had had enough; I began to cry.

"Women can only cry; this they can do very well," he remarked disdainfully.

Once more I burst out, pouring out the misery, the accusations, the bitterness, the frustration . . .

Then I looked up, for in my fury and anxiety to tell everything quickly, I had not looked at him. And I saw that his eyes were full of tears. A large tear rolled slowly down into his beard. I knew that his heart was melting and that he was full of pity for me.

I broke down into uncontrollable sobs. 'I am going,' I said, trying to get up from the chair. My knees were shaking and I nearly fell down.

'Namaskar,' I murmured, full of embarrassment, trying to smile.

At home, I tried to eat something but could not.

Felt that I cannot go on any more. Nothing left . . .

I went back at 6. They were all playing cards in the courtyard. I advanced towards him; he looked dark.

'Please,' I said,' I would like to speak to you before anyone else arrives.'

"Not now. Leave me free."

'I don't mean this very moment; but later; please.'

I sat outside, full of torture. The sunset was glorious – gold, streaks of orange; feathery clouds gradually changing to ominous dark reds, as if painted on the sky with a brush.

He came out when it was dark and I tried to speak to him.

"Don't talk to me at all; I don't want to hear anything."

I remonstrated and accused him again, demanding an apology for his behaviour. He told me that I was no better than 'the least street woman'.

"If you dare to come once more to my premises, you will be turned out." His anger was terrible.

I cried and cried. People came. Still I sat, crying.

Late in the night he said, "Go home."

'I will stay here all night as a protest against your bad treatment!'

He went inside.

After a while he came out and stood in front of me, tall, all in white, every inch of him a Master.

"It will be better for you to go," he said quietly.

'No!' I exploded in despair. 'I am not going! The whole town should know;

everybody should see what you are doing; how you are treating me. Drag me away! Kill me!'

He turned abruptly and went inside.

A little later, his wife came out and asked me to leave. I refused.

I remained alone in the dark garden The hours passed and after a while I stopped crying.

About 4 in the morning, Gandiji came (as he apparently does every day before his meditation and his bath in the Ganges), saw me sitting there, gave me a surprised glance and silently left.

Went home at about 5.30. How my heart ached . . .

9 September

He was lying on the tachat and his entire family was in the room – wife, children, grandchild, all of them laughing, talking. Nobody took the slightest notice of me. I sat near the door, apart from it all, very tired, with a sort of indifference, a kind of dull peace which one experiences after a psychological shock. I understood that he ignored me deliberately. Went home at 11.

Was there again at 6. He did not come out. Nobody came. The garden was silent. Went home and immediately fell asleep.

10 September

When I came and saw the chairs outside, but the door closed, I knew that he must be unwell. Babu told me that he was very ill – terrible heart pain and fever. Went home.

Returned at midday to enquire how he was. Allowed to enter the room. Babu was massaging his feet. He was lying motionless and very pale.

Went back at 4 p.m. Situation was the same but I was told that the doctor had been and that he is getting homoeopathic treatment.

13 September

I worry so much for him. He seems to be very ill. His face is yellow and drawn. The pain in the region of the liver and stomach is acute. He lies there, moaning.

His family takes turns to massage his body day and night. His wife is with him all the time.

I don't stay. Go home and worry. And so the hours and the days pass, full of misery.

I feel sure that the last act has begun, the final breaking down. How long it will go on I do not know . . .

⊰ 23 ⊱

This morning he seemed worse than ever. Half conscious, his eyes wide open with effort, he talked incessantly, feverishly, his hands like restless birds wandering about on the blanket.

Toxic phenomena, I thought. Told Babu that perhaps hospital treatment would be advisable but got the most resentful answer. 'At home he gets the best treatment.' When I mentioned that his wife should be told in case she does not know, that the doctor has ordered that he should not speak, Babu was positively rude and said sharply that his mother has to speak to his father. I am sure he reported this conversation to her because when she came out into the garden she stood glaring at me.

Later, Satendra told me that he had been saying, "My father, my grandfather, my brother, all died from liver trouble. I will die of it. Why not now? My time is up and I am going."

I fear that he will go into deep samadhi and not come back. And that will be that.

Satendra did not know if the doctor was coming again tonight. I suggested that he and I should go by rickshaw and fetch him. Babu was doubtful and said, 'If you like,' and the wife said nothing. So we went. 'Oh, God,' I was thinking, 'If you die, I die with you!'

The doctor lived very far beyond the slaughterhouse, in a little street behind a big temple. The street was narrow, crowded with children, cows, goats, chickens, dust and resounding with temple bells. He was sitting on a sofa in his consulting room, half-naked in the heat, conversing with a man. I told him how worried we were and that several times I had seen Bhai Sahib twitching his face, a toxic phenomena I thought.

He came with us. It was dark when we arrived. The doctor went inside and I waited, seated outside in the garden.

Babu called me in. The doctor said that he was really better, the fever was not too high, and that the homoeopathic medicines take time to act.

We sat there, the poor guru talking to the doctor, the doctor restraining him, trying to impress on him the necessity to rest. His face was strange with the effort of coughing, the eyes dilated, not seeming to understand a half of what was going on.

Later, sitting in the garden, I was distressed to hear him vomiting several times. And the cough tormenting him continually.

Went home not at all reassured. Could not sleep.

'If you go, what will become of me? You *must* take me with you. I have

135

nothing left. How can I live an empty life as I did before – without you? I don't want this world anymore. It is dead for me!'

So I wept, and prayed to him; for to God I could not pray.

15 September

He was lying in the veranda of the courtyard. Quite motionless. His wife was fanning him. He was almost unrecognisable – so thin, so hollow under the cheekbones.

A great hubbub was going on inside. A telegram was being composed to Ragunath Prasad, his best disciple, who was living not far away in the next town. And another one to his son-in-law; and one to his eldest son in Allahabad.

His wife was called in to the room for consultation. I picked up the fan she had put down and began to fan him gently. How he managed to look so beautiful even when half-dead I could not understand. Tired, ethereal, the face transparent, pale yellow. He opened his eyes and saw me.

'You said yesterday that you are going and that your time is up. If you mean it, if you are serious about it, take me with you!' He closed his eyes for a moment. 'Please,' I pleaded, 'take me with you! I mean every word of it. You cannot leave me behind.'

He nodded imperceptibly, gave me a quick glance and turned his head away as if in pain. His wife came in, talking rapidly about the telegram. She took the fan out of my hands. I sat down, crying bitterly.

Later, he was sitting in the big chair in the room. I sat there in silence, looking at him from time to time.

So thin . . . so beautiful . . . so dear to me . . .

16 September

Last night, Ramji, son of Ragunath Prasad, arrived and this morning Durghesh and her husband; and in the afternoon his eldest son.

Every time someone of the family arrived he cried and got very emotional. He very easily has tears in his eyes.

The doctor said he must not talk at all, otherwise he will have fever. But how can it be avoided with a house full of people?

God give him health, that's all I want.

17 September

Days of nightmare they are . . . Coming and going, to and from his place like a restless soul. The longing is such that I seem to break under it.

This morning when I arrived he nodded ever so slightly in acknowledgement of my greeting. A disciple who was fanning him told me that he was feeling a little better.

18 September

Still has high fever all the time. And I keep coming and going, but now at least there are responsible people here – his eldest son and Durghesh, who looks after him well.

19 September

Hardly saw him; avoided going in. So many people were in the room and such a din. And the doctor said he must have quiet! He does not look at me at all. His wife and Durghesh laugh about me. It is healthy for my ego.

20 September

His eldest son, Ravindra, told me that his father had asked him about me when he was massaging him and they were alone.

He had a better night, slept peacefully, at least for a few hours.

I stayed only a few minutes. The wife came in and sat in front of him so that I should not see his face. She is resentful because I mentioned hospital treatment a while ago.

21 September

I think he does not want to live. His son told me this morning that he had said:

"There is no fixed time how long one must remain in this world. Some remain for twenty, some for thirty, some for sixty or more. You should not worry."

23 September

This morning I did not see him. He was asleep, face turned towards the wall.

One of his disciples from Allahabad is here. I saw him for the first time in the morning, when he was massaging the guru's feet. In the evening he told me that Bhai Sahib had asked if I was there. He told me that he had been a disciple since 1948.

'I am quite new,' I said.

'There is no question of new or old,' he answered. 'It is a question of nearness; it is a question of love. You have seen me for the first time; if you love me, I will be near to you. On the other hand, one can live near a neighbour for many years and he is as far away as anything. One hardly knows him. It is all a question of love.'

25 September

Woke up about 1 a.m. The longing was dreadful. I don't think I have suffered so acutely, so terribly, in my life.

How can I live now, if he should go?

It has been raining from early morning and it is cool.

He is better. I know by the churning in my inside.

'Let me look at you,' I said to him yesterday. 'I didn't dare to look in all those days!'

He turned his head slowly in my direction and regarded me seriously.

'I hope you are not angry with me,' I said softly, my heart so full that I could hardly speak. 'You could be angry I know because I said and did things which I should not have done, but I ask your forgiveness.'

He did not answer.

1 *October*

He is much better.

I see him for a few moments in the morning and a few moments in the evening. Usually, as soon as I arrive, he asks for hot water to be brought for washing and the wife sends me out by pointing at the door. I am sure that it is done on purpose so that I shall hardly see him at all.

The days are lonely, dragging endlessly. It is so difficult to bear and the mind is in the most hopeless state.

So the days slide by. The rainy season is over, I am told.

2 *October*

I went to the shop in the bazaar this morning and bought some Indian sweets, a whole box of them, the best ones, and enclosed a note: 'Today it is exactly one year since I have been with you. It was the most difficult year of my whole life. May God bless you and give you many years of good health.'

6 *October*

I saw him dusting the shelves in his room. I approached the open door and it seemed to me that he would not mind me going in. But soon I saw that I was not welcome. So I sat outside and then went back again later.

'May I come in?'

He was still dusting, with his back to the door, and he very slowly and deliberately turned round and gave me an ironic look without answering.

I stayed for about fifteen minutes and then the hot water was brought in for him to wash. The wife pointed at the door once again and I left.

8 *October*

I saw him sitting alone in the garden; but, as I came in through the gate, he got up, went inside and closed the door.

The mind is not working. Difficulty in thinking the most elementary things; periodically blankness, complete emptiness. Events from the past keep coming into my consciousness – stupidities, blunders, things so far away, when I was a schoolgirl. Humiliating situations, when I was hurt, and had no sense of proportion, and suffered from it. I regretted all those faults and blunders; and I felt worthless.

9 October

I changed the hours of going to him in the morning. At 8 he is being washed and has his breakfast. So I go about 11. But it is no use; it is the same story; after a few moments he calls for water and the wife comes with it and I have to leave.

Today, I came at 11.30 and sat there, looking at him so pitifully weak. A few minutes later he said to his wife in Hindi (I understand enough Hindi now to be able to grasp simple conversations):

"Bring the children."

'They won't come; they are afraid of her,' said the wife.

"Then send her out!"

Walking down the street, I thought that it did not hurt much any more. I was only sad because I was not allowed to see him for more than a few moments at a time. The children are there all day long . . . But obviously it has to be like this.

In the evening, after a few minutes, I was sent out because his tea was brought in. Even to drink tea is now an excuse to send me out. Sat outside on the tachat; no chairs were out. Nobody bothers to do anything for me now. Even the servant, seeing the treatment I am getting, treats me with contempt – grins impertinently at me each time he has the chance. But he does not do it when someone else is present.

Looking up at the evening sky, softly coloured with the dying light of sunset, I was suddenly aware of the deepest peace. It was wonderful; I keep forgetting what happiness is, for my memory is so weak lately. And when it comes, when it is like this, it seems that it will last for ever.

The worse he treats me, the nearer I am to him . . .

"The time will come when you won't want to speak to me anymore," he said many months ago. This had seemed very improbable at the time.

10 October

I went in later, thinking that because his son-in-law was with him he would not mind. But he told him to send me out. I saw that the son-in-law was very embarrassed, obviously reluctant to do so. But the wife came in and she pointed to the door as usual.

11 October

At one time he told me:

"My Revered Guru never spoke to me for many years unless to give an order or to scold me. The people thought that he hated me. I also thought it at one time. Only later, just five years before his death, I came to know how much he loved me ..."

So, his guru did it to him and he does it to me. Now it is my turn. Nobody is treated like I am. And it should give me hope.

Did not even try to go inside; he clearly does not want me to. Sat in the garden and through the open gate saw him walking in the courtyard with the help of a stick. He looked frail and fascinating, in a slightly frightening way.

Later, sitting in the dark, I reflected that in spite of the difficulties I have great peace sometimes. But I foresee that, in the months ahead, more than ever this dusty garden will be my only domain; and probably I will see very little of him.

12 October

Nobody else was there. He walked up and down, a ghost of a smile on his face. He did not look human ... the light in him ... he becomes more and more like a being not of this world ...

Workmen arrived to whitewash and redecorate his bungalow. In the evening, he sat outside surrounded by his family – wife, sons, the grandchildren and Durghesh with the baby in her arms. I was sitting far away from them, under the trees.

27 October

"Yes," he said, looking up from deep samadhi, "I was ill, very ill; the illness was about to be fatal. But I was Hinted that I still have to live. I will live for a while more ..."

Later he said, softly shaking his head in answer to a remark of mine about the row:

"No, I was not angry, never angry, never. No such feelings are there for you in my heart ... Now I will stay here for a while. If you will be ordered to stay behind and finish the work, you will do; if not ..." and he made a gesture with his hands pointing skywards as if to indicate that I will go with him. His kindly smile was something to be seen.

Yes, Bhai Sahib, *I know*; you will be with me always ... and I will be with you.

28 October

He came out and walked up and down. He gave me a quick look and then went inside. Something had been done while he was walking. The flow of shakti increased again. Such power was rushing through the whole of my body; like a storm blowing right through; but there was peace inside.

He came out soon after I arrived. He talked to Sageji and the one-eyed Takur.

"Posted the letter?" he began as an opening. I said that· long ago I had done it – but was not sure which letter he meant. I managed to tell him that the shakti vibration has moved to the soles of the feet.

"It has a reason," he said quickly, "everything has a reason. Sometimes there is an increase of sex feeling, sometimes the mind is affected, sometimes something else."

I pondered. I knew that these vibrations have to do with *ida, pingala* and *shushumna** (although he uses different names). But what is the vibration supposed to do in the soles of the feet?

I said that the vibration is a kind of hand-maiden who does the cleaning work; a kind of purifying process. If it is in the heart, the heart goes wild; if it is in the throat, there is a sense of choking or suffocation; if it is at the base of the spine, there is a sensation of heat; but I could not understand it being in the feet?

He smiled, with half-closed eyes. "I never cover my feet," he said; and closed his eyes.

For half an hour we sat in silence. There was the most perfect peace. And I reflected how the situation had changed for me; before I would have wanted to say this or that to him, to question him, or perhaps wondered why he did not speak. Now . . .

1 *November*

The vibration continues in the soles of my feet, and somewhat stronger in the left foot. It is going on softly and I have to sleep with my feet uncovered, so hot they are even though the night is very cool. What could it be? There are small chakras at the soles of the feet, as there are in the middle of the palms of the hand. But why should the vibration go there? What purpose?

In the morning he came out and sat in the sun for quite a while. But he did not say anything to me and I don't speak to him lately when he does not address me.

The whole family crowded round him discussing all sorts of matters. I just sat looking at the garden, the chipmunks running up and down the tree trunks making funny chirping noises.

2 *November*

He sat outside but did not talk to me. A young disciple was there – one who had come to see him after a long absence – so he was talking to him all the time.

* *Ida, pingala* and *shushumna* are the principal *nadis* or conduits of *pranic* force in the human body. Of the three, *shushumna* is the most important, situated in the interior of the cerebro-spinal column. *Pingala* is on the right side of it and is the conduit for the positive, solar current of *prana* whilst *ida*, on the left side, is that of the negative, lunar current.

Then he got up to go to his room and asked me if I wished to remain or wanted to go home. I said that if he did not mind I would like to stay. So I went inside with the others. Realized that I had not been in the room for weeks. It was badly distempered in green, as before.

3 November

The young disciple came again and they were talking.

I asked if I could ask a question. He looked at me kindly and said, "Yes".

Told him that, as he already knows, for the last four days the vibration has been in my feet, but yesterday it stopped. And that it had been much stronger in the left foot. 'Has it anything to do with my being a woman?'

"Things come and go. And that it was felt stronger on the left has to do with the circulation of the blood. It has nothing to do with your being a woman. Some forces are different with men and women, some vibrations too, but not this one. If there is no circulation, there would be no vibration. If one is healthy, one feels these things much quicker. A healthy body does not mean a fat one; one can be thin but healthy. There must be nothing wrong with the heart; this is important. If there is, how can the Guide find the Way into the Heart of Hearts?"

Then he proceeded to tell us how many astrologers had predicted his death, especially in the year when he had received his *adhikara* [initiation] from his guru, and were astonished that he was still alive.

I told him that, according to some books, when one is on the Path all the predictions are wrong because the human being takes his destiny in his own hands.

"Maybe, maybe," he said thoughtfully. "But it could also be that the question of death was wrongly interpreted."

I understood. Adhikara would mean the death of the self . . . not that of the body.

Told him that I think that through his illness he himself crossed another barrier.

"You are right; it is so."

And he looked far, with a distant expression in his wonderful eyes.

That afternoon I saw him sweeping his room; he does it for the sake of exercise. Then he came out to direct the boys who were sweeping the garden, creating a great display of dust.

'Bhai Sahib, may I say something to you?'

"Do."

'Since you have been ill, I am acutely aware of the fact that you are not really here.'

"I am never here," he smiled faintly.

'No; it is not quite what I mean. What I mean to say is that what is here, what we see, is a sort of *mayavirupa* [body of illusion] and only one part of you is functioning on this plane.'

"You are right; you are quite right."

'It is as if you need to keep this body for a certain time, to serve as a necessary link, but you yourself are no more here.'

"Quite right."

How young he looked again; how golden was his skin in the fading sunlight ...

4 November

This morning he was talking to Tulsi Ram, the man with the large family in the *kaprail* [goat shed]. It was so unpleasant to listen to this croaking, excited voice which jarred on my nerves. He is fat, his mind is unbalanced, he cannot keep a job and has a child every year. Oh, Bhai Sahib, I am by far not surrendered yet! I should not suffer so much because of such futile things. Am full of terrible longing and restlessness. Heaven knows why. I am doing the most difficult thing in the world.

❦ 24 ❧

7 November

"Karmas are for those who are with them." I looked at him trying to understand.

"Only those who are already beyond karma have the right to investigate the laws of karma. Only when you reach a certain stage have you the right to enquire into the Laws of Nature.

"While we are in the karmic laws, we had better leave them alone, because otherwise we might do things to produce good karmic results and it would mean that the self would reappear on the higher level. We may plant a huge weed, and to eradicate it would be practically impossible for us. We should do good for the sake of doing it, and not to produce good karma."

9 November

'There is something that worries me a lot: I seem sometimes to hate everything and everybody. Hate them thoroughly and completely. Everyone seems to be irritating, ugly, even horrible. A constant irritation about practically everything surrounding me. I seem to have become barren and arid. Surely this is not an improvement?'

He smiled. "It is a stage one is passing. There was a time when I too hated everybody."

'But L. told me she feels universal love.'

"This is something else. Once you love God, you love His Creation, and then you do not hate anymore."

'But for the moment when the heart is occupied with the One, how can it love anything else? Everything is felt as an intrusion; everything is rejected.'

"Yes, it is so, at the beginning. It is a passing stage, as I just told you."

10 *November*

Sat in the sun in his garden. Very peaceful.

He came and sat in his chair. When he spoke, the peace was shattered . . .

"I am trying to quicken you, speed you up, in order that you should go for two or three years and work while I am alive. Then you will come back."

'But how?' I stammered, frightened at the sudden prospect of having to leave him. 'How will I do that? I am a beggar now. The journey is expensive!'

"Oh, I will arrange for you. It will be done. But you should go now and work for a while. Otherwise how will I know whether you are successful or not?

"I also have been sent away by my Revered Guru, and I have met many people – *mahatmas* [great souls], sages, all sorts of people; but I never wanted to be with anybody but him."

He looked straight at me, smiling. "People will come to you. Some will try to get you on the wrong Path. When one is on the Path, reaching a certain stage, temptations will come and one has difficulties which have to be overcome."

I was so thunderstruck that I could hardly speak.

'But if I have to go, I will never see you again. You know that your health is not good.'

"You will; you surely will. But now you must go. Here you cannot work, and you must work. Remember, we are not given for ourselves – never. We are given for others. And the more you give, the more you will receive. This is how the Essence works."

'What work do you want me to do?' I asked blankly, terrified at the prospect of trying to find work at my age.

"Anything. Any work which is offered you, you will do. Whatever comes your way."

'But it will be so difficult. I will be helpless without you.' My head was spinning and the chair seemed to rock under me.

"Yes; if you forget me," he said slowly, his eyes veiled as if in samadhi. "It can only be so if you forget me. Only then can you go wrong. Keep writing to me always and you will be with me."

Went home crying and cried for a long time into the night.

11 *November*

"If you obey implicitly, respect absolutely, are faithful, you are bound to succeed. That is why you will have to go. Who remains with me all the time does not progress; not those who are put on the Path you have to take.

144

"When you are away, you are alone; you will have to control yourself. Later you will come back, and progress again. When I am inside, you think I am doing nothing? I do something to you who are sitting outside, to those who are here, to those who are far away ... It is so done ... This is my work."

'When do you want me to go?' I asked, as if in a dream.

"In the spring. Perhaps March or April. We will see."

March is so near! Only four months or so away!

'But is it not a pity to interrupt the training; just now when I seem to be getting some new experiences?' I asked, not knowing what else to say, for I was lost completely ...

"Do you really think that time and space matter to me?" he demanded, looking straight at me. I lowered my eyes. "Hundreds of thousands of people do every year the pilgrimage to Kaaba. Says the Poet, 'None of them cares to win one heart ...' Because to win somebody's heart is more than all the *hajas* [pilgrimages] in the world!"

13 *November*

All is so insecure now ...

I made up my mind to stay here for many years; and now ...

The whole horror of being sent back to England, penniless, was dawning on me clearer and clearer.

'You are subjecting me to a very severe test,' I said quietly, but I was trembling inside. He went very still, tilted his head slightly backwards and nodded slowly.

'You are sending me away just shortly after taking all my money from me. You want to see what difference it will make to my attitude. But I can tell you already that it will make no difference. I made a promise – it is all yours. I will go – and trust you.

'Once I challenged you in unbelief and arrogance. This is also a challenge; but of a different sort. I am challenging destiny and you – by complete trust this time ...'

He kept nodding, slowly, gravely. But for his head, he was absolutely motionless, like a statue.

All the while I was speaking, I kept crying. But, for reasons I am unable to explain, his very motionlessness and silence seemed to confirm me in my faith, to keep the doubts away from my mind ...

16 *November*

Early in the morning, Pushpa came to take me to the satsang of a great Saint who is here from Delhi. We went by rickshaw.

In a large marquee, such as those used here for wedding ceremonies, *dharries* [cotton carpets] were laid out on the floor and hundreds of people were sitting on them.

145

The Saint, an old man of dignified appearance, sat on a platform with microphones in front of him. He was supposed to be a very important man in the Sikh religion but to me he was just a very ordinary-looking old man. He kept spitting on the carpet in front of him, then rubbing it in with his fingers. I thought it was disgusting ... but in India such things seem to matter little, if at all. Then he kept rubbing his teeth with his forefinger as if to clean them from the remains of food ... He gave a talk in Hindi and then sat in meditation. All the time, the audience was restless; much coughing going on.

17 *November*

"Money;" he said with a sigh, "I get hundreds of rupees every month, and it all goes. It is like this in our Line. Money comes like water and flows away like water. Money is less than dust. What I do with the money nobody knows, not even my wife."

I showed him the pamphlet of the Saint I saw yesterday with Pushpa. He read it through. Shook his head with disapproval.

"Propaganda, advertisement; this is not good. We don't work this way. No, this is not done."

'It is like an agony, a terror, to think that I may never see you again.'

Looking into the distance he said, "About November, in 1965, not before, there is a holiday. Then I would want you to come back."

Suddenly it was like a flood of love in my heart.

'Give me humility, and your blessing, and I will go anywhere.'

"Why ask for humility? Why do you want to limit yourself? It is an obstacle between us! If the Beloved would ask you, 'Become naked before me,' and you say, 'Yes; but only for one hour,' then it is a limitation, is it not? You put conditions. No such ideas should remain in your mind."

20 *November*

To talk to him becomes more and more difficult as the days slide by. I sort of dissolve when I am before him. Such subtle feelings. How can they be expressed when I only feel like falling at his feet? Is it surrender?

He sang again today. It does something to me when I hear him sing; it reaches right beyond the mind. Tears ran down my cheeks for I remembered that when he was so ill I thought that I would never hear him sing again.

It was a Persian verse which was translated for me afterwards:

"If somebody speaks ill of you, give him the place of honour in your courtyard; for he will be the cause of your being able to better yourself.

"A friend will not tell you the truth, but an enemy will; and it is a Grace and a Good Fortune to have a Master for it is due to him that you will be able to bear the cutting remarks and become better."

146

⊰ 25 ⊱

9 *December*

I have been in a strange mood for days.

I suppose I have done the usual things – like eating, drinking, sleeping, doing the daily chores, going to his place – but I have hardly any recollection of it.

Remember dimly that I have been worried because he does not come out.

He is clearly not well again. So my fear that he was ill is proved correct. He has fever and I hear him coughing pitifully.

Looking at a tree outside my bungalow, a sort of mimosa full of white flowers, I thought that only one year ago I would have loved to see it. Now I understand fully what he said last year, "Your heart is like a hotel; you love this and that. Only One can, must, be loved."

Now there is only the longing . . . such a longing.

12 *December*

This morning there was nobody about, and nobody came out of the house. I suspect that he is very ill.

Suddenly Satendra came out of his room and said, 'Father wants you inside.'

My heart melted. He looked so frail.

"How are you?" he asked.

'I am well, Bhai Sahib. But how are you?'

"I am better."

He made a movement with his hand for me to sit down. There was a sudden light of a smile in his eyes, illuminating his face, and disappearing into his beard. It is usually his eyes which smile first. He spoke of a poem by Jalalu'd-din Rumi:

"If I am what I am, if people admire and respect me, it is all due to my guru. It is due to the Grace of the Saint if we realise God. The soul is in the body from head to foot. When one realizes the Self, the body becomes quite stiff; so if the body is stiff it is all soul; so go to those Saints whose body is the Body of Realised Souls . . ."

Told him that it was not clear to me what this meant.

"It is because of the vibrations. They become so strong that the body cannot bear it. At a certain stage of development, the body is ill continuously. This is a secret people do not know. They think the more perfect one is, the healthier one becomes. It is so at the beginning; but not at the later stages. We must not forget we have an ordinary body meant to serve us in this world. When we are

147

on the Path at first, we are still able to take care of the body and the mind; but later body and mind are left behind as quite unimportant."

14 *December*

His Presence is constant. To live with God as a Reality is a great happiness.

As I understand it now, one does not surrender to the Master at all; for in reality the surrender is *through* the Master to God. The Master is only the focus of attention on the physical plane. In other words, the outer guru points to the inner guru, the Self.

"It is a Gift, but it is not given for oneself; it is given for others." He closed his eyes for a moment; and then, "At first love is created; it is not done to everyone. Not everyone's heart is made in such a way that it can be done. If there is much feeling quality, love is created.

"If the person lives on the mental level and there is hardly any feeling, first feeling is awakened and love afterwards. In the ordinary way, love comes slowly. In the state of dhyana, a state of pure being is felt first; then currents of love and bliss. But it is a slow process. It takes time.

"Things are done according to human beings, according to the necessities of every one of them. No two are alike.

"Surrender, I told you, has to be on all levels, to form a closed circle. If the mind is surrendered, the body is surrendered too, for the mind is the master of the body. The body is surrendered *through* the mind. Everything has to be included. Surrender is surrender."

25 *December*

"The Nakshmandia Dynasty – the Golden Sufis – descends from the Prophet. The first Deputy was the father-in-law of the Prophet; but Sufis were before the Prophet. Sufism always was: it is the Ancient Wisdom. Only before the Prophet they were not called Sufis and did not come to be called so until a few centuries after his death.

"Long before, they were a sect called *Kamal Posh* [blanket-wearers]. They went to every prophet. A tradition goes that they went to Jesus. No one could satisfy them; every prophet told them to do this or that and they were not satisfied.

"One day Mohammed said, 'There are many Kamal Posh men coming and they will be here in so many days' . . . and they came on the day he said. And when they were with him, he only looked at them, without speaking, and they were completely satisfied . . ."

He fell silent for a moment and laughed to himself.

"He created love in their hearts. No questions are answered in the System; it is infused. You only know how it feels when the love is created. Every prophet told the Kamal Posh this or that, naturally they were not satisfied. But when love is created, what dissatisfaction can there be? So they went away fully satisfied."

30 *December*

Hour after hour for over a year I have been sitting outside while he is inside with others, but I cannot go in without being asked. It can be cold and windy ... and I am sitting. It can be hot and dusty ... and I am sitting. Young men pass in groups in the street, stop at the gate and laugh at me; dogs and dirty children come from everywhere around.

But he came out today, even if very late. All went still inside me. He was wrapped in a white blanket, his head wrapped in a towel. He looked tired ... hollow cheeks, burning eyes, like strange lights ... with those high cheekbones he is like an old wooden carving ... so Tibetan ... so Eastern.

He sat in the sun; but not for long. He did not speak to me.

1 *January* 1963

"Everybody has built his home on shifting sands in this world. Everybody in the System comes to the point where they lose all beliefs and are confused, and say they are nowhere.

"Until one forgets everything, samskara will remain ... The Teacher will never tell the disciple that the teaching is finished and that he knows all that there is to know ... in order that the disciple shall not be proud."

He came out today dressed so flimsily; it seems he does it on purpose. It was bitterly cold with a sharp wind blowing from the north. Told him that my senses seemed to be working in an unusual way – as if they are not able to record impressions properly.

"The *indrias* [senses] do not seem to convey the correct impressions because you are in a state of spiritual constipation. It sometimes happens like this."

'Is it bad?'

"No. Very good. Spiritual constipation is a good thing; it means that you will make a jump forward afterwards."

2 *January*

He only looked briefly out of his room; to give me some cards to post.

7 *January*

This morning, such was the loneliness that I began to weep; the situation looked hopeless. How can I go on?

He came out in a dark mood. My heart grew heavy. I did not want to complain and yet somehow the urge to tell him overwhelmed me.

"You don't know how to love! This is not love! Did you try to serve me when I was ill? Did you sit up all night?"

I was horrified at this accusation.

'What would your family have said if I had? Once I tried to fan you but the fan was taken from my hands. Once I tried to massage your feet when you were unconscious and was stopped immediately. It is an unjust accusation!'

149

"I am never unjust!" he snapped.

When I said to him that he never subjected his wife or his daughter to such treatment, he said angrily, "You are impertinent! How can you compare yourself to my wife and my daughter? They are good women."

'They are women like me; what's the difference?'

And so it went on for a long time and I became so desperate that I said to him that death would be better than this life of such misery.

"What effort are you making? You must make effort."

I said I thought I was making superhuman effort.

"It is nothing!" he said angrily. "Nothing! What are you doing? A bit of hot weather you have had to bear; that is all." He blew disdainfully. "Why do you compare yourself with my shishyas? You are not my shishya; and you never will be at this rate; never, never!"

The depression is terrible. Absolute despair. I am useless; I am a failure; I will never make it; I cannot go on . . .

I went in the evening. I did not want to go. But could not stay away. There was nothing else . . . and I was too tired to resist.

I sat alone in the garden. Bhai Sahib appeared in the doorway and talked to a man. When the man left, to my surprise he approached me.

"How are you?" he asked in a friendly way.

'Well,' I answered, getting up. He is not angry, I thought with relief.

"It is done for the sake of training; I am never really harsh, but harsh attitude is maintained with lovers. Otherwise, how can I give a stroke if the mind gives trouble?"

'Oh, I was thinking this afternoon that you are quite right. I am still full of the self.'

"Why don't you say that I am *always* right?" He laughed gaily, as if nothing had happened. He suggested that we went inside. He sat and adjusted his legs into a comfortable posture.

"The trouble started because you took objection to my saying that women cannot reach the highest state in the same way as men. Men have a substance in them that women have not. It makes men absorb the very essence of the Master. But men have to control *prakriti* [primal or root matter] in themselves and for this purpose practices are given to them.

"Women, because they are nearer to prakriti, are fertilized by the Divine Energy which they retain in their chakras and, because of this, very few practices are needed. Women are taken up through the Path of Love, for love is feminine mystery. Woman is the cup waiting to be filled, offering herself up in her longing which is her very being.

"Souls have different qualities and according to those qualities they are directed . . .

"I can give you dhyana in a moment; it is not at all difficult for me. But I myself do not attach any importance to that. To produce love is difficult in other schools of yoga; not in ours; in ours it is easy.

"Love is a great suffering in the beginning and in the middle; later it is all joy, or nearly all."

He will not tell me the truth; all his behaviour shows it to me – that is the *only* road. I have to reach a state of faith such that if he should say this chair is a dog, I will think, yes, it is a dog.

10 *January*

"Logic will not help you; it is only a matter of lack of faith. If faith is great enough it will carry you through. If not, mind will revolt always.

"I never, never contradict myself. We never do in our System. All my statements are correct, seen from different levels.

"How can there be effort with Divine things? They are given, *infused*.

"And the Guru can *never* be forced. If you say so, you will deceive others and deceive yourself. The Divine is given as a gift ... one cannot force God."

13 *January*

Some men came and he was very angry because the sawdust they had delivered was of poor quality.

"Cheats," he grumbled after they had left.

I said, smiling, that until I came to him I did not know a Saint could get angry.

"The world is full of wrong ideas, and full of foolish people.

"A Saint is an ordinary man; only he does not indulge in anything. He has desires as every other human being; only he is not after desires. If they are fulfilled, there is no pleasure. If not, there is indifference and no pain. That's all.

"He is on the same platform as any other human being. People say the Saint has to be hungry, must not eat, only drink twice a week, and so on. This mis-- conception arises because of Hatha Yogis who often do that sort of thing – and the world thinks it is the highest thing. Hatha Yoga means one who has not been accepted; it is not a high state.

"The Almighty is full of desires; otherwise what was the necessity of creating the world? Nobody can ever remain without desires; they must be fewer, that's all. Some desires are needs – like eating and drinking – needs necessary for daily living.

"Understanding alone is not enough; if you have understood something, it must become part of your thinking."

14 *January*

It is a strange thing with Love: that it is the Beloved who merges into the Lover.

It rained all night. And when I went there in the morning it was still raining. So, I sat in the doorway. It was cold and draughty. My feet were wet. For one moment I began to think whether it was right to let an elderly woman sit in a cold doorway on a rainy day. But I stilled the mind. A dead body, if it is put in the rain, gets wet. If it is put in the sun it gets scorched. Can it protest? It cannot. Can I protest? I cannot.

<h1 style="text-align:center">❮ 26 ❯</h1>

16 *February*

A month has slipped by. The Bandhara festival has been held and Bhai Sahib gave himself unsparingly to the crowds who came. For two of the nights he had no sleep. It has taken much from him and he seems very tired.

The golden days pass, full of the fragrance of spring. How I shall miss the sky of delicate blue, the sleeping out in the courtyard, the sunshine day after day, the smell of the wind coming from the thousands of miles of plain. The time of my departure comes closer . . .

Sometimes I have peace; sometimes I have vibrations in the chakras – the feet, the base of the spine, the heart, the throat, in the centre of my forehead.

Spoke to him about my idea to keep the flat, for I am afraid that I will not find accommodation when I come back.

"Why do you Europeans always think of the future?"

I replied that that is how we are brought up.

"Then you have to stop it. You still don't want to change? We never think of the future. If you think of the future and make plans you don't trust in God. Never think of tomorrow."

'Is the sense of oneness a reality happening somewhere and coming down into the mind; or is it an illusion?'

"It is an illusion. A superior kind of illusion. What one thinks, what one tries to explain, what one speaks is an illusion. Many are illusions – some high, some low.

"Illusions will remain until the mind goes completely."

'But what about your mind? Is it gone? It seems to be very much here.'

"What a useless question! You don't know how to talk to the Elders. Why don't you listen more carefully to what I say? Why don't you grasp it? For the third time I say to you: when there is a little interest, it can be done. Without a sacrifice, how can it be?"

I said I was discouraged.

"Why do you say that you are discouraged? It only shows that you are at the mercy of discouragement. Like a straw tossed by the waves. Emotions are nothing; they are not at all the sign of spirituality."

'You have said that I will not progress here.'

He nodded. "You are sent back to atone for the life you have led previously and which was not justified.

"If you want Truth, Truth wants you."

20 February

Today I said I did not care if I had success when I return to England.

"You have to care," he answered. "You must want to be successful. If you do something, you must want to do it as best as you can. You will be letting down Sufism if you don't care."

Of course he is right. Another time he said:

"At the beginning and in the middle one wants to work, to share, to teach. Later this desire also goes. It is then that one really begins to teach. If you feel the need to teach, you are not ready to be a teacher. Wait till the need is no more, then you can teach and only then will there be success.

"The road to Him is to forget all, to leave all preoccupations behind, to let go; put yourself in His hands, trust and *you will know*. To be after knowledge is to create a veil between Him and 'me'. Even this has to go. The less one desires the better. It is the desire which prevents us from perceiving the Hint. It clouds our perception.

"After all, were not the Church Fathers very wise in suppressing all the ideas of reincarnation? Because otherwise we will not make the effort in this life! Why not realise here and now, in this life? Why think of later? Only the moment of NOW matters; the future is far away ... True we all work for the future, ultimately, what else? Otherwise you wouldn't be here. But think only of NOW, forget tomorrow."

How right he was again ...

He came out dressed in a thin longhi and a singlet. A cold wind was blowing. It had become cool for the last few days. I was horrified and asked him if I could bring a blanket; he had had a fever for three days. No, he wanted no blanket. And he sat there for two solid hours, listening to a horrid, ugly, selfish man who kept talking about his court case. Finally I could not bear it, stood up and asked him to move his chair in the sun or to allow me to bring his blanket. No, he shook his head.

"No, I don't want one."

21 February

He did not come out last night. He had a high fever. No wonder.

23 February

He has been ill for three days. But at last he now takes some medicine. At least, so Virendra told me.

Last night his temperature was 102°. My heart was aching; what an agony it is to sit outside and hear his painful, dry cough. Am sick with worry and apprehension.

25 February

When I went to him in the afternoon, the wife made me a sign to go in. Was horrified to see how weak he looked and how grey. He was lying on the bed, a wet compress was on his forehead. My heart fell. So many people were around. Poor Bhai Sahib. He never has a moment to himself. He looked as though he was dying now! How can he survive for the years I am away?

26 *February*

He came out this morning which I had not expected. As usual my heart stood still as he suddenly appeared. He was very pale, and he looked absolutely glorious. The light around him was so interesting. A ghost of a smile appeared on his lips as if he knew why I had moved further away from him. I knew that he was there just to test me if I wanted to speak, but I had no such intention. I will not address you, I thought; I know what you expect. I wanted only to look at him. He kept combing his beard with his fingers as he often does when he is thinking. When everybody had left he was still standing there.

28 *February*

He appeared today so thin and tired, pale yellow in colour, with hollow cheeks. He began to talk in Hindi but mostly he kept quiet because his brother never stopped talking; on the Chinese question, frontier incidents, politics. His eyes had a glow like burning coals, deep set and fiery. Did not feel like speaking to him at all. Simply because everything had been said, and I had nothing to ask either. Even the desire for knowledge is a veil between Him and 'me'. These are the reasons, or so it seemed to me, but perhaps something was done that it became like this. Love has drowned it perhaps.

Nigam came out and gave him a small rose. He took it, smelt it and was holding it in his hands. I wanted this rose and was wondering if he would give it to me as he did before. But no, he will not.

From time to time I had to close my eyes. It was interesting how the feeling of nothingness seems to increase as the time goes on ... The great nearness to him, like a secret complicity of which nobody knows. I want to be nothing. The greatest bliss is in Nothingness ...

Everybody left, one after another. He got up, stood for a short while, then threw the rose into the dust, turned and went inside. Quickly I got up and took the rose before he could open the door of the room and could see me doing it. It was a small, pink rose that smelt sweet and I could feel the cool petals against my skin. Sweet-smelling flower he had held in his hands. He knew, of course, that I wanted it; that's why he threw it away so deliberately.

2 *March*

In the evening many people were inside. I heard much laughter. People like the horrible pandit who don't even respect him properly. Recently, he kept complaining to me about having to speak too much; yet I constantly heard his voice telling jokes, laughing, just being merry. Heavier and heavier became my heart. I resolved to sit it out and wait till they had left. They should see me sitting outside alone in the darkness before the closed door ... They came out and pretended not to see me; passed by, talking to each other. I hope they felt guilty. Behind them he closed the door of the room with a bang. He had seen me, of course. Went home and cried; and prayed much to be helped because I cannot do it alone.

4 March

This morning the depression was great, the pain of love so deep and unending ... Kept thinking how will I live without him for years? It seemed impossible.

13 March

There has been nothing to tell except terrible pain in the heart, longing and longing so terrible that I cried non-stop. And he was inside with others and I was outside and I felt like a lonely wolf howling to the moon ...

Was sorry when Professor Batnagar came and went inside, for he speaks English and when he is here I have the chance to speak a little. He is sympathetic and shows some interest in me. I am glad of a little attention; it is difficult to sit, unloved, unnoticed ... But he remained inside and I sat outside the door. Much merriment was inside, much laughter. It is useless; the less rebellious I am, the quicker it will be over. There is not much longer; soon I will be gone and the burning days of Kanpur will be over.

Professor Batnagar came out when it was already dark; and Guruji came out too. He was coughing and moaning softly and I was thinking sadly, don't speak and laugh so much and you will cough less. He looked unfriendly, spoke for a long time with his wife and she never stopped talking.

Hatred against everybody was terrible.

14 March

This morning he did not come out at all; was pottering about in his room, arranging shelves, dusting the books. Hardly an hygienic occupation with this cough of his. Left shortly.

When entering my semi-dark room, still blinking after the blinding glare of the courtyard, I caught a glimpse of a mouse scampering under the bed. A sudden fury seized me. Wait, I thought, that will be the end of you. I quickly closed the doors of both communicating rooms. Got hold of a broom. In a vain, futile attempt to escape, the mouse was wheeling around the room jumping up the walls, squeaking, while I chased it mercilessly. But the more it tried to escape, the hotter my hatred, my fury, became. Beside myself, I kept hitting and missing and hitting, till at last it fell down; but I kept beating, hammering at it lying there already dead, till it was reduced to a bloody pulp on the concrete floor ...

Only then I stopped dead, horrified. I looked at the mess. Why? Why this uncontrollable fury rising in me and for what? For a little mouse who entered my room, perhaps in the hope of finding something to eat. The magnitude of this feeling had been so disproportionate; it had absolutely no justification, if there could ever be any justification for fury.

The truth was that I became afraid of myself, of my own reactions. For a long time I stood and stared almost afraid to move. Then fetched a rag and a pail, some disinfectant and began to clear up the mess. And then stood for a long time staring at the broom, the cold water from the tap running over it ... How much evil is hidden in us ... I realized, of course, that the intensity of feeling was such that I could easily have killed a human being, and with the pleasure of destruction into the bargain, and for no reason at all, just as there was no reason to generate such a cataract of emotions all because of a tiny creature caught in my room.

I suddenly realized that I knew nothing of myself, of the real me, that which lay somewhere I could not reach with my conscious understanding. I was ashamed, perplexed and very much afraid.

Must tell him. Why did it happen at all?

15 *March*

I saw Satendra strolling towards me soon after I arrived.

'Father says you can go home if you want; Poonam has smallpox.' I was vaccinated so I remained. I was alone; nobody came. Soon the guru came out, looking very pale. I asked how Poonam was and if she would be sent to an isolation hospital. He lifted his eyebrows.

"She will be all right; I gave her a glass of water."

But he himself looked as weak as a kitten. He will die. Only God knows with what feelings I will leave here.

Told him about the mouse incident. He nodded gravely.

"Sometimes it happens like that. Certain powers are aroused in the human being and they bring out all the evils; like dirty bubbles of foam appearing on the surface of the water when the mud at the bottom is stirred up. It is not bad," he added, continuing to pray.

Not bad? Good heavens, I killed. I know now I can kill, and he says it is not bad!

16 *March*

Today I told him about the hatred which worries me; it is so deep and strong.

"It is pride. You think yourself better than the others and you hate them."

And here I was thinking that it is the other side of love; the parallel current of it; and it was simply pride! How deluded one can become! But what to do?

"It will go away;" he smiled, "things are done slowly."

And left it at that.

156

"I speak only as I am directed and only as much as I am told; not a word more. When does gold ore become pure gold? When it is put through a process of fire. So the human being, during the training, becomes as pure as gold, through suffering. It is the burning away of the dross. I told you that suffering has a great redeeming quality. Like a drop of water falling on the desert sand is sucked up immediately, so we have to be. Nothing and nowhere, we must disappear."

He was talking to me kindly this afternoon, the first time for a month.

"The little you know will be enough for you to speak of for years. Like the child who sucks the milk of its mother and becomes strong and grows, so the disciple absorbs from the guru. The disciple is nourished with the essence of the guru."

Later he said, "Yes, you have work to do. Training is something which you acquire; talent or ability is something which you cannot help having, as a cock cannot help crowing. But training is something different, it changes the human being. Some sort of doubt will always remain. The mind is made this way."

⚹ 27 ⚹

21 *March*

Nothing much to say. The same story – pain, loneliness, worry. Snatches of conversation I remember:

"Surrender? Surrender does not mean conversion. L. thought that I wanted to convert her to our way of life and she began to wear saris. But I told her our Revered Guru did not convert us, so why should I? We are not like that; we are broad-minded; surrender is something else. Beliefs can be great traps; they imprison us, and facts are not reliable, we outgrow them. But there is such a thing as a Supreme Fact, only to that we must arrive by a long road and it can take a lifetime. One does injustice to people by comparing them. Nobody can be compared to anybody else.

"Nothing can be measured by the same time measurement. The time of a cell in your body, your own time, the time of the solar system, are different, and equal in proportion.

"And always remember that some sort of doubt, some sort of imperfection, will always remain."

22 *March*

He was relating to us some happenings which occurred in his household recently. Somehow, during the conversation, I came out with the remark he had made a few weeks ago that God is full of desires. Otherwise why should He have created the universe if He had no desire to do so?

"God is full of desires?" He looked at me in surprise. "I am supposed to have said it?"

I told him he certainly did; it was when we were discussing the desires of a Saint and him not getting angry. I noted it down in my diary as I usually do. He had also added then that I must not say it ever; nobody would accept it presented in that form.

"God is full of desires . . ." he mused, stroking his beard thoughtfully.

"I must have been in a strange mood when I said so . . . I don't remember it at all. Yes, He has Qualities, and functions of those Qualities. Perhaps it is here that one can say that He is full of desires. But the Supreme Power has nothing to do with it. How can we know why He created the universe? The world?

"Life springs without a seed; things come up. It does not mean that the earth desires them to come up. When there is mucus in the eye in the morning when you wake up, it does not mean that the eye desires it.

"If God is full of desires, what's the use of getting rid of ours? True, it is said somewhere in the Hindu scriptures that *Ishvara* [The Creator] sees the *Parabrahm* [Absolute Reality] through the veil of *Maya* [Illusion]. That is to say, immersed in prakriti, His vision is somewhat blurred. That is why I told you once that, in order to reach the Supreme Reality, we must renounce the fruits we have gained in samadhi. The state of samadhi is still within the limits of prakriti."

Later he said: "You don't always catch my thought. I did not say that women cannot reach the highest state. I said they can – only the road is different."

I answered that all I want is to be with him always. I cannot bear the idea of not being with him forever.

He smiled faintly. "There is a question of speed," he said. "Even I cannot be with my Revered Guru Maharaj."

He fell silent.

'But I want to see you, to be able to reach you from time to time, as you do with your Revered Guru.'

"That can be done; it is not so difficult. Follow the System and you will remain with me. The System will remain *always*; individuals come and go.

"Always remember that you belong somewhere; then you cannot go wrong.

"If we have to use the yogic powers, it means that we come down to the level of the individual. I tell only as much as I am allowed to tell, and only the strictly necessary, no more."

He went on to describe how one must always give good example. We are judged by the life we lead. We teach by being what we are.

"Truth which is not said gently is not Truth. Why? Because the person in question will not accept it. But if someone persists in doing evil, then you can hit; but *never* if you have any personal advantage from it. When duty-bound and there is no personal advantage for you, then there is no sin, and if they get offended it is just too bad ... If the doctor operates, and cuts and hurts the patient, does it mean that he will injure himself? No; he is duty-bound.

"You can say or do what is necessary but you have to clear the point as well as you possibly can, otherwise you will injure the feelings. If you make yourself understood, the feelings will not be injured.

"You never injure the feelings of others when you have merged. Then you will know that all souls are one. You will know why he did it, how he feels about it, what he thinks, and you will put it in such a way as not to injure his feelings.

"And I repeat: never say anything for the sake of personal gain and advantage. Be careful about that. That is a platform to stand upon and from where to start; one cannot go wrong.

"To hurt others is to hurt yourself because before you do it you think badly of them, and so you are hurt yourself."

23 March

He came out in Sufi dress – long kurta, white pyjama trousers. So radiant, so immaculate. I felt I could not bear to look at him.

He sat down, with his small, pale green jade mala in his hand. One bead after another began to slide through his slender fingers. The attitude ... full of grace. Golden skin. White garment. Green mala. The face radiant. What a sight, I thought ... I wish I could remember it forever.

I had had a letter from Madras (about my travel arrangements) but thought that I would not tell him unless he asked.

"Have you written to Madras?" he asked after a while, giving his mala a flick with a movement of his wrist. I answered that I had and gave him the letter.

When he had read it in silence and given it back to me, I said, 'There remains nothing to do except to send the money and get the ticket. Everything seems to be settled.'

He did not answer; his lips were moving in soundless prayer. An occasional click of the beads. An ox-cart rattling by. The end is approaching. A new page in my life will be turned soon ...

24 March

Went to the hospital to have my last cholera injection. Three young doctors were sitting around and we began to talk. I suddenly began to speak about him. Felt as though I had been directed to do so – what to say and what not. Sometimes I felt: don't say that, so I did not. Or I had the urge to say something, so I did. Strangely, when I left, I could not remember exactly what I had said.

When I went to him I told him about it, and said that I thought I had been saying too much.

"Never think what you have said is wrong," he replied. "If you feel the impulse to say something, say it. To act on inspiration, without a particular desire, is the thing."

'Please tell me, why do you suffer? I have seen you suffer greatly. Even if you don't complain, it is evident that you suffer much. You have no sins, so why should there be suffering for you?'

"Who tells you that I have no sins? Imperfections are everywhere! I did sometimes hurt people's feelings, so I have to suffer for it. Sometimes I did hurt your feelings . . ."

'Oh!' I interrupted. His wife laughed. 'Even your wife is laughing. You did not hurt my feelings. You crushed them. You left nothing behind!'

"If it is done for the sake of training, all is good and well. But sometimes I do not do it for this reason only. So I have to suffer.

"Never hurt anybody's feelings, never."

Later he said, "Not all things can be answered as to how and why. It is all a question of surrender – if you have faith, if you are surrendered to His will. His will becomes your will. And what needs to be done will be done.

"People say, 'Why should I have faith?' It is silly to think this way. Even to cross the street we need faith. If you say to yourself, 'I cannot cross this street,' you will not be able to do it. But experience has shown you that you can cross the street. Experience has shown you that you can go from one room into another to pick up an object, for instance. But just convince yourself that you are not able to do it and see what will happen."

He looked out of the window. A sparrow, pursued by another, flew into the room chirping noisily. They saw us seated there and flew out again, to continue their quarrel on the tree opposite. He followed them with his eyes and then said:

"Now I will tell you the secret of creation. Sex is the same in men and women; the ultimate moment of ecstasy in sexual relationship is the same in both. It may vary in intensity according to temperament and mood, but it is the same stuff. It is *ananda* [bliss], the only moment of real ananda on the physical plane in existence. It is the sweetest thing on earth; nothing is sweeter than that. And it is given to man for the sake of procreation."

I understood that the sacred gift which manifests in human beings as the bliss experienced in sexual union is but a reflection of the bliss experienced at the level of Atman. Indeed, the physical state stands no comparison to that which is the very essence of the divine, creative dynamism – the exalting and shattering power that quickens, nurtures and dissolves – the divine *will-to-be* which can only be described in terms of *fire*, and which in every creature expresses itself as the desire for existence. Hence, that bliss and the life-giving or procreative energy are one. This fire descends and is mirrored in one way or another throughout all the planes of manifestation, inter-linking them all through that one *will*, which is bliss because it is at the very core of every creature, every thing, every atom. It is the *alpha* and *omega*, the Heart of Hearts. In surrendering ourselves to that Heart, we partake of, indeed we *become*, that divine bliss. The great renunciation signifies, in human terms, the great atonement – and therefore the conscious receiving and the conscious radiating of the divine *grace* at the Heart of Hearts.

"When the period of renunciation is passed, no words can describe what can be given, no imagination. Now you are one-sided and you pick up from the atmosphere all thoughts which are on the same current, the same line as yours. They are sorted out and the ones which are your own, you are made to renounce them.

"That is why you are to return to England. There you will come into contact with people who knew you before and, if they see you have everything but are indifferent about everything, they will wonder and they will respect you and follow you. When you have renounced everything, what cannot be given?

"When complete control of the mind has been achieved, you will know which thoughts are your own and which you pick up from the atmosphere around you. And you can keep the ones you want to keep and throw out those you don't want. Then one becomes master of the mind and not the helpless plaything of it, as most human beings are."

When it was dark, Guruji got up and began to walk up and down the garden in front of the house, walking with elastic step, swiftly, as if obeying an inner rhythm ... Slender, tall, a white figure in the moonlight, crossing from patches of light into shade and back again, up and down ... Unreal he looked, so ancient, a priest of days gone by, a mysterious, arcane being older than my remotest dreams ...

⟨ 28 ⟩

16 *April*

We have been to Bhogoun to visit the grave of his Revered Guru Maharaj.

Of Bhogoun I remember practically nothing. There was a long and tedious train journey. Somebody paid for my ticket. A stranger joined our party in the carriage and spoke to Guruji in an impertinent, almost derisive way. He argued endlessly. Bhai Sahib answered him gently, with great patience. Nobody else spoke. I sat there boiling with indignation.

At last, unable to bear it any longer, I asked the young man if, being an Indian, he had not learned from his parents how to respect his elders. He stared at me in amazement, but Bhai Sahib attacked me viciously, asking me how, being only a woman, I could speak to a man in this way. He practically shouted at me and I was taken aback and hurt.

The young man was also amazed at Guruji's outburst, perhaps feeling somewhat guilty because he had been the cause of my ill-treatment, or perhaps realising that he had lacked respect for the old man. He kept quiet from then on

161

and got out after a few more stations. All I know is that it was hot ... oh, so hot.

We stayed first at his aunt's house and then with a Muslim doctor who sang his prayers most beautifully – at 4 in the morning – his magnificent baritone voice ringing far and wide across the village.

I remember our procession to the group of trees across cultivated fields where the grave was to be found. And that is all! No memory of anything else. I think we stayed three days.

20 April

My birthday today; 56. An old lady! But the body feels young and healthy, full of energy. And the heart is full of this terrible thing which people call 'love' ... but I would call it 'longing'.

Beginning to pack up my things.

Only one week left ... and he will be a memory.

23 April

Told him that it had been my birthday on Saturday ... and that it had been the loneliest birthday of my life.

'And you are throwing me out ... not only out of your house and town but out of India altogether. What a wonderful birthday present for an old lady!'

"A woman is never old; sexually she is ever young. A man is supposed to become old."

'But I am not after sex.'

"No. Never mind if one is not after sex. What I say has nothing to do with it. If woman becomes old, the whole creation would disintegrate. The law is that the physical body becomes weaker."

'Do you mean that prakriti is eternal, ever young?'

He nodded.

"The more sex-power the human being has, the easier he will reach God or Truth. Impotent people, men or women, cannot have *brahma vidya* [absolute, supreme wisdom]. Great sex-power is a great help in spiritual life. The emanation of brahma vidya comes down into manifestation as *viriya shakti*, the Creative Energy of God.

"On the lowest plane of manifestation, it appears as seminal fluid in men; in women it is preserved in the chakras. That is why the yogic training on the etheric level is different for men and women. For men I sometimes give many practices; for woman it is only necessary to get rid of her greater attachment to maya, because she is by nature nearer to matter. In her, the ties to material things like children, possessions, security, are very strong, stronger than in men."

'You said that one day even love has to be renounced. It is going to be a sad day, because love is the only thing I have left.'

"Love will always remain. One day the self will go; then only Love will remain. You will not then say 'I love'. Where will the 'I' be?"

'But how could we live without the centre, the 'I'? There would be no consciousness, for instance.'

"Yes. One lives in the self. In my case I can go out of the body at any time. When in the body, the self is present; one suffers, feels like everybody else."

'But your self is not the same as in others.'

"The Real Self belongs to the Soul. Once one is established in it, the life on the physical plane becomes of small, relative importance."

26 April

'May I ask you a question?'

"Yes," he said, smiling encouragingly.

'You said yesterday, "Let it be!" when I mentioned that London has a bad atmosphere. Does it mean that one gets protection when one is sent out into the world?'

"Why should London be worse that any other place? People say this town is a bad place. The world is the world; good and bad are everywhere. One should not dwell on it ... and it will have no effect. A beautiful flower has a thorn. People pluck the flower; they don't touch the thorn. I walk in the street; so do many other people. I am not concerned with the street, nor with the crowd which passes by."

'Does that mean that Sufis should notice good things around them?'

"With Sufis it is different. They are absorbed somewhere all the time. They don't notice good or bad. We were in Bhogoun. No fans were there. We all slept on the floor. Were we affected by it? Certainly not. We should be able to sleep in the street when there is no other possibility. Why not? The street is also part of Him, made by Him. Sufis don't say, 'I do this or that.' *They do it.* If you think that you did a great thing, then it goes; it has no value. Why not think you did it because it was your duty? Duty has a permanent value. Never think that you did something great, something special. Think you did your duty."

'You told me that your Revered Guru was short-tempered with you and spoke to you only briefly, only to give you orders?'

"Yes; so it was for years. It is true."

'Did you not suffer very much? You must have!'

"Why should I?" he asked, narrowing his eyes.

'You must have suffered greatly.'

"Why should I?" he repeated, looking straight at me. And then he said, slowly, "I was after him; not after suffering. I wanted to please him. Why should I have suffered?"

What an answer, I thought ...

Later he said, "To be intellectual, to have much knowledge, is a hindrance. For people who are not, it is easier. The ones with knowledge know all the rules – what is written in the scriptures. But they are not able to lose them-

163

selves. They may get up at four in the morning, go to the Ganges, do this exercise, that abhyasa. They don't understand that it is only an external thing; not at all important . . .

"For instance, if I am a vegetarian and he is not (pointing at a man sitting nearby), why should I tell him to be a vegetarian, or to do this or that, and hurt his feelings? The time will come when he himself will know what to do. Why should I bother?

"Intellectuals split themselves into so many exterior things; but the only essential is to be able to lose oneself. To be absorbed somewhere . . ."

27 *April*

"The parents of everybody are great; and I mean absolutely everybody. The parents keep the Gate of Heaven open for you. Respect is due to them. Otherwise, when you are dead, and come face to face with the Absolute Truth, you may be asked, 'Did you not even respect your parents?' Then it can become really difficult."

'How will I live without seeing you?' I said, with sinking heart.

"One answer only: keep me in the Heart of Hearts."

He had a stony, sphinx-like expression.

"Only two days," he said slowly, "and the physical nearness will be no more. The physical nearness . . ."

'Your physical body will change much; you will not be the same,' I said, thinking of his illness.

"I change every moment; every second I am not the same. Time passes and nobody can assess time. It passes for ever . . . One cannot bring it back.

"Remember: we discourage everything which has nothing to do with the Absolute Truth. Anything. *Only this* has to be the goal."

⤞ 29 ⤝

29 *April*

He sent Satendra and Sitla Prasad with a handcart to move my furniture to his house.

I got annoyed because they were so clumsy and banged the wardrobe against the stone wall so that the varnish was scratched. I lost my temper with them; they were worse than two little boys.

At last the wardrobe was gone and the tachat. I remained behind to collect a few things which could be useful to his household.

When I entered the gate, I saw him sitting outside alone. He looked dark, his eyes flashing angrily. Fear sprang up from somewhere deep . . .

I saluted and was about to enter the courtyard to deposit the few belongings when he stopped me.

"How did you dare to speak in such a way to my son! . . . He is a man and you are only a woman! And Mrs Ghose's daughters laughed because you lost your temper with him!"

'But they both handled the wardrobe in such a clumsy way, banging it against the wall. If you will examine it, you will see that it is badly scratched. If you too had been present, you would have lost your patience!'

"What do I care about the wardrobe? You idiot old woman! I am glad that you are going at last! You have no respect towards my children. You are good for nothing, old and stupid!"

I was so taken aback at this unexpected attack that I sat down, stunned. I don't even remember whether I cried or not. Paralysed, I saw Satendra standing in the doorway regarding the scene with evident satisfaction.

"Go!" Bhai Sahib shouted. "I don't want to see your face again! Go away!"

I went and, when in the street, looked back. He was still sitting in the same place, bent double as though weighed down with a heavy burden.

The last impression of him in my mind . . .

Evening train to Delhi . . . plane to Madras . . . then Bombay . . . then, high over the Arabian desert, the sacred land, the birthplace of Sufism. How I cried! . . . and so to London.

I took a small room, five feet by ten, £2.00 per week. A bed, a stool, a wash basin and a small wardrobe. Outside the traffic roared up and down Holland Park Avenue; and his words came to my mind, "You must be able to sleep in the street. Why not? Is the street not also His?"

After a while, I wrote to him regularly, two or three times a week. After three months I received a letter, not from him, saying that he had been very ill for two months.

I kept writing for two and a half years. I never had a direct answer; just a few lines . . . very rarely; about unimportant matters.

And then he told me to return in December 1965 . . .

PART II

⚔ 30 ⚔

December 1965

I returned on December 15th, 1965.

Babu and Satendra with their new wives met us at the airport. My heart longed to be at Guruji's place.

He came to meet me and I fell at his feet. I was so moved that I nearly fainted . . .

I was given accommodation in the home of one of his disciples, Mr Sharma, an important man in the town. I had a lovely room on the top floor. I began at once to go to him each day . . . to be with him, and hear his words.

1 *January* 1966

When we came to him yesterday afternoon, H. and I, Bhai Sahib was writing something on small pieces of paper.

"The four children of this man are suffering from smallpox. I am giving them *yantras* [magical formulae written or drawn on paper]. It is absolutely sure; death cannot come near, death goes away. The yantra is dipped in wax and put into a cotton cloth so that it cannot get wet while bathing, and then tied on: with children round the neck, for a woman under the left armpit, for a man under the right. Never, even for a moment, should the yantra be removed or the person will die. So, if the person is intended to die, somebody will remove the yantra. You see two orders are running parallel . . .

"Never, never change anything for this sort of thing, not even a *nayapaise* [small Indian coin]."

2 *January*

"If you are addicted to music there is no progress. Why? If you cannot go into dhyana or samadhi without music, it means that you are addicted; cannot do without it. It became an obstacle. In our Yoga System nothing is needed. My Revered Father was of the Chishtia Dynasty, but even then, because His Guru was not of this Dynasty, he gave it up."

3 January

'Since I have been here, my heart is singing, singing before you; it goes on all the time ceaselessly. Is this singing the constant remembrance of God?'

"It is," he nodded. "But later the remembrance will be there all the time and one will not notice it. And this state can last for many years."

4 January

'What is the difference between a Saint and a Sage?'

"There is a great difference between a Saint and a Sage. A Saint, a wali, is taken up to a certain stage – is made like his Master. Then he progresses automatically; he goes with his Master. He does not come back. A Saint is pure love. They do not give laws like the Prophets. They do not rule. They obey and are content with the Will of God. They are the instruments of God. If a Saint commits a mistake, God will always give the opportunity to correct it, because he is completely surrendered. He has no will except the Will of God. But the Sage, if he commits a mistake, he has to come back . . ."

'Merging into the Master,' I said. '*Fana fi Sheikh* [merging into the Teacher]; then *Fana fi Rasul* [merging into Mohammed, not as a man but as a primal essence]; and finally *Fana fi Allah* [merging in God]?' He nodded.

'And the first stage is the most difficult of all. Most difficult.' He nodded again, thoughtfully.

6 January

"Love is quenching the thirst on the physical plane; this is not love. The human being is Love and Love loves the human being. To realize Love is to realize God. If we sit before an open fire it warms us; there is no effort on our part. Those who have realized God are like this fire. Keep in their company. God realizes Himself in the Heart of Hearts of the human being. When we realize, Love disappears. We cannot give shape or name to Love. The deeper we go the more it disappears. It radiates from every part of the body and the last transfer which takes place from the Master to the disciple is from heart to heart. Where the trouble comes from, help is there also. People forget it; that's why they are in trouble.

"I know nothing. I flow where I am directed. The river does not know if it is flowing. If we know something we have to throw it away, to throw it back. We have to forget it because it is worthless.

"Only He knows everything. Remember: WE KNOW NOTHING. If people speak highly of you, beware of pride. Pray. If people do speak highly of you, it is only He who speaks highly of Himself. It is He who in their shape does it. If you are abused it is the same. He is abusing Himself. We should not abuse people; we should bear it.

"The relationship between the Teacher and his disciple can be compared only to the relationship of a father to his children. Only a father wants his son to be more than himself. The Teacher knows no envy; there is no jealousy in him. He is glad when the disciple is on a higher stage than himself. It is a chain of love, the love to the Master.

"Nobody is a beginner. Or we are all beginners. I am a beginner from my stage; you are a beginner from your stage. Swimming in the Infinite Ocean, who is nearer the shore?

"One day I will tell you how to help people, and how they are helped, how they receive it. There is a way to know the mind of an audience by one glance. A higher stage is if you want to help and know all about a friend far away in America, for instance. But the highest stage is when you can transfer the powers to another human being. Only Great People can do that . . ."

10 *January*

I was thinking today of the difference between this time and the last time, nearly three years ago. Then I was heart-broken that I had to go and did not know whether I would see Bhai Sahib again. I wanted spiritual life so badly. And now? It seems to me that I want nothing. Nothing at all . . . What is spiritual life? Perhaps it is a delusion. To desire something is a delusion. The only thing that seems to remain now is my love for God, which is Truth.

I sat with him in peace desiring nothing. And all around me were the plains and the palm trees, with the vultures settling in them for the night. The sun was setting in a glory of gold – that serene, infinitely serene and majestic sunset of the Indian plains.

He closed his eyes. Such a stream of love flowed strongly from him towards my heart . . .

12 *January*

'What is the difference between a bad Teacher and a good Teacher?'

"A bad Teacher will always behave as his followers expect him to behave. If he is after personal prestige, or even money or honours, he will always be kind, benevolent, compassionate, uttering at all times wise, profound sentences; that is the conventional idea. But a good Teacher obeys a law of which the world knows nothing. As it is the nature of the fire to burn or consume, or the wind to blow, so it is with the Sat Guru; he just is.

"He may do things which people don't understand, or may even condemn. Love does not conform to conventional ideas; Love can appear in the shape of great cruelty, great injustice, even calamity. In this respect the Sat Guru is similar to God. He cannot be judged or measured . . ."

"Knowledge comes through the heart. From the heart to the mind. Knowledge is always good.

"If you come to know something about someone – either the future, or the

169

past, or some other things – give help where it is needed and then forget; throw it behind you. And do not disclose it; otherwise it will be taken from you and the self will never go. And if the self remains there will be no spiritual life. But, by throwing away, you are not the doer. Samskaras do not remain. Throw away everything.

"I really know nothing; but I will say or do the right thing for every occasion."

That is why he has been repeating ever since I came back that forgetfulness is the great qualification. Not in the sense of forgetting what one needs to know in the moment, but in the sense of forgetting *what ought to be forgotten*.

In the evening, he sat there as serene as eternity. The cranes were returning from the Ganges, as I have seen them so often in past years. A large, bluish star hung in the west on the pale, yellow horizon. It became dark quickly and I watched his face in the fading light. My heart was singing to him.

13 *January*

He had a severe vomiting condition in the night. It was like death; he could not catch his breath for several minutes. Hardly saw him all day.

16 *January*

"You might say, 'What about those millions of people who will never find a guru?' But one could ask, 'Do they want a guru?'

"The soul of man comes into manifestation to have certain experiences. We get so deluded by them; we are covered by so many sheaths of all kinds of delusion. If they are satisfied with them they will never want a guru. But if you have 'lit the lamp' as it is said in the scriptures, if you want a Teacher, as soon as you are ready he will be there for you. I told you before, it is the Law and it works on all the levels right through from the lowest to the highest. When we call out, the response will be.

"The words of the *Upanishads* hold good always, 'If you want the Truth as badly as a drowning man wants air, you will realize it in a moment.'

"Pray for forgiveness if you have injured the feelings of anybody and for the power to avoid doing it in the future. This is called in Persian *toba* and means repentance – a promise not to do it again, a vow, a resolution. If you don't pray like this for the power, if you don't do the toba, you will fall back again and repeat the sins."

20 *January*

"There is a great difference between a devotee and a disciple. A disciple is following the Teacher in order to acquire knowledge. The duality always remains. There are always two of them – Master and disciple. Among the disciples, a few are devotees. Among these, there are even fewer who stick and are faithful. Even less follow the Line. And perhaps there can only be one found to continue the System.

"Between the Master and the devotee the duality disappears. Devotees have to sacrifice themselves. Completely. When there is duality there can be no realization.

"To surrender all possessions is relatively easy but to surrender the mind is very difficult. It means one has no mind of one's own. One is like a dead body in the hands of the Master. How is the dead body? It cannot protest.

"A disciple can only sacrifice himself to a certain degree. If you want something, the duality will always remain. A devotee wants nothing; he is pure Love ..."

30 *January*

He has spoken to me over the days about tremendously important things. And I cannot write them down. My mind is nowhere . . . I cannot remember ...

1 *February*

He is sitting in a deep state ... and likewise everybody around is in deep dhyana. I alone am wide awake, writing, looking up from time to time. He has an unearthly look about him.

Two chipmunks are chasing each other round the trunk of the mango tree. Two magnificent pale-grey oxen, huge, and with large humps, are passing in the street, trailing behind them an oxcart fitted with lorry tyres. A tiny old man is excitedly shouting at them, swinging a thin rod against their massive impassivity ...

This morning he said, "We were always taught, 'Think before you speak.' This is for others. I never think beforehand. I say the first thing which comes into my head. The first thought is from God."

4 *February*

What a difference there is in being able to sit alone in his garden with the feeling of luxurious peace in my heart. This morning he came out and saw me sitting.

"One cannot have faith until the time is ripe; nobody can have faith. Complete surrender is absolute faith. He is Absolute. I was given *adhikara*, permission to teach, when I was twenty-seven. But I was nothing. Until his death, until the last moment of his death, he kept testing me. He said, 'Now you have caught the thread; now you can give to anybody you like.' The power of Transference was given."

'What is full adhikara?'

171

"Complete or full adhikara is to be made a Deputy. A permission to teach everything according to need.

"You may think that I know everything, but really I know nothing."

I said that he seems to be able to tune in at will to the Universal Mind and he will know what he needs to know.

"Yes it is so," he said. "I know all I want to know; but to be master of it, more is needed."

8 February

I mentioned that Babu Ram told me a story which seems quite pointless to me. The story of a guru of Raipur who had beaten a young disciple to death; and then resurrected him to be a wali.

"I was present then, when it happened, and my Revered Guru and others were there too. The boy was the son of a disciple and the whole family were disciples of his; father, mother, uncles, all of them. They were all sitting there and also the Master, the Teacher of the boy. The boy had a natural smiling face; he seemed always to smile like my Revered Father who also had this expression. The Master looked at the boy and said, 'Why are you smiling?' And the boy kept smiling.

"So, with his stick in his hand, the Master began to beat the boy till the stick was broken. The boy kept the smile on his face. When the stick broke, the Master grabbed the heavy piece of wood with which wrestlers practise; and he continued to beat and beat till the head entered the shoulders and the shoulders entered the body. One could not recognise who it was; nothing was there; just a mass of broken bones and flesh and blood everywhere.

"Then he stopped and said to the relatives of the boy, 'What is this? Am I not at liberty to do as I like?'

" 'Yes,' they said, 'we belong to you for life or death; you can do with us as you like.'

" 'Yes,' he said, 'I can do what I like,' and went inside. Some say he was sitting chewing betel nut.

"Then he came out. 'What is this?' he asked. 'Who is lying there?'

"Pointing to the mass of flesh which had been a human being, the guru ordered with commanding voice, 'Get up!'

"And the boy got up and was whole and not a scar was seen on him. And he was told by his Teacher that from now on he would be a wali. He was a wali all his life."

I said that it seemed pointless to kill a man to make him a Saint.

"Oh no," he said with vivacity. "You see, to make a wali, it takes thirty or forty years. The physical body, the heart, the mind are subjected to great suffering to clear out all the evils which are in the human being. And here the work was done in half an hour. How many evils were cleared away completely through such terrible suffering! The boy loved him so much, was always sitting and looking at him; never spoke to him. So he was killed. Of course, he was ready to be a wali. Things are done in different ways according to the time and the people of the time.

"But with ordinary people, after such a violent death or explosion or burning alive, there is no peace for a while after such a death. I saw people burned to death; it cannot be imagined what terrible suffering it was. How can there be peace after that?"

'And what about Great People like Christ or Mansur. Surely they had peace?'

"One should not compare Great People; for they have died before the physical death. Such people are born to die; not once, but many times. That is why they are beyond comparison. You should not ask such questions."

He concluded and fell silent, narrowing his eyes, looking far into the distance.

11 *February*

On the front of Mrs. Sharma's bungalow there are two creepers coming high up to the flat, roof terraces. One has orange, large, tubular flowers, and the other rich scarlet. Poinsettia is flowering at the bottom of the gardens and the beds are full of roses . . . A large, scarlet creeper is tightly hugging one of the columns of the veranda near the table where we take our meals. It is such a lovely thing, covered with bunches of rich scarlet and dark green, glossy leaves.

Early in the morning, the sky in the east was robed in the colours of the dawn, grey stripes of clouds cutting across it. Far on the horizon, the dome-shaped temple stood like a sentinel watching; watching over the awakening town. I sniffed the wind; gorgeous smell of India's endless distances. Sky everywhere and the daily drama of sunrises and sunsets . . .

"In dhyana the mind is thrown somewhere. Where does it go? The smaller is supposed to be absorbed in the Greater. And what is this Greater? One should not say God, not even Almighty. It is Absolute Truth. Truth as such is Absolute and it is everywhere. The mind itself forms part of this Absolute Truth. Imagine an earthen jug; air is contained in it. When the jug is broken the air will merge again into the atmosphere. If the jug is mended, some air again will be imprisoned in it. But will the surrounding atmosphere be affected? Surely not. You have seen how it is done.

"People ask me, 'Have you realized God? Have you realized the Self?' I have not realized the Self; I have not realized God, I answer."

'Bhai Sahib,' I laughed, 'that is a lie.'

"Why a lie? If I am nowhere, how can I realize something? To realize something there must be somebody to realize; if I am nothing, if I am nowhere, how can I have realized something?"

I was amused at the cleverness of the answer and how philosophically correct it was.

"I often say to my family, 'You are nowhere.' It is a nice thing to say; it is helping people. My Father used to tell me the same; 'You know nothing; you are nowhere.' "

Walking home, I reflected how subtle the training is; a passing remark; a sentence here and there; sometimes said in a casual way and easily forgotten ...

On the physical plane, or the worldly platform as Guruji likes to put it, the Sufi training is chiefly a test of endurance. How much can one endure for the sake of Love? How much and for how long can one tolerate it?

14 *February*

Yesterday morning when I came, he was already outside doing his mala.

When he is in his official Sufi dress, all in white *and* doing his mala, it means he will give a sitting to someone. In other words, he is on 'official duty'.

What a beautiful sight it is to see a Saint praying. As his slender, strong fingers passed one bead after another, I began to repeat *La-il-llillah* mentally.

He looked up. "I didn't give you any practice to do. If I would teach you *La-il-llillah* correctly, the world would be yours. It is powerful when it is given by a living soul. Power can be abused; what then? With ladies we send vibrations of love, that is all. But it does not mean that ladies never need any practice; it is according to the necessity of each human being."

It was raining last night and this morning it is dark and stormy. The sun rose among threatening grey clouds in blood-red and crimson. My room was filled with red light. It was quite uncanny. I will go there now; sitting in the draughty doorway, it will be cold and uncomfortable.

As soon as I walked through the garden gate, the brother told me that he was not well. Shortly after I had left last night he had had a heart attack, or a weakness; as usual nobody knew for sure what it was. Virendra asked us inside. The sound of singing was coming from the room. Bhai Sahib lay on the tachat. At his feet, on the floor, in kneeling asana was the young man who sang so beautifully at the Bandhara. He was singing now and his voice was so tender, so devoted, that it brought tears to my eyes. I looked at Guruji. A strange face. Pale. With large nostrils as if hungry for air ... The same face as when he was so ill a few years ago. His eyes, veiled with samadhi, were full of tears.

Ragunath Prasad came and took his pulse. Later I was told that he hardly had any pulse. He opened his eyes for a moment and looked straight at me.

15 *February*

It was a heart attack. He is very weak; we can lose him at any moment, the doctor said. I don't believe it; a Saint of his calibre KNOWS when he will go and will arrange his work accordingly ... Perhaps it is the Will of God that my training should not be finished. Who knows? And now I have this fear in my bones ...

In the night, such was the agony that I howled like a wounded dog to the moon . . .

17 *February*

I went out on the terrace this morning at dawn. The sky was an ominous dark red in the east, like the underground fire of a volcano beyond the horizon, its deep purple full of stars. A young crescent moon was shining unusually brightly against the deep red, and not far from it, an outsize star shone like a diamond. Venus, planet of Love? Fresh wind was blowing from the west. Soon this same wind from the deserts of Pakistan will become the Loo. Blissfully I sniffed the air. Oh, the glorious smell of the Indian plains in the mornings at dawn. Exhilarating freshness in the air; the smell of coal fires; and the bitter, pungent smell of burning cow-dung cakes which they use for fuel.

Last night he came out looking tired and frail.

"My Father kept having heart attacks for eleven years; but before the last one he said to me, 'If I have this trouble again, I die.' But I did not believe it. I thought, he is such a Great Man he will not go yet."

'I will die if you go; I cannot imagine life without you. I will lose the will to live.'

"Then pray that I should stay. Go on praying and do the practice of *La-il-llillah* when you sit here alone in the garden, and when walking, so that nobody should notice what you are doing."

Later I said to him, 'Sometimes, when I have to ask you something, I feel a barrier within me, and know I should not ask.'

"The self is the barrier; the self who wants. If you have no self, if the self is diminished, you can ask.'

I will not ask any more questions. Surrender is the acceptance of everything *without exception*. I ACCEPT. I will go to the end of the bitter road. Will sit, endlessly sit, and ask nothing any more. And now, because I accept it voluntarily, the mind will not give me trouble and restlessness any more. Not from this side anyway. Acceptance of 'everything' means also acceptance of deliberate falsehood and cruelty, to which he still treats me freely.

And so, this morning I was alone with him and asked nothing. He looked friendly, as if to encourage me to speak. But I kept quiet.

Speaking of his Father he said:

"My Uncle was the rising sun; my Father was the midday sun; he was shining, just as radiant as the midday sun. Who will be the setting sun? God only knows."

'Do you mean that then it will be the end of the System?' I asked, thinking that by the setting sun he meant himself.

"Oh, no!" he laughed. "How can that be? Never! If there is no sun there is the moon!"

I went all cold. Such a clear hint ... By the expression of my face he must have gathered that I understood the meaning. He gave me a quick glance and then looked out of the window.

"Sun and moon eclipse; stars never eclipse."

'How is this to be understood?'

"Saints undergo obscurations," he amplified. "They undergo great suffering; lose the respect of people."

Then he went in.

⟨ 31 ⟩

Mid-March

'For the last eleven days I have managed to control my mind a little. I see that it can be done.'

A flicker of a smile, like a ray of sudden sunshine, passed over his tired face. "Gooood," he said cheerfully, drawing out the 'oo'.

'But I find that I encounter two major difficulties; the first is memory.'

"How is that?" he enquired.

"By sitting in your garden, many situations crop up which remind me of past sufferings. Terrible things have been done and they come up and stand before me like ghosts. I was afraid that it might happen, and I wrote to you about it from London. It happened as I feared. And then the resentment comes. Now to get rid of the resentment I have to remember that it was, and it is, the Will of God. The other obstacle is that I live in surroundings of suspicion. How to know which doubts are mine and which are reflected from somebody else?'

A shadow of compassion showed in his eyes; he picked up his mala. "Thoughts come and go," he said softly.

He came out and I did not notice until he passed me by going to his chair. I got up and saluted him hurriedly. 'Strange that for a few times I did not notice you lately.'

He had the ghost of a smile for an answer. The merging into the Master is obviously accomplished by degrees and in silence. The whole morning he was there praying and then in samadhi. He looked at my forehead two or three times when opening his eyes. All was peace. Even the garden was still; even the traffic and the busy household. For the first time I noticed that the nearness to the Master is of the *same quality* as the nearness to God; only God, or should I say Truth, is more distant.

176

He came out looking better. For a long time he was talking Hindi but from time to time gave a friendly nod in my direction. He must have noticed that I was somewhat depressed, thinking of the heat in the months ahead. It was hot already.

"How are you?" he said, after glancing at me in a kindly way.

I said that I was well and was glad that he was better.

"Better, yes. Hard times are ahead. Please don't sit always outside; come inside at any time. You can sit in the room. Go inside, don't even ask: nobody is here to check you. I myself sometimes don't come into this room for hours."

'Thank you,' I said. And then with a smile I added, 'This is a great change; you know what I mean,' alluding to the past when I could never go inside, heat or no heat . . . His eyes smilingly said, yes, I know, and he nodded.

"Last night when you had left, Bhalla and others were speaking so highly of you. They were saying, 'She is coming every day, sitting here for many hours. And she does not know why and for what she is coming, but she sits. But we know that we come here to talk only; we don't want to sacrifice; we don't make any efforts . . .' And, when people speak like this, I feel ashamed," he continued.

'But why should you feel ashamed?'

"Had I been a greater man, I would have taken you," – and he made a gesture to indicate infinite horizons. "God knows where I could have taken you, but I cannot do it."

'Good heavens! You cannot do it because of my limitations. I am still full of self.'

All the time he was speaking he was looking me straight in the eyes. It flashed through my mind that the talk was a test; he wants to see if I am resentful that he is not taking me higher.

'Bhai Sahib, when will the self go?'

"When the smaller merges into the Greater. But something will always remain. I told you this before. Even in Great People something *always* remains; so that people will say, 'Look here; how many faults are there!' While we are in the physical bodies something *must remain*. If we are absolutely perfect, we cannot remain in this world. And never mind what people will say; never mind at all what is said about one; let us do our duty, live according to our lights, and let the rest take care of itself."

When I was resting after lunch the wind already smelt of the hot breath of the Indian plains. It is the forerunner of the Loo. Hot, unbearably hot, is the breath of the plains. I saw them once from an aircraft, stretching for thousands of miles, ochre-coloured and endless; tiny villages and a few trees scattered and lost amongst this arid vastness. What a life of privation it must be. How can they live? The bougainvillea on the terrace is in glory. Crimson and scarlet. I looked at it for a long time, feeling the scorching wind on my face. I know that in the future it will always mean India to me; the heat of the plains, the smells; all the memories will come crowding back with unbearable yearning and longing.

17 March

Last night he exchanged a few friendly words with me. And then I sat in the darkening garden, listening to the Hindi conversation and looking at the sudden flashes of his eyes in the light of the street lamp. The feeling of nearness was perfect. Lately, when I dream of him, we are sitting alone, either near each other, or he is telling me something. I wonder, could it mean that the merging has begun? Last night I was very lonely. There is a kind of ... foreboding. I am not sure ...

This morning he was squatting near the water pipe and the Sikh was cleaning a cycle. I just stood there quietly.

When the Sikh departed, taking the cycle with him, he got up and said, "I gave the cycle to him. When the human being is in trouble, who will help? Even animals help each other. Shall we be less than animals?"

He began to walk up and down, talking about plants and irrigation; simple everyday things. There was oneness and I never experienced it to such an extent as today. The garden had been sprinkled. A lovely smell of moist earth was in the air. People came and went. The chairs were put out. The usual crowd arrived. The talk began in Hindi ... Odd sentences in English, for my benefit, floated over to me on the hot night air.

"Luminaries set, but when the sun has set, the moon shines like the sun ...

"One should always answer letters of doubts. Always try to disperse doubts in human beings. When the doubt goes, there is progress ...

"Until the time has arrived, nobody accepts anything. But when the time comes, only a little hint is needed and the human being accepts ...

"Who has renounced, God will provide for his needs."

Early April

He was so kind when I was ill with renal colic at the end of March, even visiting me as I lay in bed. But then it was the other face. My mind gave me trouble. He kept attacking me. I was contradicting him, telling him that there is no greatness in being so harsh and I cannot speak to him; the usual story of rebellion. And so he told me that he is not my guru, took up his towel, went out and closed the door.

I left. And at home I cried. What a difficult path! Treated with harshness; cannot speak to him when I want; and he is not my guru. Then I remembered a quotation from some Buddhist scripture:

'I have no home, I have no father, I have no mother, I have no guru, I am not a disciple; all is taken away from me ...'

Nothing will remain at the end ... It is Easter. I had forgotten it ... And, in the night under the stars, calling to Him in loneliness and longing. The neem tree nearby was so fragrant. Strong, sweet smell, coming gently on the whiffs of breeze.

I said to him, 'Our relationship to God is something entirely different from what we usually imagine it to be. We think that the relationship of God and Man is a duality. But it is not so. I have found that our relationship to God is something quite different. It is a merging, without words, without thought even; into 'something'. Something so tremendous, so endless, merging in Infinite Love, physical body and all, disappearing in it. And the physical body is under suffering; it is taut like a string in this process of annihilation. This is our experience of God and it cannot be otherwise.'

"What you have said is absolutely correct," he nodded gravely.

Mid-April
He is not well. He ignores me completely. Before the others came I asked him how he was feeling; he seemed breathless and gloomy. He said he was not well.

'No wonder you can never be well. You talk too much. Every doctor will tell you that a heart patient must not speak much and you talk for hours. And for what? And to whom? To people who are here only for discussion.' He did not answer but turned away in disgust.

Sweet are the nights of the waning moon; full of strong fragrance. I am calling on Him day and night ...

"Between you and what you are doing, your practice, there is a veil, a barrier, caused by the flood of ideas which bring confusion into your mind. The flood comes; the flood will go ... But you cannot wait ... To turn against the Guide is to cut off the link ... The wiring is there; the bulbs are there; but there is no current.

"When you eat a sweet for instance, what happens? When you swallow it, the taste is gone but the memory remains. So it is with the desires of the mind and of the body. Even if the desire is not here any more, the memory is still there and the mind can give trouble. Every human being is full of desires of the mind and body. The training I am giving you is of such a kind that in this life you will be away completely from your body and mind ..."

This arose from my telling him how troublesome it is for others when people don't wash. They don't wash their dhotis, or their bodies; they smell. Such a man had just left.

"Yes, this is true. It is very troublesome. But there are people who are dressed nicely and are clean; but they are full of inner dirt. Greed, vanity, sex and other things too ... They come and sit here and what shall I say who am the sweeper of everybody?"

I felt small.

"Yes," he repeated kindly, "you have only that – the physical smells – and I know it is very disagreeable. I cannot stand cigarette smoke, or the smell of drink, but if I hate them will they give it up? No, never. I will not hate anybody because, if I hate him, how can I help him to better himself?"

"If people come for help, help should be given. But I am not after anyone. If one is after Absolute Truth one cannot be after people. They should come and merge themselves. Divine Providence will guide them to me ... Anger, the real anger, cuts us away from Reality, sometimes for months. For years I did not get really angry. But sometimes I make myself angry and look at myself if I am after a thing or not ... It is beyond the power of the human being to control anger. But, after the anger, look at it, from where it came, why and how it came, and what it did to you. You might learn many things. When the mind is merged nothing can come in. Nothing can disturb it ..."

'Even when the disturbance comes, it is less than before.'

"Yes, it is quite true. But if this lesser disturbance comes after a long time, it has great power and would disturb much. Don't let it come in at all. Prayer, meditation and the remembrance of the Name are the only things worthwhile doing in this world, because you will not stay here forever. In the night, pray. Pray much.

"Many things you will understand only when I have gone. I myself understood so many things only when my Revered Guru Maharaj was not alive any more."

'When you are not alive any more, I would like to go too . . . I cannot remain here, it would be unbearable.'

"Somebody has to remain; the System must go on. The training I give you is to continue my work. *Do not care about anything ever; the grace of God is in every shape around.*"

Late April

Mrs Sharma told me she has a big wedding on 29th and I must try and find other accommodation as she will need my room and the terraces upstairs. I felt very lonely and upset. Sometimes I feel I am not welcome anywhere.

Last night he had another attack. A terrible one apparently. He is very breathless and I am deeply worried.

He was already sitting on the charpoy in the garden, looking frail and very pale, dressed all in white.

'Mr Sharma thinks that if you don't see the heart specialist and don't do something about it, it will carry you away in less than one year,' I said.

He was standing in front of me and suddenly let out a laugh which sounded most cruel.

"He is right!" He turned away to go inside; then stopped for a moment before going into the doorway passage.

"He is quite, quite right!" He emphasized the words, laughed this strange laughter, and disappeared inside. I felt stunned. And cold. Staggered by this mocking statement so brutally thrown at me. I sat down alone. Suddenly it occurred to me that each time he has to test me, or do something important from the point of view of his Line, he is always dressed in white.

Days later, when he was speaking to me again, I told Guruji that I had noticed this fact.

"You are quite right," he said and laughed, clearly pleased and amused at the same time.

It is now nearly 110° in the shade, practically every day; and it will be much more in May. The Loo – the breath of the deserts – is blowing hot and it will push up the temperature even more.

Tomorrow I go to the new accommodation that Nigam Sahib has found for me. So I slept for the last time on the Sharma's terrace and saw from there, for the last time, the pale dawn of the hot season. I watch the sky getting pale pink. Bats are flitting around, black against the sky, sole masters of space. Then the croaking crows, flying with much noise from the trees, and the black Indian swallows darting swiftly with piercing cries. The birds at dawn are lovely. There is a yellow and black one who has the sweetest voice and sings only at dawn. Birds of the morning, goodbye . . .

A night of nightmare; the fan humming its maddening song, all closed in the oven-hot cement box of the room that I now have at Mrs Scott's. One door, one window opening onto a crowded courtyard. The courtyard full of sleeping people. The sheet under me wet with perspiration, like lying in a pool of steaming water.

Again did not sleep. Sweating. Could not even do the *jap* [repeating the name of God] properly, such was the suffering of the body. At Guruji's place; unsung, unnoticed; and I have no money at all.

"You came here to suffer, so suffer," he said yesterday, when we were discussing the money question. And he said it softly, his eyes full of compassion, dark and sorrowful.

In the afternoon I sat alone in the darkened room. Suddenly he came in and lay down on the tachat. I felt a slight surprise; he never came in like this for my sake alone. Then a great activity in the heart chakra began. Something is being done, I thought. He was lying on his back; his eyes were closed. I was listening to the somersaults of my heart, the soft hum of the fan, noises from the street. In the room was great stillness and peace. Then he got up as quickly as he had come and went out. Not once did he glance at me, and not a word was exchanged.

I remembered him saying, "The rose does not say, 'I am fragrant.' The fra-

181

grance reveals itself; it is the very nature. The God-Realized Man will never say, 'I realized God.' All he needs to do is just to be. His very being will reveal what he is . . ."

❦ 32 ❧

Unsung and unnoticed. I must admit that I admire the control he has over his eyes . . . I was sitting opposite him in the room. He was lying on the tachat facing me, scarcely three feet away. Not even once, not even by mistake did he happen to glance at me . . . It is very difficult. How often have I decided not to look at somebody in an audience when lecturing, but found my eyes wandering there, to my annoyance. But it never happens to him. Even if I sit in front of his very nose.

He does not speak to me. Today is Thursday. I have four rupees left and it looks as if I will have to go on living on them if money is not given to me tomorrow.

Then there was a question of my touching the water-jar without taking off my shoes; he remarked on it rather severely, and then began to tell me off when I took some water for drinking. I was puzzled.

'But I did not come with my shoes even near the jar!' I protested. What sort of hygiene is it when the servant who fills the jar keeps his dirty fingers in it, but I am not allowed to touch even the brim of the glass, standing at a distance?

"This is our Aryan culture," he declared, throwing a card on the table – they were playing cards as usual at this time of year. I saw that even his wife seemed to think he was too hard on me; she gave him a disapproving look and made an impatient gesture.

Stretching himself comfortably on the tachat in the garden (which had been watered, for it was dreadfully hot), he began to talk kindly to me again. I came nearer to him, to an empty chair, and told him how lately I have strange feelings when I am with him or even just thinking of him.

"And what precisely are those?" He was drawing the words out ironically. Told him that it becomes more and more difficult to look at him. I have a sinking feeling in the stomach and feel like fainting. It is a kind of not-being, very bewildering . . .

"This is quite good," he said slowly. "It is, rather, very good." And he talked to me for one and a half hours on the importance of time, on wasting time. Who wastes time? Those who don't catch the thread or those who love not!

I tried to explain some states I have been in lately, but the mind was void, I stammered and could not formulate the sentences properly. And he talked about so many things . . .

"Did you get the idea?" he kept asking. At that moment it seemed to me that I got it and said so; but when at home in bed I tried to remember, I could not.

"If a golden chair is put on auction what happens? People will bid for it and whoever offers the highest price will get it."

He was alluding to the training of course.

"When you are before the audience, you are the master. You are the sun; nobody can shine before you . . . Before my own guru I was an idiot." He smiled, looking at me closely.

I complained that I cannot speak and cannot think two coherent thoughts in his presence and he laughed. I know he gave me a few hints but I don't remember them.

10 *May*

Sat alone in the garden till 10 a.m. Bhai Sahib was in the room. I asked permission to come in and sit under the fan. I attempted to express what I felt.

'Bewildering! This is perhaps the best definition of it. The mind does not understand. It seems to be gasping and getting hold of this and that like a drowning man. It is the nearest state to dissolution. After all, you are a human being; why I should feel like this before you is beyond my understanding . . .'

All the while I was speaking in disconnected, hesitant sentences, he kept nodding quietly. And suddenly I knew that I was not afraid because somewhere he is holding me. I should have fear but I have not, because there is faith. Dissolution, non-being, is death for the mind. The mind should be afraid; but strangely enough it is not.

He asked me to close the door and windows and then turned his face to the wall and went into samadhi. Watching him closely I saw that he did not breathe. Then I remembered that he said lately that breathing sometimes disturbs and prevents one from going into a deep state.

"So I simply stop it. It is called *ghat pranayam*, 'inward breathing'. I sometimes don't breathe for hours. The heart goes on beating . . ."

The room was still. A Yogi in deep samadhi; and I mindless but full of great peace.

"Yes?" he said, suddenly sitting up and turning to me! "Please open the door!"

As I went to do so, thinking he probably had heard somebody outside (though I did not hear anything), he said, "Collector Sahib."

But nobody was outside. I went out, looked around; empty chairs stood in a semi-circle in the sun.

'The garden is empty; nobody is here,' I said returning.

He sat cross-legged blinking in the light which came through the open door.

At this moment a car stopped; Collector Sahib got out.

'You knew it before it happened,' I said.

'This is nothing unusual,' grinned Babu, who was having his lunch in the next room.

For some reason which I cannot explain I had the uncanny feeling that the training is taking on a different form; some turning point is ahead.

11 *May*

Testing time ... He does not speak to me. Nor does he ask anything. When I lived at Sharma's place, he often asked me if I was short of money; then he knew perfectly well that I wasn't. Everything which arrived I gave to him or nearly everything, because I needed so little, had a roof over my head and food too at that time. I was suprised that he was asking me. Now I understand why. He knew that soon the time would come when he would not ask; and the contrast will be greater and more painful.

Of course, he must know that I had to borrow fifty rupees from his eldest son when taking the new room, to pay the rent in advance. I live on potato soup. The little bit of rice I had was finished a few days ago, as well as a little flour. Have still some sugar left and a little tea.

On Friday the temperature was 112° and yesterday it must have been more. It was quite unbearable last night when they watered the place where the chairs are put out. I kept wandering up and down avoiding the servant throwing buckets of water. Hot steam rose from the sun-baked soil. Bhai Sahib, squatting on the brick elevation, was organising the watering and gave directions to the gardener.

I left soon. Had a bath. I ate the last three boiled potatoes with all the skin on, and finished the last, small flour pancake.

There was wind on the roof. Prayed to the blinking stars. My heart was full of Him. Soon the wind became stronger and, about 9 p.m., became a dust storm. Clouds of dust whirled in the air. Nobody moved. So I remained where I was and covered my head completely. Could not face the idea of going down into the oven-hot room which would also be full of dust. The whole night the wind blew in strong blasts, shaking the bed, trying to tear off the sheets. I had to tuck them under me tightly so as not to lose them. When I collected my bedding in the pale dawn, the sheets were grey with dust.

12 *May*

I came later this morning, about 8. He came out almost immediately and gave me a sharp look and a faint smile. I knew that he was pleased with the state of my mind; he was watching for trouble. There was none.

He was seated in Sat Guru asana; suddenly he had the flickering radiant look which denotes that his consciousness is not on this earth. He began to recite and to sing poems of Kabir, and Persian songs. His voice ... A fortnight ago I could not bear to listen to it; it was too much for me. I kept running away, going home or to the bazaar, so disturbing was this feeling of non-being before him. Most of those present were now in dhyana. Only two or three listened.

'With your permission I would like to go home.' He turned his head in my direction with his strange samadhi look which pierced my heart like a sword with its power and magnetism.

"Yes, yes," he smiled. But I knew it was an automatic reaction; he was not there. I got up and saluted, touched his left foot, and walked to the door.

"My feet are full of dust; you took the dust with you!" I heard his laughing voice. He was radiant.

'To become less than this dust of your feet; this is the right thing is it not?' I said slowly, as one hypnotized. I heard the murmur of assent and approval from those present and I left with the ring of his kind laughter in my ears and the light of his eyes haunting me.

13 *May*

I had told him that it seems to me that he has much more power than a few years ago. He did not answer; his face was stern and stony. Thinking it over in the night felt a slight bitterness. Nothing is explained. He does not give me the slightest satisfaction.

I had money to buy half a kilo of potatoes. Again potatoes? I felt nauseated only to think of them. I had better buy some *nimbus* [limes] and have them with water. Potatoes in this heat would be poison. So I bought nimbus; had mugs of water with half a nimbu in each; eight in all; and I thought that would be good enough. I have headaches but not unbearable ones.

Guruji does not look at me and does not speak to me. I hope he will not ask anything. The Test of Hunger. The whole situation and his attitude seemed to point clearly that that was it. It is quite according to the Ancient Tradition of Yoga training. The Test of Hunger; and then the next one – the Acceptance of Death. What does it mean? Complete surrender, of course. The Test of Hunger is not the very last one, but it is one of the last. I have to hold out at any cost. Help me! Help me not to be resentful! Help me to pass it! I am determined to persevere ...

15 *May*

Went to Guruji's place at about 7.30 this morning. He was not in the garden. The heat was already unbearable; the air did not stir.

Later he said, "You can go; it is eleven." And then added, "You cook your food?" I looked at him.

"How long does it take you to prepare your food?" He looked up at me gently.

185

'Very little time,' I answered.

"Good. Go now!"

I left sightly puzzled. He gave an opening in case I could not bear it. He tested me. Or was it pity? No, it was a test. If I had said that I have nothing to eat, then it would have meant that I had not accepted the situation. He would have offered some food immediately. But no, my Master; I offer it to you, the Test of Hunger; and I will go through with it whatever happens. I will not die. And if I do, in this condition, it would mean Salvation at once ... I will have won in any case ...

"Not in financial difficulty?" he asked.

It made me smile. 'As you ask me directly, I must answer.' And I told him that on Monday, ten days ago, I had had only four rupees left. Had carried on for as long as they lasted; and then began to fast; water and some nimbu juice; and then only water. 'But let me go on. It is no hardship. I have no sensation of hunger even. I had no intention of telling you if you had not asked.'

"No, you should have told me; I forgot completely."

'I cannot believe it; and I don't believe it,' I laughed. 'If you are the man I know you to be, you must have known. There were little signs that you knew.'

He did not reply directly, but said, "Go to my wife. She will give you something to eat and tomorrow I will give you ten rupees."

I went into the courtyard and his wife put several dishes before me. I took only one chappathi and a little dahl. I knew that after a fast it would be dangerous to overload the stomach. Besides, I was not hungry ...

And so he has given me ten rupees!

⊰ 33 ⊱

16 *May*

I cannot bear to look at him it hurts so much, hurts somewhere ... There are times when I cannot bear to hear him laugh.

Today, while talking to others, he looked at me from time to time. Serious, deep, right into my soul. There is an unearthly light in his liquid, hazel eyes; like drops of water dancing in the sunshine, strange fire suddenly flashing in his eyes; those eyes which have seen the three worlds ...

The feeling of nothingness before him grows deeper and deeper.

17 *May*

Went there at 6.45 a.m. His brother came out immediately and informed me that he had had a severe heart attack in the night. Oxygen was given. It was the worst one he had had so far.

He was lying on the tachat in the middle of the courtyard. His face was pale, full of the deepest peace. He seemed to be asleep. My heart flew to him in mute sorrow. His wife had the look of such anxiety in her dark eyes that I felt deep sympathy for her.

I suddenly felt great peace. I know he cannot go yet.

After some time he turned his head in my direction and beckoned to me.

"You are all right?" he whispered, hardly audible. My throat was in a cramp I could not speak. He nodded. "My wife and my children will look after you," he said, and turned his head to the other side. I stood for a moment, profoundly puzzled by this statement.

'You will be all right,' I said quickly, not knowing what to think.

18 *May*

About 2 a.m., could not sleep. Dressed quickly. The street was full of yapping dogs hunting in dangerous packs.

At his place, all was still. Munshiji slept in the garden, and the servant too. I sat down near the door, against the wall, in the Sufi praying posture and began to pray and do jap. And the thought of what he had meant did not leave me in peace.

About 4 a.m., the doctor got up, measured his blood pressure, gave him medicine and left.

I heard Guruji asking Ravindra, "When did Mem Sahib come?" He answered at 2 a.m. "Let her sit here," he said, pointing to a chair near his bedside. He turned to the other side with his back to me. I left about 5 a.m.

I was at his place again at 7 a.m. He was already in the room. Stood at the door and looked at him for quite a while, from a distance. He slowly turned his head in my direction and gave one, long, deep look. I turned away and went quickly. I was choking; tears were running down my face. Such was the longing. Do not go, prayed my heart. I will go too; what will become of me?

The whole day passed in anxiety. The doctor came at 12 a.m. and took an electro-cardiogram.

20 *May*

Went with Ravindra to the heart specialist. There we learned that only the right side of the heart is working and that he is seriously ill.

"It was a hopeless night," he said yesterday. What did he mean?

"My family will look after you," he said again. Does he mean, "Here my responsibility ends"?

When I see the large shining star rising in the east I know dawn is near. From here, Guruji's bungalow lies in the path of the rising sun. The large star is above it. Is it symbolic? As soon as I open my eyes the longing leaps up like a flame; burning with terrible yearning. I pray under the shimmering velvet of the Indian sky that my heart can bear the pain.

25 May

The week creeps and creeps; it never seems to end. See him for a moment from afar; salute him. He solemnly nods; sometimes ignores me. Then I go and sit either in the doorway passage or somewhere where I can find a bit of shade. The temperature is 117°. How much he must suffer under this heat. If I could take some of his suffering upon me ... Grant that my misery relieves him at least a little. I am a broken woman, tired, feeling sick; death would be better. A scorching wind is blowing, it is unbearably hot.

I will not return to the West. What would be the good of it? I will be a failure. His family, his disciples – they have something or somebody to hold on to, but I have nothing left. I will go to the Himalayas. I know it will mean dying by inches. What alternative have I got?

26 May

When I arrived before 7 he sat on a chair, his feet drawn up; so weak, so pale. My heart was trembling.

"How are you?" he asked audibly. I told him my cold was much better and sat opposite him on the tachat.

'But how are you?'

"Better." He was nodding softly. He was so weak; and he was in samadhi. He soon went inside, walking with difficulty; he nearly fell at the threshold of the room. Ravindra sprang to help him. A few minutes later he was lying on his back moving his hand as if following an inaudible rhythm. I left after saluting him.

Some days ago, he said, "Unbelievable suffering of the mind and the body are necessary in order to become a wali. Absolute Truth is difficult to attain. In a subtle way the Master will put one against himself; and then put the disciple under a severe test. And if he accepts it, thinking, 'I cannot do more but die,' then he is ready for the high state."

The test of the Acceptance of Death. Merciful God, how lonely is the road.

28 May

Yesterday afternoon the room was full of people, all talking. I sat at his feet. I stretched out my hand and very, very gently touched his right foot. The Lotus Feet of the Guru. Merciful God, grant him time to help me to reach him when he is no more.

His blood condition has deteriorated and the anti-coagulant has been increased to a double dose. But they feed him all the wrong foods – *pokoras* and *puries,* all fried; and I can say nothing; yet the doctors have forbidden it.

He walked a little this morning but is unsteady on his feet; then he was in the other room in deep samadhi. At one moment he opened his eyes and saw me. I folded my hands in salute. A sudden beautiful smile lit up his pale face. That was all. But it was enough for me. I had peace.

30 *May*

Yesterday afternoon I went there at 4.30. The wife made a sign to me to go into the front room. It was in darkness. I sat there doing my jap. Suddenly the servant came in and barred the outer doors and windows. I heard Guruji's voice ordering to close everything. In the next moment, I felt the impact of the storm on the bungalow.

The building was hit as if with an explosion and trembled; in a moment it became quite dark. Tropical dust storm, I thought, and wanted to watch it outside. 'Come out with me,' said Ravindra and held open the door against the impact of the wind.

The courtyard was already covered with dust and it was completely dark. The sky was strangely deep red; a threatening dark-red light which soon became bright yellow. The impact of the storm on the trees was tremendous. The ashoka tree was bending and shaking dangerously; the whole world was a madly whirling grey chaos. I was so fascinated I didn't care how covered with dust I was. It was the biggest storm I had seen till now in India.

In the front room, Guruji was squatting on the tachat clasping the sides of his head with both hands, as if in pain. All these upheavals in nature are felt much more when one is so ill. My heart cried out in agony for him.

1 *June*

In the morning I went there and my heart was heavy with some sort of impending disaster, a kind of fear. He was on the tachat in the garden. Many people were sitting around with funereal faces. Learned later that the vomiting condition had begun again. The medicines they were giving him for his heart condition upset his enlarged liver. He have me a long searching look which made me feel like nothing at all before him.

2 *June*

Seated in the big chair, the wife was chanting the *Ramayana*. A disciple was massaging his feet. A truly traditional Indian scene; the sky covered with thin clouds and a pale light coming from the doors and the windows. The voice of the woman, the ringing rhythm of the chant, the deep devotion of the young man, the buzzing of large flies, the chatter of the chipmunks ... And the smell of India; dust, some distant exotic fragrance of incense and flowers ...

Then a man came and talked for over an hour in a loud aggressive voice. Guruji also talked a lot. What suffering it is to know that every one is led in to talk and talk and tire him out. He will die, I thought.

3 June

Somehow I have the feeling that he is winding up his earthly affairs. It is just a feeling. I have no proof, but this morning he was talking in a lowered voice to his wife. I detected the word *memsahib* so they were discussing something concerning me. He mentioned the word *shishya*; perhaps he is just testing me.

10 June

This morning when I came he was taking his bath at the pipe in the garden. He will catch a cold I thought and a cold would be his death. There is always for me this hard, cold, stony face again. And he was dressed all in white; perhaps he was thinking that I would want to speak to him; but lately I have no such desire.

11 June

We were in the room alone. He looked stern but not unfriendly. Perhaps I will try and speak to him. I leaned forward.

'May I speak to you?'

"Hmmm?" He turned his head in my direction, with a vacant expression as if pretending not to understand. Instantly my mind left me. Somehow I began to speak in a strained, unnatural voice:

'It is this pain ... This terrible pain which is drying up my body. The longing day and night causing even physical pain, and it makes me feel so weak; it is a kind of pathological state. I cry nearly all the time.

'Then there is this feeling of non-being. I am nothing before you. It is not that I mean because you are so great; that can be flattery; the self is still there. That is not what I mean. But in this feeling of nothingness there is NOTHING ... Just that, nothing at all, a void! When I speak to you as I do now, for instance, I know that I am speaking, but when I just sit here in silence, I notice that there is only you, nobody else seems to be here. Please tell me, is this surrender?'

He remained motionless while I was speaking. He did not speak. Slowly the mala began to slide through his fingers. It was the one he used on special occasions, belonging to his Guru Maharaj. Clearly something is being done ...

20 June

This morning his breathing was difficult and his voice raucous. He caught a cold. He will never listen to anybody. This morning, for instance, he stood in the doorway, in the full draught, clad only in a thin singlet and a flimsy longhi.

"Hard times," he said suddenly, "in one way or another, are passing away."

My heart gave a quick beat of joy.

'But it seems to me that hard times are only beginning. This increased long-ing is leading somewhere . . .'

A quick, kind smile passed over his face.

25 *June*

In the west the sun was setting in a sea of shimmering golden clouds. The whole world seemed to be illumined by this vivid gold, was transformed by it. I had to cross the *chowraha* [circus] to get to the baker's shop. Before entering, I stopped and turned and saw that right across the chowraha was a magnifi-cent rainbow. So clear, vivid and bright, against the golden sky; and I must have walked right under it. I stood for a while, enchanted. There is a Russian saying that when one walks under a rainbow it means that if one has a wish or a desire it will be fulfilled. What an omen! My Master told me that my troubles are passing away. I don't think that I ever was so happy in my life . . . with this special happiness never experienced before . . .

30 *June*

Deepest peace. And I nearly fall down when I salute him lately. And the feeling of nothingness before him represents such happiness. He will be resting, his eyes closed or open; and I sit, bent in two (a comfortable position for me in his presence) under the blow from the two fans; he and I alone somewhere, where nothing is but peace.

Lately it becomes increasingly lovely. Deep happiness welling from within. From the deepest depth . . . Also at home, when I think of him, it comes over me . . . soft, gentle. A bliss of non-being; not existing at all. It is difficult to believe, unless one has experienced it, that it is so glorious 'not to be'.

15 *July*

"There is nothing but Nothingness," he said yesterday. And the way he said it, repeating it with emphasis, and the echo it awakened in my heart, made me think it was the most wonderful sentence, and it made me glad.

Speaking of this astonishing state of Nothingness, I said that at the begin-ning it was just Nothing. Later there was a kind of sorrowful happiness with much longing in it; but now it was just wonderful; a feeling too new and diffi-cult to analyse.

'I sometimes suspect that this feeling of not-being can put the body to death.'

"The body can die; you will never die," he replied.

He told me important things about the Nakshmandia Dynasty. To my ques-tion if in the Chishtia Dynasty they also have *Param Para* [spiritual succession] he replied:

191

"Yes, of course they have. And in all the Sufi Systems the surrender to the Teacher is demanded. Chishtias are very magnetic, because many things they do through the physical body. So the body becomes very magnetic. It is the body which attracts the body and through it the soul. In our System, it is the soul which attracts the soul and the soul speaks to the soul. The Chishtias need music for instance; without music they can do nothing. They use ceremonies, sometimes breathing practices, and other things. We need nothing. We are not limited. Music is bondage. Ceremonials, worship, when done collectively, can also be bondage. But we are free. We go to the Absolute Truth in Silence, for it can be found only in silence, and it is Silence. That is why we are called the Silent Sufis. If some practices are given, they are performed always in silence."

Then I asked if, in the Chishtia System, love is also created, as in our System.

"No. This is done only with us. Nobody else has this method."

16 July

In the morning we were sitting opposite each other in perfect silence. He wore his devic expression and I just looked and looked, speechless and with much reverence. Later, in the room, he spoke a few words and this gave me the opportunity to say:

'This feeling of Nothingness deepens and deepens. It is so deep that I need only to keep my mind in it consciously; it is beyond description.'

I glanced at him and saw that his eyes were closed; his face was carved of stone. A sign for me to stop talking. I did. Reclined my head on my knees and remained so . . .

There has been nothing much to write in recent weeks. I go there, sit immersed in Nothingness. And this evening he was in a very deep state. How the Divinity shines through his frail human form when he is in samadhi.

18 July

We were sitting outside and it was dusk. A fresh wind was blowing after a hot and sultry day. It was very pleasant. An old man asked about me and offered me his chair.

"No," Guruji said, "she is used to sit on this wooden chair; she wants to lose herself in every way."

Then he proceeded to tell the old man that the first time I stayed with him for nearly two years. "Then she went back and did much work." And he smiled his strange enigmatic smile.

"There was something in her and she had to come back. Now she will stay with me, till . . ." He stopped.

'Till she is perfect?' the old man asked. He shook his head softly.

"Who am I to make anybody perfect? Only God can do that."

⚔ *34* ⚔

24 *July*

It is the third day since my Sheikh has left his physical body ... And I still cannot believe it ...

When I am at his place it seems that at any moment I will hear his swift step, his ringing voice, his laughter ...

A few days ago I was thinking that since he had his last heart attack, his voice has changed. I was thinking it in the morning, listening to his voice in the next room. But in the evening he was singing Persian songs to the old man and his voice was clear and bell-like as I always knew it. And I looked at him hoping so much that he would translate something for me, but he did not ... It was the last time. Never again ...

Until the last moment he did the usual, ordinary things. Nobody at that time had even the smallest hint of what was going to happen. On the 20th in the afternoon he went out into the garden and stood there talking to those who had come. The chairs were not put out yet; it began drizzling softly. The sun came out; it was still drizzling. There must be a rainbow under these conditions. I thought. I looked for it; and there it was between the trees to the south-east.

'Sheikh, Bhai Sahib, please look!' I shouted. 'Look at the beautiful rainbow! Please come here; from here you can see it!' He smiled and came to stand beside me. He looked at it with a smile saying something in Hindi to the others who all commented on it. The colours were very vivid.

'There are two rainbows,' Virendra said. 'A double rainbow!'

Right across the sky towards the south-east were two magnificent rainbows; they seemed to span from one side of the horizon to another. One very clear and bright and the other above, paler, delicate, ethereal; but both complete, parallel to each other.

I did not notice anything unusual. It did not occur to me to look and see if all the colours were there. But Satendra said next morning that his father went into the room for a moment and said to his wife:

"See, the Great Painter, what wonderful colours he paints ... But the yellow colour is missing ..."

And in the night, when Satendra was massaging his feet, he suddenly sat up, his eyes blazing, and said, as if speaking to himself:

"The yellow colour was missing ... my colour was gone ..."

Once more that day it was one of those exceptional sunsets and I continued to watch the colours change. Then I noticed something rare, never seen in my life before – small, perfectly circular clouds stood motionless, right above the bungalow, seemingly very low. They were of purest, tender amethyst, sur-rounded by the great flood of orange and pink from the setting sun. I suddenly realized to my surprise that they were not clouds at all, but perfectly round openings in the surrounding clouds, like little windows through which the blue of the sky was visible. They gradually changed shape, becoming pale blue, and one could see clearly that they were indeed holes, not clouds at all. The film of vivid crimson reflected by the clouds turned the blue-black sky into infinite, purest mauve.

Then suddenly the whole garden, nay, the whole world, seemed to glow with an incredible golden-pink light. I got up and went further away, stood by the door to take in fully the golden garden in this strange, and somehow ominous, light. He was sitting there, the white garment glowing, his skin also; his disciples seated around him. He looked like a golden Deva. Such an oriental scene as one might see in dreams. It was incredibly lovely. The white walls of the bungalow reflected, emphasized, and deepened the effect. It was so much India.

I thought to myself, 'How beautiful you look in this golden light; your skin seems to glow with it from within.'

He gave me a glance, but his face was serious and he looked far away into the blinding light, shimmering with the setting sun. His strange eyes had an expression which I could not interpret and were faithfully reflecting the clouds and the sky and the colours. I did not know at that moment that the Greatest Painter painted the sky in Glory and bathed the garden in Golden Light because a Great Soul of a Golden Sufi was leaving this world forever.

It was his last sunset, the last greeting; he would never see another one. He would never have another physical body; it was his last. So Nature greeted her Great Son for the last time . . .

I stood up to leave at my usual time.

"You want to go now?" he murmered.

'With your permission,' I said, and he nodded briefly. My heart became quite small . . . There was something . . . As if . . . As if some kind of regret in his voice . . . I felt disturbed. I did not know it was his last evening . . .

That night was cool. I slept fairly well. Woke up early; it was still dark. Felt such deep serenity.

Walking to his place amongst the busy morning traffic, the noise of children going to school, cows wandering aimlessly, rikshaws driving at greatest speed, dogs fighting and the sky covered with white clouds, I reflected that the feeling of Nothingness is not only now in his presence. It stays with me . . . I feel like that before God, before life; it seems slowly to have become my very being.

He came out. His torso was naked and he began to walk up and down on the brick elevation; then he sat down. His wife came out and discussed some-thing; the newspaper was handed to him. I brought his glasses. He began to read; he had read the paper every morning lately.

A Muslim barber entered the gate. Guruji's chair was put in the shade of the mango tree and the ceremony of cutting the hair and the beard began. For it was quite a ceremony and I loved to watch it. Today it was especially particular.

"A little here, and here, and here," he kept saying, pointing to the places he wanted to be cut or shaved, either more, or in a different way. I was amused. Poor barber, I thought, it already lasts over an hour; I wonder how much he intends to give him? I will pay, I thought.

'How much is it? Please let me pay for it.'

He smiled. "Put on the chair what you think he should get." I did. He smiled again and, turning to the barber who was still putting all his paraphernalia away into the box, "Here is your money." The barber left thanking profusely.

When I arrived in the afternoon he was reclining on the tachat, talking animatedly, telling a story to his wife, sons and brother, all sitting in the front room. I noticed nothing unusual. I remember I only thought that he talks too much; it will do him harm ...

At one moment we were asked to go out. Closing the door behind me, I enquired from his brother if Bhai Sahib was not feeling well. 'No,' he said, 'he does not feel well.'

I was not really worried. After a few minutes the door was opened. I waited a little; then went into the room. He was squatting on the edge of the tachat, holding his head with both hands.

'May I come in?' He gave me a cold look, not answering. 'Your brother told me that you are not well.'

He turned his face sideways away from me and nodded quickly. But I managed to catch a glimpse of such compassion and tenderness and it puzzled me. I kept quiet. His wife came in and sat opposite him, looking at him with concern. I heard him say to her in Hindi: "I have great trouble with breathing."

In fact his breathing was rapid and obviously painful. Cardiac asthma, I thought, and become alarmed. Babu was sent to fetch the doctor. I could see he was obviously in distress. The body seemed to labour with each breath. I asked him, 'Shall I go to Dr Ram Singh?' This was the heart specialist who had helped him through all the previous heart attacks. He made an indefinite movement with his right hand as if to say, "What is the use?"

His wife said, 'Yes.' So I got up quickly; Virendra said he would come too.

The journey seemed endless to both of us. The sky was heavy and grey with clouds. Dr Ram Singh was at home fortunately. He came at once, driving us in his car.

'It is an attack all right, and this time the same left ventricle is affected. There is also cardiac asthma.'

I went to the side door. Guruji was reclining, his elbow on the pillow, supporting his head with the right hand. I stood outside the door for a few seconds. My eyes, my face, must have expressed that all my being was crying out to him. My heart was full of anxiety. Without lifting his head, he gave me a deep, unsmiling look; lowered his eyes for a brief second and then looked again.

It was the look of a divine lover ... My heart stood still as though pierced. Even then I did not realize that it was his last look, and it was his special look for me ...

The doctor went inside and gave the injection. I sat outside with the others. Virendra said that he was sleeping now.

Suddenly we heard a strange sound like a kind of roar. Virendra stood near the door. I joined him. I saw that Ravindra, his eldest son, was sitting on the bed behind him, supporting him.

I looked at Bhai Sahib, half-supported by the pillows. I saw to my surprise that his abdomen was going up and down in a strange, unusual way, working like bellows. I pointed it out to Virendra, whose large dark eyes were wide open with anxiety.

'He is breathing with the abdomen,' he answered. I did not like it. I felt it was quite abnormal. His wife came into the room with several women, uttered a piercing cry, and threw herself on the bed, weeping loudly. Virendra rushed into the room, took one look at him and came running back:

'He is dead!' he cried, 'He is dead!'

I ran into the room. He was lying supine, heavy on Ravindra's arm. His face was as if swollen with effort, and red ... I went out, dumbfounded. So many people were streaming in; they seemed to have suddenly appeared; they had not been here before ... Dead? I could not believe it ... How is it possible?

Women began to howl, like hungry wolves at the moon. Horrible habit that, I thought; such a dreadful noise, and so useless. Surely he cannot be dead ...

But he was.

I went in and knelt down at the end of the tachat and pressed my forehead against his feet. Their coldness seemed to burn my skin. A lamp had been set in the recess where he kept his books. It was the only light, and in its dim glow his face assumed a strangeness, no more of this world. I kept coming and going. All was silent in the room now.

Went home at 11.00 and cried myself to sleep; but in my heart was stillness and eternal peace ...

Went there about 5 the following morning. Sat outside with the others. When it became sufficiently light, I approached the side door and went inside the room. And to my surprise I saw that his face bore a smiling expression. A strange, mysterious smile with closed lips. The mystery of *pax aeternam* ... It was so wonderful, so unexpected that I could not take my eyes from his face. And my heart was beating so violently that I heard it pulse in the whole of my body ... The tender curve of his lips ... The beard which was cut yesterday with so much care and attention ... His magnificent forehead.

'Goodbye, Sheikh. Never again,' cried my heart.

I wanted to remain, but if I had to sit on the floor amongst all the women I would not see his face. So I kept coming and going, looking with avid eyes, trying to remember this face forever, so long as my physical body would last … This face, so beautiful, so serene, so full of eternal peace …

The funeral was to be at about 1 p.m. Many people were sitting outside; the garden was full of a milling, talking crowd. Then all the male members of the family went inside to wash him. We heard loud wailing and crying coming from the room. When he was dressed, the women were shepherded in and the great howling began again, rising to a crescendo. His face was still the same; smiling enigmatically, tender; but already there was a kind of remoteness, a 'going away'.

Prof. Batnagar said to me, 'Courage! he is not dead; they make a noise for nothing.' I smiled. It was so true. And except for a fleeting glimpse when they lowered him into the grave, it was the last time I saw his face …

I don't remember the moment when we reached the Samadhi. He wanted to be buried at the feet of his father. I noticed that his grave was much deeper than in the West. And it had on the left side a niche, like a drawer for the body to be put into, which later would be sealed off with bricks, before the earth was filled in.

There was such peace around; so much sunshine; clouds in the sky; the wide Indian plains and the wind … Sheikh, my Sheikh …

'Take off the sheath from the face,' somebody said. For a second, a glimpse of this serene face which seemed so fresh and only sleeping … And then it was all over, except for the sound of the moist earth being filled in.

Sheikh … my Sheikh, my mind kept repeating. And the sky was transparent with the white clouds. And the wind smelt good. I took a little earth, blessed earth from a Saint's grave … This represents your body to me … but you, you for me, will live for ever …

PART III

⚜ *35* ⚜

October 1966

Dearest,

This letter comes to you from a solitary retreat in the Himalayan hills. I am writing seated on my doorstep, facing the snows. They are clear this morning. And last evening too; the whole range was coral pink, the glow after the setting sun dying gently away on the glaciers. And so near they seem . . .

It is a glorious morning. The ashram garden is a riot of colours. Sunflowers, zinnias, dahlias and, above all, cosmos and marigolds. The air is vibrating with the hum of the bees and the crickets are busy filling the garden with the gay monotonous sound which seems to belong to the sunshine. Sheer joy of living, bringing back childhood memories of summer days, blue sky and much hot, lovely sunshine.

Everything grows so tall here; as if the vegetation is trying to compete with the high hills around and the huge mountains. Sunflowers are nine to ten feet high; the nearest one to my door has thirty-two blooms and at least the same amount of buds. There are shrub-like zinnias covered with large blooms rather like dahlias, four inches across. And cosmos! I have never seen anything like it! They grow wild here on the slopes, and in the clearings of the jungle, and in our garden we must have several thousand plants in crimson, white, deep pink, pale pink, and pink with a crimson heart. There is a marigold six feet tall near the veranda!

Our ashram garden looks like a valley of flowers just now. The other day I went into the pine forest on the opposite hill, from where there is an enchanting view into the three valleys. The valley of Garur with the snows behind it; then of Kausani and of the Chenoda river. All round are high hills, the famous Kumaon Hills, covered with pine forests at this altitude and with jungle lower down on the slopes. The ashram is at 6,075 feet above sea level. Kausani, a village of only one thousand inhabitants, is in the centre, about six hundred feet below. Once a week I go down to the village to do my shopping, although at present most things come from the ashram garden.

I seem to live on my doorstep lately, since the snows are clearly visible. Every morning I am up long before sunrise. The green, livid transparency of the sky changes gradually into a pale yellow, the harbinger of dawn. It is perfectly still. The snows are sombre, forbidding. No sound from anywhere.

Nature is waiting. Then from the village below sounds begin to come, of life awakening. Children's voices, laughter, dogs barking, an occasional snatch of song. The sound of water running into the buckets. Smoke begins to rise, the lovely acrid smell of wood fire.

But the forest and jungle are still. Then suddenly, as if obeying the signal of an unseen conductor, the birds begin to sing on the slopes and in the valleys. At first hesitantly, a lonely sound, a soft modulation. Then all join in. As in the West, the blackbirds are the first to begin; and here in the Himalayas they have yellow bills as our own blackbirds do.

And I sit and listen and the sky is orange with shafts of light behind the peaks. Each day these shafts are more to the south. Now the most dramatic moment arrives: the tips of the snows get the first glow. It is as if a Deva lights a crimson lantern on the tip of the highest mountain and, one by one, all the other tips begin to glow. The deep, red light slides lower and lower, and the tips of the peaks become coral-red. Then by magic, the whole range becomes coral-red, then deep gold, then brilliant yellow, and, becoming paler and paler, they will stand white, glistening, unreal in their purity; first against a livid, yellowish sky and later as though suspended in the blue. Seemingly so light and ethereal that one cannot believe one's eyes.

The nights are completely windstill; and there is something very special about the silence of the Himalayas. I have never experienced anything quite like it. I mean the Sound ... Everywhere I went, in Darjeeling, in Kashmir on the borders of Nepal, and here of course, I have heard it louder than ever. The Sound, like a distant melodious roar. Something between the whistle of a bat and the singing of telegraph wires. It seems to come from afar, and at the same time it is very near, outside one and inside the head also. When the Silence is Absolute, it has Sound. It must be the same with Light. For it is said that Absolute Light represents Absolute Darkness. So the Rishis call God 'The Dark Light'. I call it the Roar of Silence, *Nada*, the first and the last Sound of Creation.

As soon as I arrived here from the plains on the 5th August I heard it. I woke up in the night; it was pitch dark. There was stillness and the Sound. And my heart was suddenly glad; it was like a greeting from the homeland ... The silence is so compact, so dense, almost physically felt; it seems to descend on and envelop one; one is lost, immersed in it, drowned; and there is nothing else beside it in the whole wide world ... The Sound is deep, endless, eternal.

The Yogis in Rishikesh say that it is the *Nada*, the Breath of Brahma, who can never sleep, can never rest, otherwise the Creation will disappear into Nothingness. And they also say that you can hear it in the Himalayas much more easily than anywhere else in the world, because so many Rishis have meditated in those hills for thousands of years, creating a special, favourable atmosphere. Perhaps it is true; certainly the Sound is true and very real. It is impossible to say from where it comes; from very far; from very near and yet from all around.

I am so deeply happy here, a happiness never before experienced. That peace which Guruji left with us all. Prayer is easy and God is near . . .

My Love to you . . .

8 *November*

I have been here for three months. Almost sixteen weeks have passed since Guruji's death. So much has happened within me; slowly, gradually, by degrees the world begins to look differently, to change imperceptibly.

The sunrise, the sunset, the garden, the people, the whole daily life seems outwardly the same. But the values have changed. The meaning underlying it all is not the same as before. Something which seemed intangible, unattainable, slowly, very slowly becomes a permanent reality. There is nothing but Him. At the beginning it was sporadic; later of shorter or longer duration, when I was acutely conscious of it. But now . . . The infinite, endless Him . . . Nothing else is there. And all the beauty of nature which surrounds me is as if only on the edge of my consciousness. Deep within I am resting in the peace of His Heart. The body feels so light at times. As if it were made of the pure, thin air of the snow peaks. This constant vision of the One is deepening and increasing in the mind, giving eternal peace.

Memories come crowding in. Unexpectedly I hear his voice again, remember his kindness.

I recalled particularly, on a day of trembling luminosity, of sparkling transparency, that he was already seated outside when an Indian village woman came to him.

She was small, very thin, her face wrinkled and shrunken, as if dried up by the merciless sun and the hot winds of the plains.

She was telling an endless, sorrowful litany of her troubles. Illnesses, misery, the death of her husband and most of her children. Now she was alone, useless, nobody needed her, she had nothing to hope for, nothing to live for . . .

And she came out with the question which seemed to burn, scorching her trembling lips:

'Maharaj, why did God create this world so full of troubles? Why did He create me to endure all these sufferings?'

I saw him lean forward, a shimmering light in his eyes, the light of compassion I knew and loved so well. His voice was soft when he answered:

"Why has He created the world? That you should be in it! Why has He created you? He is alone; He needs you!"

Never will I forget the broad, blissful smile on that lined emaciated face when she was walking away. She went happy in the knowledge that she was not alone, not really, for God needed her to keep Him company because He too was alone . . .

Never will I forget the love that I felt then. Only a very Great Soul could have expressed so simply and convincingly one of the greatest Mysteries to a naïve, childlike village woman. The Ultimate Metaphysical Truth; that He who is Alone and Perfect, in order to realize His Perfection, created the Universe . . .

Mid-November

Since I have been here in Kausani, from the beginning when the states of consciousness began to change considerably, I felt that I was nearing the end of the road. I mean the end of the road to the Real Home. There is nothing else to do. He takes over. When the devotee becomes His, everything ends there. Yes, I am only at the beginning of this state; there will be many ups and downs. But this is really the beginning of the end. This feeling of belonging to Him, every breath, every pore of the body, every thought, every little cell – it is wonderful! There is such security in it, such tenderness; and yet it is Nothingness itself. Like a perfume rising from the innermost sweetness is this still joy . . .

December

The Realization that every act, every word, every thought of ours not only influences our environment but mysteriously forms an integral part of the Universe, fits into it as if by necessity, in the very moment we do or say or think it, is an overwhelming and even shattering experience.

If we only knew deeply, absolutely, that our smallest act, our smallest thought, has such far-reaching effects; setting forces in motion; reaching out to the galaxy; how carefully we would act and speak and think. How precious life would become in its integral oneness.

It is wonderful and frightening. The responsibility is terrifying and fascinating in its depth and completeness, containing as it does the perplexing insecurity of being unique and the profound consolation of forming part of the Eternal Undivided Whole. And we all have the right to, and can achieve, the realization of this wonderful meaning of life; one is *quite simply* part of it all; a single vision of Wholeness.

Very acute it became after Guruji's passing away. And I could not reconcile the torment of the heat, the mangy dogs, the filthy children, the sweat, the smells; for they were THAT too . . .

But it was here, in the stillness of the mountains, that it gradually crystallized; distilled itself from a different dimension into the waking consciousness. And now I must live with the Glory and the Terror of it . . . It is merciless, inescapable; an intensely virile, intoxicating Presence, so utterly joyous, boundless and free. It is blasphemy to attempt to put it into words.

I know that the states of Nearness will increase, will become more permanent; but also the state of separation will become more painful, more lonely, the nearer one comes to Reality.

I know that I go back to a life of fire; for you, dear Guruji, told me what to expect. I know that sometimes my health will fail, and that I shall be burned. But I know also that I can never be alone any more, for you are with me always. I know that God is Silence, and can be reached only in silence; the Nearness to Thee will remain and give me the strength to go on.

Goodbye days of peace; and days of wrestling with myself. Days of incredible beauty with Nature at its best; days of glorious states of consciousness, wherein the divine heart within myself was the Divine Heart within the cosmos. When I knew the meaning of Oneness because I lived it. You did not deceive me, Guruji. You pointed out the Way, and now the Way has taken hold of me . . . fully . . . irrevocably.

Glossary

abhyasa Spiritual practice
adhikara Initiation, permission to teach
ahimsa Doctrine of not killing or injuring
ananda Bliss
anandamayakosha One of the five sheaths of illusion covering the Truth (see p. 74)
annamayakosha One of the five sheaths of illusion covering the Truth (see p. 74)
asana Posture
ashram Place of religious retreat
Atma The higher of true Self
Bandhara Public religious ceremony
Bhai Sahib Elder Brother (term of address)
bhakta Devotee
bhut Ghost
brahma vidya Absolute wisdom
Brahman The Absolute
Brahmarandhra chakra Chakra at the crown of the head
buddhi Intuition, pure intelligence, wisdom
chakra Centre of psychic energy. The main ones are associated with particular locations along the spinal column
charpoy Rope bed
chik Blind made from bamboo
chitta Universal intelligence
deva Angel
dhoti Indian dress; a kind of sarong
dhyana Contemplation followed by complete abstraction of all outward impressions
ghat Elevated bank of a river, used for bathing and cremation
ghat pranayam 'Inward' breathing
manamayakosha One of the five sheaths of illusion covering the Truth (see p. 74)
guru Spiritual teacher
haja Pilgrimage
indrias The senses
Ishvara The Creator
jap Prayer, repeating the name of God
kaprail Goat shed
karma Law of cause and effect
khanna Food
Kirtan Singing of devotional hymns
kundalini Energy, pictured as an 'inner fire coiled like a serpent at the base of the spine' when dormant
kurta Indian dress, a collarless shirt
loka A form of repetitive thought-desire causing reincarnation
longhi Indian dress, a straight piece of material tied round the waist
Loo Hot wind from the desert
Mahatma Great Soul
mala A kind of rosary

manamayakosha One of the five sheaths of illusion covering the Truth (see p. 74)
manas Mind
mantra Word of power
maya Illusion
mayavirupa Body of illusion
moha Attachment
muladhara chakra Chakra at the base of the spine
Parabrahm Absolute Reality
Param Para Spiritual succession
prakriti Primal, root or universal matter or substance
prana Life force
pranamayakosha One of the five sheaths of illusion covering the Truth (see p. 74)
prasad Food which has been blessed
Puja Devotional service
sadhu Holy man
sahaj samadhi Effortless samadhi
Samadhi Grave, place of rest
samadhi A superconscious state; merging into Universal Consciousness
samsara Wheel of birth and death caused by illusion
samskara Impressions of actions which lead to rebirth
sankalpa-vikalpa Projections, distractions of the mind
sannyasi An ascetic or devotee, a wandering monk
satsang Being in the presence of the spiritual teacher
shaitan Evil spirit
shakti Power
shishya Disciple
siddhi Spiritual power
suf Wool
swami Teacher
tabla Drum
tachat Wooden bench used as a bed
tapas Penance
tonga Two-wheeled carriage
tyaga Complete renunciation
vasana Locality
Vedas Holy texts of Hinduism
viriya shakti Creative energy
wali Sufi saint